Reasoning About Program Transformations

Springer
New York
Berlin
Heidelberg
Hong Kong
London
Milan
Paris
Tokyo

Jean-François Collard

Reasoning About Program Transformations
Imperative Programming and Flow of Data

With 125 Illustrations

 Springer

Jean-François Collard
Compiler Research Laboratory
Intel Corporation
2200 Mission College Blvd
SC12-305
Santa Clara, CA 95052-8119
USA
jean-francois-jcollard@intel.com

Library of Congress Cataloging-in-Publication Data
Collard, Jean-François.
    Reasoning about program transformations : imperative programming and flow of data /
Jean-François Collard.
    p. cm.
    Includes bibliographical references and index.

    1. Programming languages (Electronic computers)   I. Title.
QA76.7 .C645 2002
005.13—dc21   2002017378

ISBN 978-1-4419-2981-5   e-ISBN 978-0-387-22461-9

Printed in the United States of America.

9 8 7 6 5 4 3 2 1

www.springer-ny.com

Springer-Verlag   New York Berlin Heidelberg
A member of BertelsmannSpringer Science+Business Media GmbH

To Sonia and Alison
To my parents

Preface

Overview

The motivation of this text lies in what we believe is the inadequacy of current frameworks to reason about the flow of data in imperative programs. This inadequacy clearly shows up when dealing with the individual side effects of loop iterations. Indeed, we face a paradoxical situation where, on the one hand, a typical program spends most of its execution time iterating or recursing on a few lines of codes, and, on the other hand, current optimization frameworks are clumsy when trying to capture the effects of each incarnation of these few lines—frameworks we inherited from designs made decades ago.

The reasons are manyfold, but one of them stands out: The same concepts have been used, on the one hand, to represent and manipulate programs internally in compilers and, on the other hand, to allow us humans to reason about optimizations. Unfortunately, these two uses have different aims and constraints. An example of such a situation is given by control-flow graphs of basic blocks, which have been extremely useful in practice as an internal representation of programs, but which are not always adequate or convenient to formally think about programs and specify their transformations. In some cases, definitions based on control-flow graphs can be overly restrictive. Dominance, studied in Chapter 4, is a good example.

The consequence of these low-level representations is that many analyses and optimizations are defined constructively, by giving an algorithm instead of defining what the goal is: Instead of first telling *what*, they tell *how*. Then there is no specification against which the implementation can be checked.

In addition, implementation-oriented definitions of analyses and optimizations are often clumsy at representing one key aspect of programs: data flow. The flow of data is one key characteristic of algorithms, which programs implement. Unfortunately, because of its intrinsic reuse of memory, imperative programming blurs the data flow and hides the algorithm it implements even more so. If the compiler could extract the algorithm from the text of the program, it could apply extremely sophisticated optimizations. We argue that the closer a compiler (or we humans) gets to the underlying algorithm, the wider the spectrum of transformations it can apply. And indeed, one sure way to understand the algorithm is to first understand the data flow.

Another important concept we would like to advocate for is the use of symbolic computations. In many current analyses, possible values of results—like lattice elements in data-flow analysis—are predefined (or are *synthesized* [10], which just delays the problem). In other words, the information of interest has to belong to a predefined set, and this set has to be described *in extension*, that is, element by element. On the contrary, *closed-form expressions* allow us to describe a (possibly infinite) set *in intention*, that is, by describing the common properties that bind its elements, rather than enumerating these elements.

Similarly, several analyses contrast data elements by their *lexical names* only. Clearly, this is fine for scalar variables, but not, for example, for arrays. Again, a more general and natural approach is to use some type of symbolic computation on names. We try to show in this book that symbolic computations provide a very interesting alternative to several usual frameworks.

With this in mind, this book introduces a framework that is reasonably simple and yet allows us to contrast and compare a relatively large family of analyses and optimizations. Symbols and mathematical formulas are avoided as much as possible while we still try to retain the formality of mathematical reasoning. The math used in this book does not go beyond logic formulas, basic concepts on sets (such as minima and maxima), and basic linear algebra.

This framework is not meant only as pen-and-pencil notations: Several academic compilers, including the PAF compiler at the University of Versailles, France, rely on similar frameworks and implement some of the analyses presented in this book (in particular, instancewise reaching definition analysis and conversion to single-assignment form). We also provide many hands-on exercises that use the Omega calculator developed by Prof. Pugh at the University of Maryland. This software can be found at

http://www.cs.umd.edu/projects/omega/index.html

We strictly adhere to the syntax of the interface except when indicated.

Because this framework is centered around the flow of data, it cannot capture several types of classical compiler concepts. In particular, all syntactical optimizations (like PRE, to give just one example) fall out of its scope. For the same reason, this framework is irrelevant to most machine-dependent code-generation optimizations. Still, the alert reader will notice that there are obvious subjective biases in the choice of analyses and optimizations described in this book. However, throughout this book, we try to make explicit the paths we did take and those we decided not to take. We also hope this book will provide students and people interested in computer languages a gentle introduction to compilation, automatic parallelization, and optimization.

Organization and Features

Chapter 1 presents the key concepts and issues this book addresses. In the chapter, we intentionally prefer to give an intuitive flavor to the text, "hand-waving" rather than formally defining. This simple introduction may look naive to experts in the field, and these readers might be tempted to skip this chapter. However, we recommend them not to, and instead to try and guess, beyond the apparent naiveté of descriptions, the direction the rest of this book will take.

The rest of the book is divided into three parts: The first part introduces our framework; the second revisits classical programming language concepts and classical compiler optimizations; and the third addresses memory optimizations in sequential and parallel languages.

Part I consists of Chapters 2 and 3. Chapter 2 specifies what we want to describe, and Chapter 3 provides such a description. Because Chapter 2 introduces the notations, reading it is probably required. For those familiar with loop nests, however, Chapter 3 may be skipped.

In Part II, Chapter 4 shows how several classical topics in compiler design and programming languages can be defined using our framework. To make your own judgment, compare these definitions with the traditional ones. Chapter 5 elaborates on one of these classical topics: reaching definition analysis. Because the definition of a value, when it reaches a use, conveys a part of the data flow, reaching definition analysis is detailed with great care. Chapter 5 also provides a detailed explanation on how to automatically compute reaching definitions using symbolic solvers. Chapter 6 presents applications of reaching definition analysis. Finally, Chapter 7 revisits more classical concepts related to data flow.

Part III consists of three chapters detailing the interplay between memory usage and the expression of the data flow. One way to make data flow more explicit is to expand data structures. The most aggressive type of expansion is single-assignment, which enforces that a memory location be assigned at most once. Chapter 8 discusses single-assignment forms: plain single-assignment, and what is known in the literature as static single assignment (SSA). Less aggressive expansions are also discussed. Chapter 9 details a restricted form of single assignment called maximal static expansion (MSE). MSE is presented in the last core chapter only because it applies and leverages most concepts discussed throughout the book. It should not be understood as the panacea to all parallelism-versus-memory tradeoff issues, but only as one answer to this general problem. This discussion is also extended to parallel programs in Chapter 10, which chapter shows how reaching definitions and singleassignment forms can be derived for parallel programs using similar frameworks. Finally, Chapter 11 gives a conclusion to our presentation.

One key feature of this book is a detailed description of state-of-the-art symbolic analyses that handle array elements and statement instances individually. The benefit of these analyses is that they achieve much better precision than their classical counterparts. This book also features many examples and exercises, nearly all with solutions, to make this book easy to read and use and a good bookshelf reference. As said, most of these examples offer hands-on experiments using a freely available symbolic solver. Also, to the best of my knowledge, these techniques have never before been presented in a single volume, using a single framework and consistent notation—only dispersed technical publications were available.

Audience

This book is written for professionals and students interested in code optimization or verification, whether manual or automatic. Writers of compilers or program checkers will find new ideas for development, and users of these tools will better understand what compilers and checkers can and cannot do. The numerous examples should not only make it easy for developers and users to try their own experiments, but also make this book ideal teaching material.

Acknowledgments

I would like to thank Paul Feautrier and Luc Bougé for their mentoring during my tenure at the National Center for Scientific Research (CNRS). Many results presented in this book were first investigated and published by Paul Feautrier. Also, I would like to thank Martin Griebl, whose friendship and joint work have been invaluable. Many thanks as well to Albert Cohen, whose research on recursive programs is presented in this book. Sincere thanks also to Rob Schreiber and David Wonnacott for reviewing this text and for their numerous comments and suggestions that greatly enhanced the manuscript.

Contents

III Data Flow and Expansion   163

List of Figures

Chapter 1

Introduction

Algorithms were invented thousands of years ago, when the only thinkable machine to do computations were human beings' own gray cells. And since this book is mainly about algorithms (and how imperative programming hides them), we start with a simple experiment involving some generic concept of a "computing device." Indeed, the term "computing device" is intentionally fuzzy to stress the fact that most of the discussion in this chapter—and throughout this book—is not restricted to computers as we currently know them.

With this conceptual device, let us think about an extremely simple example of a computation. Such an example is given in Figure 1.1, where three multiplication called 1, 2, and 3, are applied to four values, a, b, c, and d. We try to make as few assumptions as possible on the "computing device" we use to perform this computation or on the way the computation is conducted. Therefore, we simply consider "values," depicted by square boxes labeled with letters, and "operations," denoted with their usual symbols (here, multiply) surrounded by circles and labeled with numbers.

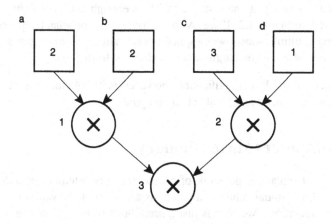

Figure 1.1. A simple computation.

The rule of our little game is as follows: Try and imagine as many ways as possible to actually perform the computation. Here are a few ideas:

- There are three possible orders in which the computations in Figure 1.1 can be done: first, the multiply operation labeled 1, then the one labeled 2, and finally that labeled 3. Or, we start with 2, then do 1, and eventually 3; 3 has to be the last one since it needs the results of both 1 and 2 *in any order*. The last possible order is to do 1 and 2 *simultaneously*, that is, without being ordered, and then do 3. The potential benefit is obvious since, assuming we have two "machines" to compute multiplications, the end result can be completed in two steps instead of three.

- We can replace the multiply operation labeled 1 by an add, since adding 2 and 2 gives the same result as multiplying them. The idea here is that addition is much simpler than multiplication to humans and, not surprisingly, to computers, too. Being simpler, it goes faster, too: a nice property we all enjoy! We could alternatively replace the multiplication by 2 with a shift on the binary representation of the numbers. This is more complex for us, but almost trivial for (binary) computers!

  You may say, however, that this is too simple a situation, since values a and b just happen to both be equal to 2. However, there are several cases where such a simplification can be applied. For instance, computing an absolute value can be skipped if the input value is known to be positive—and even if computing an absolute value is not very time-consuming, it takes more time than doing nothing at all! Indeed, there are many cases of similar simplifications known in the literature as *strength reduction*. In the same spirit, we could discard multiplication 2 and replace it with value c, since obviously $c \times 1 = c$ for all c's.

- The need for two values, a and b, to denote the same number (2) can also be argued. Indeed, just one instance of "2" is enough, and we might simplify Figure 1.1 into Figure 1.2. If we try to precisely describe what happened, we could say that multiplication 1 was applied to two values, called "arguments," and that the *name* of the second argument was changed from b to a.

The benefit of the last simplification, however, is not obvious yet. To understand the benefit, we now need to look at actual computers.

1.1   Computers Have Memory

A key feature of actual computers is, of course, memory. Memory provides a place to store values, either initial values computations are fed with, or values produced in the course of computation. Memory is just a scratchpad where values can be stored and retrieved.

Notice that there can be constraints on the way values are stored in and retrieved from memory. In particular, the *order* in which these accesses to and from memory take place may be restricted. Observe that these restrictions may come from technological

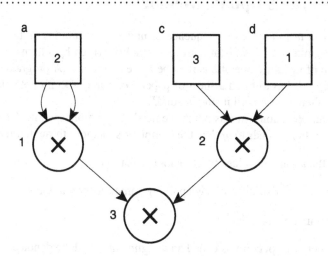

.... *Figure 1.2. Simplifying a simple computation.* ....

constraints—the way memory devices are built may limit their operation. Think of tapes, for instance: From a given position on a tape, we can only directly write to the following position. Writing to another position involves a costly repositioning delay.

Restrictions may also come from theoretical considerations: We may intentionally assume a given type of memory and study the consequences this choice implies. Throughout this book, however, we assume that memory locations can all be accessed at any time without technological ordering constraints: Namely, we assume memory with *direct access*, also known as *random access memory* (RAM).

Values are stored in memory at *locations*. The precise structure of locations depends on many technological choices. In the simple case, locations are accessed as an interval of positive integers, from 0 to billions. In more complex cases, the set of locations is structured: Some locations may be accessed faster than others (think of a caching technique); the set may be structured as a tree (think of distributed memory); etc. At this level, we are not interested in such a fine grain of detail. Rather, we consider a *flat* set of locations, without any notion of locality.

Locations are named after the variables used in the program text, such as a, b, and so forth. Variables are syntactical objects printed in courier font. Their *values* (i.e., the values contained in these memory locations) are denoted by italic names, such as a and b. We will soon see that values contained by variables change in the course of program execution (they are, after all, *variables*), so denoting by a the value of a might sometimes be ambiguous. The value of a at a given step s of the execution will be denoted by $[\![a]\!]_s$. More on this later.

The number of memory locations is, of course, finite, but we will assume that it is large enough to accommodate our needs.

1.2   Programs Update Memory

A *program* is a *text* describing a sequence of updating operations on the memory. A program is a finite text: It was (at least, potentially) written by a human. In contrast, the sequence of updating operations may be finite or infinite. A program looks like a cooking recipe. It has to fit on a sheet of paper, but it may specify potentially infinite operations: "Gently heat until it smells good."

What is an operation? At this point, we need not be more specific. The only point is that an operation intends to *update* the computer's memory through three steps:

- Read the argument values from memory locations,

- Compute a new result value by applying some function to them,

- Store it in a memory location.

Such an elementary operation is called an *assignment*. It will be denoted

```
a := f(b, c)
```

When executing that statement, memory locations b and c are read, which provides values *b* and *c* on which function f is applied. The result is then written into location a. a is called the *left-hand side* (lhs) of the assignment. f(b, c) is called its *right-hand side* (rhs). Function f may be as simple as a multiplication or as complex as predicting the weather next weekend. It may require several argument values, or only one, or possibly none as, for example, a constant function: a := 0.

Using assignments to store values in memory allows sequences of computations to execute step by step. Intermediate values are kept in memory until needed. In a sense, memory allows to implement the "arrows" of Figure 1.1. An example program implementing Figure 1.1 would be as follows:

```
a := 2 ;
b := 2 ;
c := 3 ;
d := 1 ;
tmp_1 := a * b ;
tmp_2 := c * d;
result := tmp_1 * tmp_2
```

where tmp variables serve as temporary scratchpad locations.

The *control flow* of a program is the order in which the successive operations are carried out. In this case, it is the straightforward top-down order. Control flow in the program above is very strictly defined and is, in fact, overspecified. Each semicolon is a "stop" and requires the computing device to complete execution of operations preceding a semicolon before proceeding to the operation that follows.[1] A drawing, like the one in Figure 1.1, can provide all the information on control flow we need

---

[1]Notice that a semicolon is a statement separator à la Pascal. In contrast, languages such as C use semicolons as end-of-statement markers.

without giving spurious details. Describing sequences of computations with English words or mathematical symbols may betray the original intent—or the original *lack* of intent! What we need is a syntax that just states what Figure 1.1 states: Multiplications 1 and 2 may execute in any order but must complete before multiplication 3 starts. How to express control flow in a less rigid fashion is addressed in Section 1.4.

Data flow refers to the sequence of values, or data, computed in the course of program execution. In the preceding program, the first statement does not actually produce a value: It only serves as a way to tell the computing device to use a memory location named a as a scratchpad to "remember" the value 2. The first new value actually produced is $a \times b$, which is temporarily stored in a memory location called tmp_1. The second and third data are produced in the following two instructions. The flow of data here boils down to the creation of two values computed from initial data, which are then passed to (they "flow" to) the multiplication producing the third value. Again, the program as written above prescribes the data flow in a more rigid way than the drawing in Figure 1.1. It is more operational. It also fails to make explicit the flow of data that was so clear—to a human eye at least—in Figure 1.1.

Consider this: Imperative programs compute output values from input values.[2] This process does not occur in one step, but in several (perhaps billions) steps, each taking its inputs and producing its output, contributing to the global flow of data specified by the algorithm.

But as we can see, imperative programming hides the data flow. This book focuses on how to discover and reconstruct this data flow, and how to exploit it. Sections 1.6 and 1.7 provide an introduction to these issues.

1.3 What Is a Program Transformation? When Is It Correct?

Chefs do not like following recipes too closely. Instead, they love adapting a recipe, taking advantage of the freshest available vegetables, for example. The same holds for programmers. Instead of following the specification as it is written, they may prefer implementing an equivalent behavior in a different way, because it makes a better use of available resources. This amounts to applying a *textual transformation* to a program.

The text is just the *source code* in computer-speak, or a recipe in cuisine-speak. Defining the "meaning" of a program may require involved formal frameworks, but it boils down to one rule: The end results must be preserved when transforming a program.

Since this book deals with imperative programming, the "end results," like all results, are stored in (memory locations referred to by) variables. The distinguished variables that contain end results are often called *output variables*. Therefore, the meaning of a program is preserved if, after executing the original program and the transformed one, the values of the output variables are the same. This rule gives in fact

---

[2]In contrast, logic programming works "both ways." In theory at least, users of a logic program can provide values to any data and request values of remaining data to be computed from the given information.

a lot of headroom for program transformations. For example, the values of temporary variables can be changed at will, as long as the "end results" are safe.

So a transformed program is *correct* if it computes the same output values as the original one from the same input values.[3] As we saw earlier, one possibility to do so is to change the operations being applied to values—like 2×2 instead of $2 + 2$. However, this approach is not very promising, for several reasons. First, it is not widely applicable, as there are not many interesting cases. Second, the validity of the transformation is not always guaranteed: Operators $\times$ and $+$ can be substituted in a few cases only. In addition, when using floating-point numbers instead of "natural" integers, we must do similar transformations with extreme care.

The second approach is to change the *order* in which computations are done. This approach is, indeed, much more exciting and is developed later. A third approach is to change which and how many memory locations are used, and when, in the course of program execution. The usefulness of this approach depends on technological considerations. Decades ago, when computer memories were small and expensive, making sure programs would use as little memory as possible triggered a lot of research and development. Today, when memory is a relatively cheap commodity, program optimization may take the opposite approach and trade off higher memory consumption for higher performance.

But probably the most important thing to take away here is that the last two approaches share one key property: They do not change the flow of data prescribed in the program text even if the first approach, since it changes the very individual computations made at each elementary step, indeed implies that the original algorithm is changed into another, presumably more efficient, one. Our act of faith is that understanding the flow of data provides a big part of the underlying algorithm and, therefore, provides a wide spectrum of opportunities for improvement.

1.4   Parallelism and Parallel Languages

Parallelism among computations is the property of these computations to be executed in any order.[4] The computation may be *physically* concurrent, if several independent computing devices are available, or rather *logically* concurrent if execution is actually interleaved. One usually considers that a program has no control on the relative speed of the devices or on the scheduling strategy used in interleaving. At the level of programs, parallelism can be seen as an annotation: "These two tasks may be carried out in any order, interleaved or independently: I do not care." For instance,

---

[3]Observe that this definition of correctness is very stringent. Some situations can make the problem more ambiguous. An obvious border case that pops into mind is numerical computations with floating-point numbers: Rounding may significantly change the results. But the validity of apparently different results is even deeper than that, in algorithms themselves: Consider a program whose goal is to search a root of a quadratic polynomial. Which root is actually found may well depend on the technical features of the computing device.

[4]We can argue that parallelism is the ability of a *computing device* to carry out several computations at the same time—and not a property of a program. In truth, parallelism can only be carried out by a device, and the program may prescribe more parallelism than the device can use. However, this distinction is subtle and not very fruitful. In addition, it leads to contradictions when using well-accepted terms, like "parallel language" or "parallel programming."

```
x := x + 2; y := y + 2
```

means "First increase x by 2 and then y also by 2." The composition of the two statements is a sequential composition, as underlined by the semicolon. In contrast,

```
x := x + 2 // y := y + 2
```

means "Just do both: I do not care about the order." The separator // alludes to the parallelism or concurrency of the two assignments. Variable x may be increased first and then y, or the opposite. Observe that we implicitly consider that the assignments are *atomic*, that is, operations that cannot be split.

Parallelism can apply not just to two computations, as above, but to many more. We might want to add the value 2 to 100 variables named x1 through x100, or even to an arbitrary number n of variables x1 through x_n. We might want to invent a notation to express these parallel computations in a concise way. One idea that comes to mind is to generalize // into

$$//_{i=1}^n x_i := x_i + 2$$

in the same way as $\sum$ generalizes $+$. For those reluctant to use symbols, or just because our keyboards don't offer much more than old-fashioned typewriters do, we might write it as

$$\texttt{forall } i := 1 \texttt{ to } n \texttt{ do } x_i := x_i + 2$$

In the above examples, all computations are specified to be unordered. However, parallelism can also be "incomplete," in the sense that an order may be imposed between some computations. The computations in Figure 1.1 give a good example. Only the top row of computations (multiplication 1 and multiplication 2) can be done in any order. These computations follow a treelike pattern, the image being that the last computation, at the bottom, is the *root* of a tree and that edges, looking upward, look like tree branches, until *leaves* are reached. The number of steps such a tree requires to be computed grows with the logarithm (in base 2) of the number of leaves (indeed, in Figure 1.1, we see that the four values can be multiplied together in $\log_2 4 = 2$ steps). This tree pattern is very common and is called a *scan*. It applies to many usual math operators like $\sum$ or $\prod$, and in general to any associative operator.

Parallelism can of course yield different results if the values produced by one of the computations happen to be used by the other one. Writing

```
x := 0 // x := 1
```

indicates that we accept that variable x gets value 0 or 1. Such a situation is called *nondeterminism* in the literature. Actually, the word is slightly misleading, as it intuitively refers to somebody tossing a coin. In our context, it simply means that the programmer left the result *underspecified*: Any result obtained by interleaving the atomic assignments of the two computations complies with his or her intents.

Another related issue is *memory consistency*. Consider this program:

```
x := 0; (x := 1 // y := x)
```

Two parallel threads are spawned by parallel composition (//). However, can y := x possibly read 1? In technical terms, do we have *strong* memory consistency, meaning that if x := 1 completes before the read of x in the other thread, then this read returns 1? Or do we have *weak* consistency, and the assignments by one thread cannot be seen by a sibling parallel thread? In that case, we know for a fact that the read returns 0. (Observe that, with strong consistency, y := x may read 1 *or* 0.)

1.5   Transforming a Program Into a Parallel One

The overall goal is to remove constraints that overspecify the data flow, so as to give the computing device more freedom to handle instructions in parallel. Enhancing parallelism in programs through transformations is expected to eventually yield better performance at the price of possibly larger resource consumption. In the following sections, we informally explore two such typical transformations: commutation and expansion.

Let us consider three simple programs. The first one is

```
x := 2+3;
y := f(x)
```

Could we swap, or *commute*, the two statements and yet in the end get the same values in x and y? Not in general, because value x in the second statement might then be different from the one produced by the first statement. In other words, the flow of data x from its assignment in the first statement to its use in the second would be "broken."

For a second example, consider

```
y := f(x);
x := 2+3
```

Could we now commute the two statements? Again, no, since the value stored in variable x when applying function f would then *have* to be 5.

For a third program, now consider

```
1   x := 4+y;
2   x := 2+y+2
```

Could we now swap the two statements? At first sight, one may think that the two statements describe two independent computations, because adding 4 and y does not need the result of adding 2 and y and 2, and vice versa. Therefore, one may think the two statements can execute in any order. But imagine there is a third statement that eventually reads x:

```
3   y := f(x)
```

Then swapping the first two statements would mean statement **1**, not statement **2**, now gives x its final value. Therefore, x in statement **3** may be a different value. Of course, we all know that $4 + y = 2 + y + 2$, so in this case the swap is harmless. But how do we know that? It took us years of (elementary!) algebra to take it as *obvious*. Can we expect a compiler to discover such things? Probably not with current technology. In fact, because the expression 2 + y + 2 has a y between the two 2's, the compiler probably sees it as (2 + y) + 2. The added parentheses make it harder to detect that reordering the terms of the expression (an optimization known as *reassociation*) would give, say, (2 + 2) + y. In conclusion, when two statements write into the same location, we should stay on the safe side and avoid swapping them to preserve the data flow.

Notice also the contrast between the discussion above and nondeterminism. We check if two statements commute when we cannot assume the programmer accepts nondeterminism on x. We have to assume the two statements were written in the specified order for a good reason.

1.6 Another Typical Transformation: Expansion

We have seen that reusing a variable in a program saves memory space but may hinder parallel execution, as it introduces a dependency between the statements: The second statement re-uses a memory location used by the first one.

Consider the following program skeleton:

```
1   x := ...;
2   ...   := x;
3   x := ...;
4   ...   := x
```

We assume here that the variable x does not appear in the ellipsis "...". The value of x defined in statement 1 is read in statement 2. We say Definition 1 *reaches* statement 2, or that statement 1 is the *reaching definition* of statement 2. We denote this property by

$$RD(2) = \{1\}$$

which means that the set of definitions that may reach **2** consists of one and only one element—more on this later. Then, another value is written into x in statement **3** and read in statement **4**. Clearly, the definition of x in statement **1** does not reach **4**: Only statement **3** does. Therefore, $RD(4) = \{3\}$.

Therefore, it is clear that statements **2** and **3** cannot be swapped without a potential modification of the final result. (Again, note this may not be the case for some particular instance of the ellipsis, but we do not want to depend on any deeper analysis of their contents.) The computing device has to execute **1**, then **2**, then **3**, then **4**.

However, we can introduce two new variables:

```
1   x1 := ...;
2   ...   := x1;
3   x2 := ...;
4   ...   := x2
```

Interestingly, the text of the program now makes it obvious that **1** reaches **2** and only **2**. Of course, references to x after **4** also have to be changed to references to x2 for the final values to be consistent with those in the original program. In other words, the definition of x2 in statement **3** (but not that of x1 in **1**) may reach statements following **4**.

Now, statements **1** and **2** are independent of statements **3** and **4**, and we can safely write

```
( x1 := ...  ; ...    := x1 ) //
( x2 := ...  ; ...    := x2 )
```

leaving the computing device the freedom of interleaving the execution of the two statements. We say that variable x has been *expanded* into x1 and x2. We have traded memory space for execution freedom and a potential improvement in performance.

Is that the entire story? No, of course, since the control flow may not be known when the transformation is applied or may be too complex to be analyzed. Consider, for instance, the following program:

```
1   x := ...;
2   if for then x := ...;
3   if bar then x := ...;
4   result := x
```

Here, foo and bar stand for two complex expressions whose outcome may not be predicted by simple means. Can we swap **2** and **3**? The answer is no at this state of affairs. Let us now expand x:

```
1   x := ...;
2   if foo then x1 := ...;
3   if bar then x2 := ...;
4   result := ?
```

Where should statement **4** then read from? If bar yields true, then the question mark should be x2. If bar yields false, and if foo yields true, the question mark should be x1. Otherwise, it should be x. To wrap this up, the question mark in **4** should be an expression looking like this:

$$\phi(foo, bar, x, x_1, x_2) = \begin{cases} x_2 & \text{if } bar \\ x_1 & \text{if } foo \wedge \neg bar \\ x & \text{otherwise} \end{cases}$$

Function ϕ dynamically restores the data flow that was lost by expanding variable x.[5] Now, **2** and **3** can safely be swapped, so the computing device gained some freedom and

---

[5]The similarity with ϕ-functions in the SSA framework is intentional. More on this in Chapter 8.

a potential improvement in performance. Yet the cost is higher than above: Not only did memory space increase, but also function ϕ has to be evaluated. This tradeoff between weakening constraints on the execution order and increasing resource consumption (memory space, computing power, etc.) is at the heart of this book.

1.7 Yet Another Transformation: Contraction

We have seen that we can trade constraints on the execution order against execution resources. Of course, this depends on the priority: Do we consider execution time as the primary goal, at the expense of computing resources?

In some cases, it may be valuable to apply the inverse transformation to a program: Instead of expanding it, just contract it to save memory space. This is actually a common transformation for beginning programmers and (rather dumb) compilers: Each time a temporary memory location is needed, reuse a variable.

Consider a program of the form

```
1   x1 := ...;
2   ...    := x1;
3   x2 := ...;
4   ...    := x2
```

and assume that the values of x1 and x2 are not considered as *interesting* with respect to the result of the program, that is, they are not output variables. Assume also as usual that the ellipses do not contain any reference to these variables. Therefore, one can safely *contract* this program into

```
1   x := ...;
2   ...    := x;
3   x := ...;
4   ...    := x
```

Observe that contraction, as well as expansion, refers to memory space and not to program size.

A classical example of contraction is register allocation, because compilers must indeed map an arbitrarily large data set in the source code to a fixed set of registers. Another example that takes place in source-to-source program transformation is the topic of Chapter 9.

1.8 Dealing with Statement Instances

In cooking recipes, a single line of the recipe text may specify to repeat an operation several times. Just consider the statement, "Break each of the eggs into the bowl." We have to carefully distinguish the textual description of the operation from the successive actions it implies. Each of these actions is called an *instance* of the (textual) statement.

Similarly, in all the programs we have seen so far, each statement executes at most once. However, all programming languages provide a way to go through a single program line several times using branches, loops, procedure calls, etc. In fact, popular wisdom says that 90% of the execution time of a program is spent in 10% of its source code. This means that, grossly speaking, a statement generates either a single instance or a large number of them.

A typical loop looks as follows:

```
for i := 1 to n
  S
end for
```

Each time program execution reaches the program line that contains S, the corresponding statement (or statements) executes again. The purpose of the for construct is to remind us of formulas in elementary math: $\forall i, i \leq 1 \leq n : S(i)$. However, the program above is said to be *imperative* because it requires executing what S says, whereas the mathematical formula states that S is a *fact* for all valid i's. A consequence is that the mathematical expression implies no order on the values of i. It would be meaningless to say that $S(1)$ holds *before* $S(2)$ holds. In contrast, the for construct does prescribe an order: S should be executed first when i equals 1 and *then* when i equals 2.[6] Both expressions, however, share some similarities. First, both expressions have a *bound variable* i whose value ranges from 1 to n. Very often, such a bound variable serves as a "placeholder": Its name does not mean anything; it basically helps to express a set of possibilities. Also, both expressions feature a *free variable* n, whose value is not given in the context.

Free variables appear very often in compilation. They correspond to constants, which nearly all programming languages allow to be expressed and which are often called *symbolic constants*. However, the value of these constants may not be known to the compiler or even to the programmer: The value of a constant may be provided by the user at run time or defined in a separate source file, etc. Therefore, we might not know how many times the loop above iterates (even if we know it iterates exactly n times).

Reasoning about the control and data flow of programs requires being careful about instances. Indeed, a loop may generate a fixed number of instances:

```
for i := 1 to 10 do
    a := a + 1
end
```

Another construct, while, allows us to iterate a statement but does not give the iteration count. In contrast to the for loop, it gives only the condition under which another iteration takes place:

```
while (some condition on a) do
    a := a + 1
end
```

Some languages, however, offer a version of the while loop with an explicit counter. This control structure has the following syntax in this book:

---

[6]An unordered equivalent of the for loop is the parallel forall loop we saw page on 7.

```
while (some condition on a and/or w) do w := 1 begin
    a := a + 1
end while
```

In that case, w is supposed to be a variable whose scope is the immediate surrounding scope. It is also supposed to be initialized to zero upon entering the scope. That is, if the while loop does not iterate at all, the value of w after end while is defined and equals 0.

A while loop may trigger an infinite number of iterations. An obvious example is

```
while (true) do
    a := a + 1
end
```

but many infinite while loops are not so easy to detect.

Data flow actually deals with instances, and not with textual instructions: The value written by one instance is read by another instance. Consider the following program, where instructions have been labeled for the sake of clarity.

```
1    a := 0;
2    for i := 1 to 10 do
3        a := a + 1
4    endfor
```

The one and only instance of instruction **1** is executed first, then 10 instances of instruction **3**. We haven't yet decided how to name these instances, but let's just denote them with $3^{first}, \ldots, 3^{tenth}$ for the moment. The value read by instance 3^{first} is the one written by the single instance of **1**. By contrast, the value read by the second instance 3^{second} of statement **3** is the value written by the first instance of the *same* statement **3**. This "loop-carried" data flow goes on until the value produced by 3^{ninth} is consumed by the last instance, 3^{tenth}.

This example shows that contrasting instances is important to precisely understand the dynamic behavior of a program and that being able to *name* these instances is also a must. Indeed, we intuitively feel the notations above are awkward. We have to find better ones!

1.9 Parameters

Using English words like "first" and "second" is not the reason why the above notations are awkward. Using numbers is only a tiny step forward: Indeed, writing

$$RD(3^{10}) = \{3^9\}$$

is not much clearer. More importantly, we still have to enumerate *all possible cases*, that is, to state that $RD(3^9) = \{3^8\}$, that $RD(3^8) = \{3^7\}$, and so on. Obviously, doing that would be painful if the loop iterated 1000 times.

It can be even worse. Imagine the previous loop iterates n times instead of 10. Yes, we do mean n times, where n is unspecified. This often occurs in real programs, because the iteration count may be provided by the user or computed on the fly.

So we have to find a general way of describing this relationship, a formula that captures the set of all possible cases with as few "symbols" as possible. We say we want a description *in intention* (the formula just says what the set "intends" to include), not *in extension* (the description does not show the "extent" of the set). A mathematical formula that works in intention is called a *closed form*. An example of a closed form that captures the reaching definitions in the on-going example is

$$RD(\mathbf{3}^i) = \{\mathbf{3}^{i-1}\}$$

where i is an integer greater than or equal to 2 and less than or equal to 10.

Notice that not only is the above closed form very small (if you are not convinced, write down the enumeration of all cases one by one), but it also makes immediately obvious one interesting thing: Nothing is said for i equal to 1. In general, such special cases are made obvious when checking the validity conditions of closed forms.

1.10   What This Book Is About

What you just read tries to give the intuitions guiding this book: We focus on analyses that extract the flow of data, which imperative programming hides through its use and reuse of memory. We detail some program transformations that conserve this data flow. We introduce a family of analyses, called reaching definition analyses, but also sometimes array data-flow analysis or value-based dependencies, to do this task. We show that correctness of program transformations (assuming again that functions and operations are preserved by the transformation) is guaranteed by the conservation of data flow. We study how to make data flow explicit, using single-assignment forms, and how to better use memory, using expansion and contraction, while improving performance using parallelization.

1.11   What This Book Is Not About

This book is neither an introduction to programming nor a survey of compilation techniques. On purpose, this book does not provide a single algorithm for compilers.

This book focuses on one key characteristic of programs: the flow of data. Other key features, such as which functions or operators are applied to which data are not studied, and we assume these functions are never changed. The reader should be aware that most reaching definition analyses we present are not based on iterative computations of fixed points of equation systems but on symbolic solvers. In addition, dependence tests for arrays are not discussed much in this book, and the interested reader is referred to [5, 6]. In fact, we do discuss dependence tests in Chapter 7, showing that such tests are in fact conservative but easy-to-implement ways to guarantee that the flow of data is preserved.

Also, the program transformations detailed in this book focus on how imperative programs use memory. For a comprehensive description of other transformations, an up-to-date reference is [68].

Finally, we hint in the conclusion about automatic algorithm recognition. A nice path for program transformation is to recognize an algorithm from the program text and to replace it by an equivalent, "better" algorithm. Automatic recognition and replacement of algorithms have enjoyed much popularity in recent research. However, this builds a whole separate field of computer science in its own, and readers interested in this approach are referred to the corresponding literature.

Part I

Basic Concepts

Chapter 2

Describing Program Executions

Since this book deals with reasoning about program transformations, we intend to analyze and manipulate program texts to enhance certain properties of their execution: leaving more freedom to the computing devices in ordering the individual operations, reducing the number of auxiliary memory locations needed during execution, and so on.

Choosing one imperative programming language, say C, would have perhaps been more appealing to some readers—but not to, say, Pascal fans. However, the two main reasons we use a toy language in this book are much more important. First, choosing any single language would force us to address language features not relevant to our discussion. (As an example, we want to consider real, simple for loops where the lower and upper bounds of the loop counter are evaluated once and the loop is iterated for all counter values in that interval. This would exclude the C language for instance, since its for construct is a more powerful but also more dangerous type of loop.) Addressing these specific features could be interesting, but the book would lose its focus. Second, a simple toy language that captures the salient features of imperative programming languages abstracts our discussion away from the idiosyncracies of any real language. It also provides clean support for presenting concepts and transformations that apply to imperative programming in general. The section that follows presents this toy language. Being extremely simple, the language does not take long to describe.

If the source code of a program gives each instruction to be executed, it gives little information on the sequences of computations that will actually be performed. A classical representation of a program is the control-flow graph, which indicates which instructions (or blocks of instructions) may follow any given one. Execution sequences can be obtained "one step at a time" following the links (or "edges") in this graph. We argue that this approach has two main limitations. First, a control-flow graph does not express certain useful properties of the execution of the given program, properties that can be captured and exploited by symbolic processing. Second, a control-flow graph does not differentiate instances of a given statement. When you traverse a control-flow graph, either a given instruction can be reached or it can't. We have no way, or no direct way at least, to tell whether it is the first time you reach that statement. More

19

importantly, we have no way to say this is nth instance of the statement (the nth time the statement is reached) and to reason about the $(n - 1)$th or the $(n + 1)$th time—in other words, we cannot *parameterize* executions of statements. A control-flow graph is an abstraction of a program, but an abstraction where some information is lost.

In contrast, our standpoint in this book is to leverage on recent symbolic tools. We abstract program executions as a set, the set of statement instances, augmented with an order (the execution order) and a mapping on memory states (a memory state gives values to program variables, but, due to the very nature of imperative programming, each statement instance may change this state). We see that for certain kinds of analyses and transformations, and when certain syntactical restrictions are placed on programs, we can reason about program executions using these concepts only and without the need for a control-flow graph.

We also address a key issue in program analysis that is independent of the program abstraction: compile-time approximation. Indeed, we cannot know when compiling a program (nor when staring at a program) exactly what its executions will look like. So we have to approximate a given property so that it is valid for all executions while retaining the expected level of precision.

2.1 Language and Statements

The toy language we use in this book provides a (large enough, but *finite!*) set of *variables*: x, y, etc. *Expressions* are built from variables and mathematical functions: x + y, x > y, f(x,y), etc. Observe that constants are a particular case of expressions, namely functions with arity zero.

As a special case of program variables, we consider *indexed variables*, such as t[1]. They correspond to the traditional notion of array, as found in the Pascal or Java language, for instance. Unless otherwise specified, we disregard any problem with array bounds: We just assume that we are careful enough to write sensible things. Indexes may just be any expressions, including variables, and even indexed variables themselves: t[i], t[t[i]], etc. Also, we admit multiple indexes, an abstraction for multidimensional arrays. Nonindexed variables are called *scalar* variables.

In this book we limit ourselves to only two types of values: either integers or Boolean values "true" and "false" denoted by **true** and **false**, respectively. Considering other types of values, like real numbers, would not add value to this book.

Exercise 2.1 Using indexed variables as indices, also known as indirect indexing, introduces an additional level of difficulty in reasoning about programs, very much like pointer aliasing in the C language, for instance. As an example consider the following pathological case due to Dijkstra. We assume the values of elements of x are either 0 or 1.

```
1   x[0] := 0;
2   x[1] := 0;
3   x[x[0]] := 1;
4   if (x[x[0]] = 1)
```

```
5   then b := true
6   else b := false
```

What is the value of variable *b* at the end of this program? What conclusion can you draw from this example? ■

An *assignment* is a program instruction of the form

```
x := e
```

The variable on the *left-hand side* (LHS, for short) is *written* by the assignment, and variables appearing in the expression on the *right-hand side* (RHS, for short) are read by (are read when executing) the assignment. A variable may change its value only if it is written by some assignment.

A variable may, of course, be both read and written by an assignment: `x := x+1`. Observe that the variables may be scalar variables or indexed variables: `t[i] := (t[i+1] + t[i-1])/2`. It will prove useful to provide an assignment that does nothing. It is denoted by `skip`. It neither reads nor writes any variable.

A *program* is made up of statements. A statement may consist of an assignment:

$$\text{skip} \quad \text{or} \quad \text{x := e}$$

A statement may be a choice between two statements, depending on some Boolean expression *b*:

$$\text{if b then T1 else T2}$$

It may be a *sequential composition* of two statements:

$$\text{T1; T2}$$

It may be the bounded iteration of a statement, indexed by a scalar variable i ranging between two bounds n_1 and n_2:

$$\text{for i := n1 to n2 do T end}$$

Notice that we enforce n1 and n2 to be evaluated before entering the loop.

If $n_1 > n_2$, then nothing is done, as with `skip`. Otherwise, the loop body T is executing first with *i* set to n_1, then *i* set to $n_1 + 1$, and so on, up to and including n_2. It is not allowed to *write* i within the loop body, in contrast with the `for` iteration construct of the C language, so that there are exactly $n_2 - n_1 + 1$ iterations if $n_2 \geq n_1$. Finally, a statement may consist of iterating another statement while some predicate *b* remains true:

```
while b do S endwhile
```

Of course, such an iteration may be infinite: `while true do skip end`.

This small set of possible statements is sufficient at this time. The set of statements of a *real* language such as Fortran or C is obviously much larger, but similar in spirit. They could be accommodated within such a framework with some effort.

2.2 Program States, Computations, and Paths

It is now time to provide a formal way to talk about program executions. In other words, we want a framework that captures the set of executions a computing device may generate when running the program, and we want to reason about how to transform these executions. Of course, it is out of the scope of this book to address the specific behavior of each kind of processor, memory, bus, etc. Instead, we consider a mathematical notion of computation that abstracts away most kinds of computing devices we have in mind, say, uniprocessor PCs.

The underlying mathematical theory is called *structured operational semantics*, or SOS for short. Plotkin introduced it in the early 1980s to reason about systems of communicating sequential processes (CSP). The interested reader will find an introduction to SOS in [70]. In this book we refrain from going into technical details: We only introduce the intuitive concepts, as needed for the following chapters.

A *memory state*, or just state for short, is a mapping of variables to values. A memory state maps a variable x to its value x. Memory states are modified by assignments—in this book we assume there are no other "sideeffects." At this level of abstraction, we disregard all problems of typing, just as we disregard all problems with array bounds.

An expression e is essentially a mapping from memory states to values. For instance, we can identify expression x + y with the mapping that maps the current memory state to $x + y$. Observe that this implicitly assumes that the expressions are all *pure*, that is, evaluating an expression does not modify the memory state by side effect. The variables appearing in the expression are said to be *read*: The value of the expression depends on their values only. In other terms, if we are given an expression e and two states that coincide on all variables appearing in e, then the value of e is the same in both of them.

A *point of control* (PC, for short) is a place in the program text. A *program state* is a pair made up of a PC and a memory state. A program state does not say anything about the *past* of the computation or about the way this state was reached: It does not provide any direct information about how many times loops were iterated, about which branches were selected in choices, etc. However, a program state fully determines the *future* of the computation: its *continuation*. Starting the program at this point of control and in this memory state completely determines what will happen next.

A program *execution* is a legal sequence of program states. For a deterministic program, an execution of a program is completely determined by the initial state of memory, that is, by the values of all input variables at the execution start point, which we denote $\perp$ (read "bottom") by convention.

For our purposes, however, we often forget about memory states and consider only the sequence of points of control in a given program execution. This sequence of points of control is called a (execution) *trace*. So we tend to say "program execution" when "program trace" would be more correct.

> For the sake of simplicity, we identify program executions and their traces when no confusion may arise.

There is a caveat here. This simplification can be treacherous because different program executions having the same execution trace can have very different properties.

Consider the example shown in Figure 2.1.

. . . .

```
1   read i;
2   a[i] := 0
```

. . . . *Figure 2.1. The importance of memory states.* . . . .

Statement **1** reads the value of i from the keyboard. At compile time we have no idea what this value will be. We know, however, that only one execution trace is possible (**1** then **2**, assuming no exception occurred in **1**). Still, the set of memory locations potentially modified by this program is as large as array a.

Throughout this book, the set of possible execution traces for a given program P is denoted by $\mathcal{E}_P$ or simply $\mathcal{E}$ since the program under consideration is often clear from the context. However, computing $\mathcal{E}$ for a given program can be difficult or even impossible. Yet, being able to reason about this set proves to be very useful in the sequel.

Any prefix of an execution trace corresponds to a step in executions, just after one statement instance executes and just before another execution takes place. So if we consider a given step p in execution trace e, we can be unambiguous when talking about values of variables. Now, do you remember that x denotes the value of x in the "current" memory state? "Current" was ambiguous, indeed. We can be more specific and talk about the value of a textual expression in the memory state corresponding to step p of a possible trace. We denote by

$$[\![x]\!]_p^e$$

the value of x at p during execution e. When discussing a statement, the "step" under consideration occurs just before executing that statement. Consider the program fragment below:

```
1   x := 0
2   y := x
```

For a given execution e, the value $[\![x]\!]_1^e$ is unknown—statement **1** has not been executed yet. However, we do have $[\![x]\!]_2^e = 0$.

Also,

$$[\![x+y]\!]_p^e$$

is the value of the expression x + y at p and is equal to $[\![x]\!]_p^e + [\![y]\!]_p^e$.[1] The value of a[i] at p is denoted as

$$[\![a[i]]\!]_p^e$$

Notice that a[$[\![i]\!]_p^e$] does not denote a value but instead a memory location: the element of array a whose index equals the value of i at p. The value contained in this

---

[1] With a functional language, we might also want to consider the value $[\![+]\!]_p^e$ of + itself, which is a function.

memory location is $[\![a\,[\,[\![i]\!]_p^e\,]\,]\!]_p^e$, or equivalently $[\![a\,[\,i\,]\,]\!]_p^e$. Notice also that it makes perfect sense to consider

$$[\![a\,[\,[\![i]\!]_q^e\,]\,]\!]_p^e$$

with p distinct from q. This denotes the value at p of an element of a whose index equals the value of i at q.

Reasoning on Executions

One possible way of grasping programming executions is to draw a *control-flow graph*. In a control-flow graph, a node represents a program state. Nodes are connected by edges, which represent statements—indeed, statements change one program state to another. (Alternatively, we could also take the dual definition where statements are nodes and transfer of control is represented by edges.) A trace is then materialized by a possible path in the control-flow graph.

....

```
1   if foo then
2      x := 42
3   else
4      x := 43
5   endif
```

.... *Figure 2.2. Execution traces.* ....

For instance, consider the simple program in Figure 2.2. Two traces are possible: either **125** or **145**. The set of possible execution traces, or *execution set*, is therefore $\mathcal{E} = \{125, 145\}$.

> Notice also that there are several ways to give names to execution traces. In the trace names above, explicitly mentioning statement **5** doesn't add any information because we *have* to go through this statement anyway. The same holds with statement **3** (which is not even an actual statement, but the beginning of the second part of the if statement). Indeed, we can talk without ambiguity about traces **12** and **14**.

Considering possible executions has a very strong impact on analyses explored in this book. Because of this, control-flow graphs are not enough. To see why, consider the example in Figure 2.3. Figure 2.3 also displays the program's control-flow graph: Edges are labeled by their corresponding statements. Edges **3** and **6** correspond to the "else" parts (of the fall-through) of conditionals in **1** and **4**, respectively. Following the control-flow graph blindly, we *always* end up with four possible traces in the execution set, no matter what foo is:

$$\mathcal{E} = \{012457, 012467, 013457, 013467\}$$

```
0  x := 0
1  if foo then
2      x := 2
3      (else do nothing)
   endif
4  if foo then
5      x := 3
6      (else do nothing)
   endif
7  y := x
```

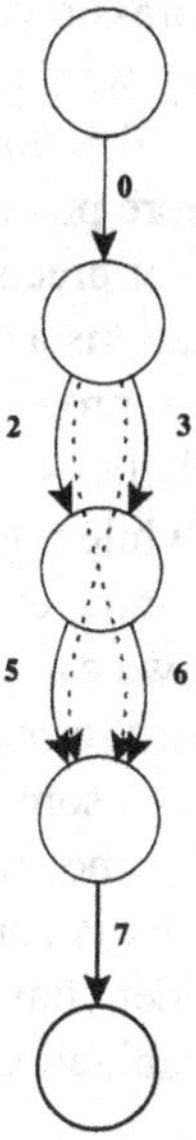

Figure 2.3. Illustrating impossible execution paths.

However, imagine foo does not read x. Then, execution flows either through both **2** and **5** or through neither of them. This is exactly the kind of property a control-flow graph can't express. Indeed, two impossible execution paths are depicted by dotted lines in the figure, but nothing in a control-flow graphs allows you to see this.

This simple example illustrates one caveat we have to face when choosing a representation for execution sets. Control-flow graphs have the advantage of being well known, but blindly relying on them is dangerous. In other words, control-flow graphs don't allow us to build the exact execution set when the above assumption holds, $\mathcal{E} = \{\mathbf{1257}, \mathbf{1367}\}$.

The Problem of Compile-Time Approximation   Being able to precisely capture which traces are possible and which are not is extremely important in compilers. The previous section showed how some frameworks to express execution sets can have an edge on others. However, this information can seldom be perfectly precise. In the example of Figure 2.3, we have, even in the best case, at least two possible execution paths to take into account.

Indeed, when a compiler compiles a program for the first time, it has no information on execution patterns this program may have. Some execution paths that seem feasible when we look at a program may happen to be unfeasible. Some program parts will always be executed, what ever the input values are, and some never will.

Going back to the example of Figure 2.3 and assuming foo does not read x, the compiler can safely eliminate the assignment x := 0 of **2** because, whenever this assignment executes, it is overwritten by **5** before x could be read anywhere. (If this code transformation does not appeal to you, just imagine the right-hand side of statement **2** is a long expression to evaluate, like x := x * x * x * x.) Another task the compiler may want to do is to try and figure out the value of x in **7**. Using the control-flow graph and following the four possible paths, the value of x in **7** is 0 *or* 2 *or* 3. Using the more precise execution set, the only possible values are 0 and 3.

The lack of precise knowledge on execution paths has an impact on all the analyses and optimizations a compiler may want to apply to a program. In other words, a compiler has to approximate some information, to remember that some information may or may not hold—and to live with it, that is, to keep optimizing the program as much as possible while preserving correctness. One perspective is to say that 0 is a possible or "maybe" value of x. Another way to consider things is to say that the most precise information we can deliver is the *union* of all possible values.

A bit more formally, one way to think about the nonpredictability of executions is to reason about some generic execution e and to consider all possible executions when implementing the analysis—that is, to consider all elements $e \in \mathcal{E}$. In mathematical symbols, if P_e is some property that depends on execution e, then a compiler writer has to consider some combination of all P_e's. If the property is defined by sets, then possible combinations include the union of all possible values of the property:

$$\bigcup_{e \in \mathcal{E}} P_e$$

and their intersection:

$$\bigcap_{e \in \mathcal{E}} P_e$$

As an example, consider the value of x at **5** in Figure 2.2, during an execution e. P_e here is $P_e = \{[\![x]\!]_5^e\}$. If we are interested in all possible values of x, the first approximation is appropriate:

$$\bigcup_{e \in \{125,145\}} P_e = \{42, 43\}$$

If we want to check if x has only one possible value, however, the property becomes

$$\bigcap_{e \in \{125,145\}} P_e = \emptyset$$

Because a compiler, or a human, does not in general have a perfect knowledge of $\mathcal{E}$, it might have to settle for a sub- or superset, that is, a set P such that either

$$\bigcup_{e \in \mathcal{E}} P_e \subseteq P$$

or

$$P \subseteq \bigcap_{e \in \mathcal{E}} P_e$$

In a sense, we already saw an example of approximation by taking the union of all possible executions: when computing the execution set $\mathcal{E}$ itself. For instance, the execution set for the program shown in Figure 2.2 was approximated as the union of $\{125\}$ and $\{145\}$, resulting in $\{125, 145\}$.

Alternatively, if P_e is a Boolean property, the combination may be the disjunction

$$\bigvee_{e \in \mathcal{E}} P_e$$

or the conjunction

$$\bigwedge_{e \in \mathcal{E}} P_e$$

This, of course, leads to a similar approximation P, defined by either

$$\bigvee_{e \in \mathcal{E}} P_e \Rightarrow P \qquad (2.1)$$

or

$$P \Rightarrow \bigwedge_{e \in \mathcal{E}} P_e \qquad (2.2)$$

depending on the intent.

....

```
1   i := 0; j := 0; k := 0;
2   while ...  do
3      i := i+4;
4      if ...
5         then j := j+4
6         else j := j+12
7      endif
8      k := k+4;
9      print i, j, k;
10  endwhile
11  print i
```

.... *Figure 2.4. An example, taken from [40].* ....

Consider again the program in Figure 2.4, which we introduced in Chapter 1. The value of i in statement **11** may be 0 for some execution, 4 for another, etc. We could then say that an approximation of the value of i is given by the set $\{0, 4, 8, \ldots\}$. By making sure the actual final value of i is included in the answer the analysis gives, we make a *conservative* or "safe" approximation.

It is important here to understand that the way a conservative approximation is done depends on the question being asked. If you ask, "Is the final value of i equal to 12?" then there are two ways to answer your question: On the one hand, we could answer "no," because we have no guarantee that, for any given program run, the value will be 12. In this case, the answer would be the conjunction (the "and" $\bigwedge$) of all possible answers for all possible executions. On the other hand, we could answer "yes," because indeed we can find *one or more* program executions, that is, at least one initial memory state, for which the final value is 12. In that case, the "or" $\bigvee$ solution has been picked. Both ways are possible and can make sense. It all depends on the question being asked and what the answer will be used for.

2.3   Statement Instances

In the last example, we discussed the possible values of i in statement **11**. Choosing statement **11** was an easy pick, because this statement has at most one instance in the course of program execution.[2] Reasoning about values of i in statement **9** is more difficult for the moment because we still haven't decided how to name statement instances. Indeed, this is on purpose: We first want to define the "specifications" the naming convention must meet before we actually settle on a convention. To do so, let us enumerate which concepts it should allow us to manipulate.

First, let us denote with $\mathcal{S}$ the set of all statements in a given program. For a given execution $e \in \mathcal{E}$ of the program, the set of instances of a given statement **S** is called the *domain* of **S** and is denoted with $\mathcal{D}_e(\mathbf{S})$. As an example, consider the program shown in Figure 2.3. For execution trace $e = \mathbf{012457}$, the domain of statement **2** is $\mathcal{D}_e(\mathbf{S}) = \{\mathbf{2}\}$. The latter equation just captures that statement **2** is executed exactly once during execution e. On the other hand, during execution $e = \mathbf{013457}$, for example, statement **2** does not execute and its domain is empty.

We can then define the set $\mathcal{I}_e$ of all instances spawned by all statements, for a given execution e: We gather all instances of all possible statements, as written formally below:

$$\mathcal{I}_e = \bigcup_{\mathbf{S} \in \mathcal{S}} \mathcal{D}_e(\mathbf{S})$$

Of course, the exact set of instances of a given statement **S** cannot always be known exactly at compile time. Therefore, a conservative approximation $\mathcal{D}(\mathbf{S})$ has to be defined. This approximate domain is a set characterized by

$$\bigcup_{e \in \mathcal{E}} \mathcal{D}_e(\mathbf{S}) \subseteq \mathcal{D}(\mathbf{S}) \tag{2.3}$$

which boils down to saying that any "collective" domain of **S** should contain at least all domains for all possible executions traces.

As an example, let us consider Figure 2.3. The domain of statement **2** must contain $\{\mathbf{2}\}$ and the empty set. Therefore, $\{\mathbf{2}\}$ is an acceptable domain for **2**. Indeed, it would be difficult to add any other element to this domain! In general, domains are obvious in programs that contain no loops and no calls. The domain of statement **2** in Figure 2.5 contains all 10 instances. In Figure 2.4, the domain of statement, say, **3** contains an unbounded number of instances.

Remember also that $\mathcal{D}(\mathbf{S})$ is in general not unique and that any approximation satisfying constraint (2.3) can be called "the domain of **S**." Obviously, the concrete form $\mathcal{D}(\mathbf{S})$ takes in a compiler depends on the precision of the program analysis.

---

[2]If the `while` loop does not terminate, it has no instance.

....

```
1   for i := 1 to 10
2     x := x + i
3   endfor
```

.... *Figure 2.5. Simple loop with a recurrence.* ....

The set $\mathcal{I}$ of all possible statement instances in a program is defined in a similar way. It is set at least as large as the union, for all possible executions, of instance sets during these executions:

$$\bigcup_{e \in \mathcal{E}} \mathcal{I}_e \subseteq \mathcal{I}$$

Without any "oracle" knowledge on execution patterns, we know that $\mathcal{I}$ is any superset of the union of all possible $\mathcal{I}_e$'s. For approximations $\mathcal{I}$ and $\mathcal{D}$ to be consistent, we require that

$$\mathcal{I} = \bigcup_{S \in \mathcal{S}} \mathcal{D}(S)$$

Notice the equality in the latter equation. Approximation, if need be, is supposed to be already "included" in sets $\mathcal{D}(S)$.

By convention, the execution's starting point $\perp$ is also an instance included in $\mathcal{I}$. Instance $\perp$ often serves as a "don't-know" answer by analyses (more on this in Chapter 5).

2.4 Memory

In a first approach, we view memory as a nonstructured set of locations denoted with set $\mathcal{M}$. Memory is updated by assignments, which we assume contain at most one write each. A generic assignment has the following form:

S `lhs := foo(rhs_1,...,rhs_n)`

This implies, in particular, that statements with double side effects, like `a[i++]=0` in C, are supposed to be split. During a given execution e, any instance u of a statement is thus associated with (at most) one element, call it m, of $\mathcal{M}$, which we denote by $\mathsf{write}_e(u) = \mathrm{m}$.

For a given execution e, this mapping write from $\mathcal{I}$ to $\mathcal{M}$ that maps an instance to (the label of) the memory location is called a *store mapping*. To sum this up in one short equation, this mapping takes an element of the set $\mathcal{E}$ of executions and an instance of some statement and yields the memory location this instance writes into:

$$\mathsf{write} : \mathcal{E} \times \mathcal{I} \to \mathcal{M}$$

Since statements are assumed to have at most one side effect (the one in the left-hand expression), the name of the variable being written is not needed. A statement with several side effects can be cut into smaller statements with one side effect each. Otherwise, the store mapping above can easily be extended to accommodate several side effects. Its signature then becomes

$$\text{write} : \ \mathcal{E} \times \mathcal{I} \times \text{Text} \rightarrow \mathcal{M}$$

An equivalent solution would be to change the granularity of our framework: Instead of reasoning on instances of *statements*, we could reason on instances of *references* to memory, or instances of any subexpression for that matter. Any evaluation of a syntactical object (a piece of program text) can be uniquely labeled with a pair

$$\langle \text{statement instance, expression} \rangle$$

and such pairs would become the basic unit of reasoning in this book. The signature of the store mapping would become

$$\text{write} : \ \mathcal{E} \times (\mathcal{I} \times \text{Text}) \rightarrow \mathcal{M}$$

which isn't much different. Actually, we use this finer granularity at some point in this book but will refrain from doing so until absolutely necessary.

As an example, again consider the program in Figure 2.5. We have $\text{write}_e(u) = \text{x}$, where u is any instance of statement **2** and $\mathcal{M}$ is the symbolic set $\{\text{i}, \text{x}\}$ of variable names. Similarly, we have to define for a given execution a read mapping **read** from each read reference to the set of memory locations $\mathcal{M}$. In contrast to **write**, we have to specify which read references we are talking about since several variables may be accessed (typically, in the right-hand side of an assignment). In mathematical words, the read mapping takes three inputs (an execution, an instance, and a textual reference) and yields one output, the memory location being read:

$$\text{read} : \ \mathcal{E} \times \mathcal{I} \times \text{Text} \rightarrow \mathcal{M}$$

If we still assume that $\mathcal{M}$ is the symbolic set of variable names, the *read mapping* for the same example is

$$\forall e \in \mathcal{E}, \ \text{read}_e(\langle u, \text{x} \rangle) = \text{x}$$

for any instance u of statement **2** and for the first reference appearing in the right-hand side.

Of course, this formula looks a bit obvious. However, remember that $\mathcal{M}$ may be more complicated–it could, for instance, be the set of addresses in virtual memory, so $\mathcal{M}$ would be (a subset of) $\mathbb{N}$. In the case of advanced data structures, $\mathcal{M}$ can be more complex.

Whenever possible, and to simplify notation, we use examples where statements have only one read reference and the second argument of read is dropped. In symbols

$$\text{read} : \ \mathcal{E} \times \mathcal{I} \rightarrow \mathcal{M}$$

Note that execution e must be, and is, taken into account. If you are not convinced, just imagine that we added a statement to Figure 2.2, as shown in Figure 2.6. For

```
1  if foo then
2     x := 42;
3  else
4     x := 43;
5  endif
6  a[x] := 0
```

.. *Figure 2.6. Execution traces and accessed memory locations are tightly linked.* ..

execution $e = \mathbf{125}$, the modified element of a is $\mathsf{write}_e(\mathbf{6}) = \mathsf{a[42]}$, whereas for execution $e = \mathbf{145}$, we have $\mathsf{write}_e(\mathbf{6}) = \mathsf{a[43]}$.

These definitions can naturally be extended to statements, that is, we might be interested more in the compound effect of a statement than in the effects of all individual statement instances. For that purpose, we can define similar mappings for any statement $\mathbf{S}$ and any execution e:

$$\mathsf{write}_e(\mathbf{S}) = \bigcup_{u \in \mathcal{D}_e(\mathbf{S})} \mathsf{write}_e(u)$$

Taking executions into account is useful but sometimes difficult, because it can be hard or even impossible to foresee all possible executions of a program. It may then be enough to reason about the set of all possible effects of a statement or a statement instance for all possible executions, or a conservative approximation of this set. To this purpose, we introduce, for any statement $\mathbf{S}$, the set $\mathsf{write}(\mathbf{S})$ of memory locations that statement may access. This set should satisfy

$$\bigcup_{e \in \mathcal{E}} \mathsf{write}_e(\mathbf{S}) \subseteq \mathsf{write}(\mathbf{S}) \tag{2.4}$$

which requires that $\mathsf{write}(\mathbf{S})$ include memory locations written during all possible executions.

We readily have a similar approximation at the instance level. The approximate set $\mathsf{write}(u)$ of side effects caused by an instance u contains all side effects appearing across all possible execution traces—provided, of course, the instance at hand executes in each of these traces:

$$\bigcup_{e \in \mathcal{E}, u \in \mathcal{I}_e} \mathsf{write}_e(u) \subseteq \mathsf{write}(u) \tag{2.5}$$

For the program in Figure 2.6, we have $\mathsf{write}(\mathbf{6}) \supseteq \{\mathsf{a[42]}, \mathsf{a[43]}\}$. Therefore, an analysis that would not track the values of x, or that would consider arrays as monolithic variables, could correctly (but imprecisely) derive that $\mathsf{write}(\mathbf{6})$ is the set of all elements of a. However, an analysis yielding just $\mathsf{write}(\mathbf{6}) = \{\mathsf{a[42]}\}$ would not be correct.

2.5 Execution Order

A program also specifies the *order* in which instances should execute. Let us denote this order with $\prec$, which is a relation on $\mathcal{I}_e \times \mathcal{I}_e$ for a given e. The execution order in sequential programs is *total*, meaning that any two computations u and v in a given program run $\mathcal{I}_e$ are executed one after the other, either $u \prec v$ or $v \prec u$. Indeed, during a given execution, statements are executed one at a time (execution goes from one point of control to the next), and instances of a statement (typically loop iterations) are also executed one at a time. As an example, in the program in Figure 2.2, two executions are possible, and the execution order is total in both cases: **1** then **2** then **5**, or **1** then **4** then **5**.

Notice that, by convention, $\perp$ belongs to any $\mathcal{I}_e$, for any e. We also postulate $\perp \prec u$ for any u of $\mathcal{I}_e$ distinct from $\perp$. In fact, we often omit $\perp$, as in the example we just gave.

This "order-centric" view of programs provides an elegant definition of parallel programs: A program is parallel if the execution order in some given program run is a *partial* order. In other words, there are an execution e and two instances u and v in $\mathcal{I}_e$ that are not *comparable* with respect to the execution order: Neither $u \prec v$ nor $v \prec u$ is true.

Order $\prec$ can be naturally extended to $\mathcal{I}$, meaning that it is also a relation on $\mathcal{I} \times \mathcal{I}$. However, $\prec$ on $\mathcal{I} \times \mathcal{I}$ may not be total even for sequential programs because there might be two statement instances not comparable with respect to execution order. There is no contradiction here: These instances simply cannot belong to the same execution e. We just "extended" order $\prec$ to $\mathcal{I}$. Consider the program in Figure 2.2 again. Statements **2** and **4** are not ordered by $\prec$, but this is just due to the fact that, even though both **2** and **4** belong to $\mathcal{I}$, there is no execution e such that both belong to $\mathcal{I}_e$.

Order $\prec$ allows us to capture several important properties of programs in a general and abstract way. Imagine, for example, that you want to define the first statement instance in a program execution e. This instance is simply defined as

$$\min_{\prec} \mathcal{I}_e \tag{2.6}$$

which by convention always equals $\perp$.

Similarly, the last program "computation" is defined as $\max_{\prec} \mathcal{I}_e$. Extrema with respect to $\prec$ can be extended to the case when the execution set is approximate. For example,

$$\max_{\prec} \mathcal{I} \tag{2.7}$$

denotes all instances that can be the last executed "computation" for some execution. Not surprisingly, the following property holds:

$$\bigcup_{e \in \mathcal{E}} \max_{\prec} \mathcal{I}_e \subseteq \max_{\prec} \mathcal{I}$$

As an example, consider again the simple program in Figure 2.2. As discussed earlier, the set $\mathcal{I}$ of instances consists of **1**, **2**, and **4** (we drop **5**). The instances that come last according to the execution order are $\max_{\prec} \mathcal{I} = \{\mathbf{2}, \mathbf{4}\}$.

Manipulating minima and maxima with respect to an execution order is not just a conceptual toy. It does have very down-to-earth applications, which we discuss throughout this book. As an example application, we use maxima on execution order to minimize the memory a program uses. Indeed, if we were to look for the last write into x in the program in Figure 2.5, we could define this problem as computing

$$\max_{\prec} \{u \: : \: u \in \mathcal{I}, \: x \in \mathsf{write}(u)\} \tag{2.8}$$

which is the 10th instance of statement **2**. More elaborate and more convincing examples will follow. Another case in point is scheduling, presented next.

2.6 Relations

So far, we have only been looking at properties holding for a given statement instance, or possibly for a set of instances (including the whole program execution). However, several problems that arise very naturally are *relative* properties valid between two instances.

Consider this question: Given an instance u and an order $\prec$, what is the set of all following instances in S? This question can be defined as finding the set mapping O:

$$O(u) = \{v \: : \: v \in S, u \prec v\}$$

This is, in fact, a relation between instances u and v, and like any relation between two "objects" u and v, this relation can be written as a set on the *tuple* (u, v)—in our example, this set is

$$\{(u, v) \: : \: u, v \in \mathcal{I}, \: u \prec v\}$$

It looks like the two sets above are alike, but in the former, u is (implicitly) given. In the second set, u comes as one of the variables.

Looking for instances writing to the same memory location is also a problem best expressed as a relation. The set of tuples corresponding to this relation may be written as

$$\{(u, v) \: : \: u, v \in \mathcal{I}, \: \mathsf{write}(u) \cap \mathsf{write}(v) \neq \emptyset\}$$

Notice that a more stringent definition could be

$$\{(u, v) \: : \: \exists e \in \mathcal{E}, \: u, v \in \mathcal{I}_e, \: \mathsf{write}_e(u) = \mathsf{write}_e(v)\}$$

The two definitions above make immediately clear what level of precision is required: In the first case, the set of all possible side effects is compared between the two instances, whereas in the second case, the side effects of both instances are compared on an execution trace basis. We come back to this point in Section 4.1.

Alternative Expressions of Extrema Minima and maxima of any set have an important property we would like to remind you of. By definition, the set of minima in a set S, with respect to an order $\prec$, is

$$\min_{\prec} S = \{x \: : \: x \in S, \: (\not\exists y : y \in S, \: y \prec x)\} \tag{2.9}$$

with a similar definition for the maximum. Equation (2.9) can be restated as

$$\min_{\prec} S = S \setminus \{x : x \in S, \ (\exists y : y \in S, \ y \prec x)\}$$

We just saw that order relation $\prec$ is also a mapping O. Then

$$(2.9) \iff \min_{\prec} S = S \setminus O(S) \qquad (2.10)$$

So we have two ways to solve an equation like (2.6): directly (using, for instance, integer linear programming), or indirectly using a symbolic solver to simplify either (2.9) or (2.10).

Taking Advantage of Associativity   It is pretty obvious to claim that the maximum element in a set is the same element as the maximum of, on the one hand, that element and, on the other hand, the maximum among all other elements in the set. This is just taking advantage of associativity. But it justifies a natural tendency when looking for the definition reaching a given instance: We tend to look at the immediately preceding write to the same memory location. If we are sure that previous instance executes, then the reaching definition is found. Otherwise, we start again *from that previous instance*. In other words, we go backward in program execution until we find a write. Then that write is a definite definition (it both definitely executes and definitely writes the memory location), or it *might be* a definition, or it definitely is not. In the last two cases, we can resume the search for reaching definitions from that point. We come back to this in Chapter 5.

2.7   Scheduling

Scheduling consists of finding a map (a schedule) from the set $\mathcal{I}$ of instances to a set of logical time stamps, typically $\mathbb{N}$ or a Cartesian product of $\mathbb{N}$. Scheduling is a field in its own, which dates back to the invention of operation research in the 1940s. For our purposes, however, only a special type of scheduling is relevant: The set to be scheduled is a parametrized set of instances defined in intention. This thread of research started with the work of Karp, Miller, and Winograd [53] on the scheduling of recurrence equations. Our book does not discuss how schedules can be computed. For the automatic computation of schedules, the reader is referred to [59, 32, 33, 24].

Let θ be a schedule derived by one of the works just cited. The *latency* $L(\theta)$ of the schedule is the difference between the "dates" of the first and last executions:

$$L(\theta) = \max\{\theta(u) : u \in \mathcal{I}\} - \min\{\theta(u) : u \in \mathcal{I}\}$$

Intuitively, the latency gives the number of steps needed to execute a program. (In fact, it gives an *upper bound* on the number of steps since the set of instances for a given execution may be a strict subset of $\mathcal{I}$.) The smaller the latency, the faster your program. In fact, minimizing latency may be the goal of scheduling. In terms of operation research, it can be the *objective function* [32, 33]: The very goal of many scheduling algorithms is to derive a schedule that gives a minimal latency.

2.8 From Math to Compilers

If now you are thinking, "Hey, defining the first or last instance is not so important. What I want is my compiler to *compute* them," then you are quite right. You are, however, missing the point of this book: We believe it is interesting, useful, and even fun to first describe objects and problems in the most abstract way possible, to look at these descriptions from as many standpoints as possible, and only *then* to try and derive the constraints a concrete implementation (data structures, algorithms, etc.) has to satisfy.

For example, effectively computing the first and last instances requires us to first *label* instances in a suitable way, then to find a concrete and suitable way to express order $\prec$, and then to design a suitable algorithm to compute $\min_{\prec}$ or $\max_{\prec}$. Similarly, to solve the aliasing problem, we have to choose "suitable" labels for memory locations and make sure computing set intersection and testing for the emptiness of sets are feasible—and efficient.

But what does "suitable" mean? What exactly are the constraints that make data structures and algorithms efficient or sufficient? As much as possible, the framework we use to define program analyses and transformations assumes *any* labeling scheme for statement instances and for elements of data structures. What this labeling scheme actually looks like is not relevant, the goal being, indeed, to reason on program transformations in an abstract way, independently of what labels actually are.

Perhaps the "philosophy" of this book is to first formally define what we want to compute and, from that, derive the design constraints we face. Therefore, any labeling is sufficient as long as it easily lends itself to *algorithmic computation* of the problems we have to solve. One typical problem is testing for equality. However, testing for the equality of two elements of a group (in the mathematical sense) is, in general, undecidable. The representation must therefore be chosen with care. Other typical problems we might want or have to solve include checking for the emptiness of a set and computing the maximum/minimum element in a set with respect to a certain order—as in, for instance, Eq. (2.7).

Chapter 3

Labels

In the previous chapter, we saw that contrasting run-time instances of program statements is the key to understanding many program properties. However, reasoning about "generic" instances is frustrating, because we need a way to connect instances to the text of the source program. This issue also arises with basic blocks: Basic block numbers do not tell from which function and source lines the block originates. For that purpose, compilers usually provide source-line numbers, typically as comments. We have a similar issue here: We need to *label* instances, that is, to give them names that clearly correspond to the source code. Obviously, source-line numbers are not enough, because by definition instances are *repetitions* of source lines—if programs had no loops and no recursion, each statement would be executed once, and program line numbers would then be enough to label instances.

We already know a few requirements labels must meet and don't need to meet. First, we'd like them to be as short as possible. Instruction traces, therefore, are ruled out since their size depends on the length of the execution. Also, instance labels have to distinguish statement instances, that is, they have to be unique. As an example, acyclic path segments, introduced in a different context in [4], are not satisfactory because they don't take into account how many times a loop back edge was taken. We also want to "parameterize" labels, so that we can speak, for example, of the ith instance of a statement for all i. A more stringent condition is that they must lend themselves to the toolbox of concepts and operators discussed in the previous chapter, like relations on instances, and extrema.

3.1 The Case of Loop Nests

Labeling for loops is easy because the loop counter provides the label we are looking for. A loop like

```
1   for i:=1 to 10 do
2       ...
3   done
```

instantiates its body S 10 times, and the 10 instances of **2** are referred to as $2^1, 2^2$, up to 2^{10}. This notation naturally lends itself to parameterization: We can refer to the ith instance of **2** as 2^i.

Nesting loops simply means that an entire loop construct is iterated by another loop. As an example, consider the program in Figure 3.1.

. . . .

```
1   for i := 1 to n
2     for j := 1 to n
3       A[i,j] := A[i-1,j] + A[i,j-1]
4     end for
5   end for
```

. . . . *Figure 3.1. An example of a nest of loops.* . . . .

Observe that statement **3** has several instances in the course of the program execution. Actually, there is one instance per possible value of its *iteration vector*, which is the vector built from the counters of surrounding loops. In the case of the program in Figure 3.1, we denote by $3^{i,j}$ the instance of **3** for a given value of counters i and j.

We saw in Section 2.3 that the *domain* of a statement is the set of its instances. For statement **3** in the loop nest in Figure 3.1, this set is

$$\mathcal{D}(3) = \{3^{1,1}, \ldots, 3^{1,n}, 3^{2,1}, \ldots, 3^{n,n}\}$$

assuming, of course, that n is greater than or equal to 1. If we try to get a pictorial view of this iteration domain, the natural way to represent each element is to draw a grid and a square of n by n lines. Each line intersection lying in the square or on its borders corresponds to a value of the iteration vector. It is easy and fun to represent iteration domains this way, especially since this domain has a nice geometrical form—a square, as depicted in Figure 3.2.

This nice geometrical property can be generalized if loop bounds are affine functions of symbolic constants (such as n) and counters of surrounding loops. Indeed, going back to statement **3** in the loop nest in Figure 3.1, its domain can be written as

$$\mathcal{D}(3) = \left\{ 3^{i,j} : i,j \in \mathbb{N}^2 : \begin{array}{c} 1 \leq i \\ i \leq n \\ 1 \leq j \\ j \leq n \end{array} \right\} \tag{3.1}$$

In this set of constraints, the lower bound 1 on j is indeed an affine combination of n and surrounding i, since $1 = 0 \times n + 0 \times i + 1$. The upper bound is also affine with respect to n and i, since $n = 1 \times n + 0 \times i + 1$.

A polyhedron is a geometrical figure built by intersecting half-planes. To represent a half-plane, just draw a line and discard the irrelevant half. If the line is a straight line, then the half-plane can be defined by an affine inequality. A $\mathbb{Z}$-*polyhedron* is the set

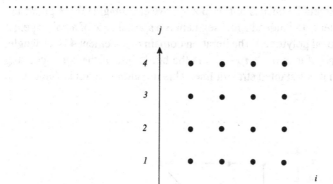

.... *Figure 3.2. Domain of statement **3** in Figure 3.1, for $n = 4$.* ....

of integer points contained in a polyhedron. The domain of **3** in (3.1) is therefore a $\mathbb{Z}$-polyhedron since it consists of integer points ($i, j \in \mathbb{N}$) enclosed within affine bounds. A *polytope* is simply a "finite" or bounded $\mathbb{Z}$-polyhedron. In the loop nest above, this polytope is the integer $n \times n$ square.

Of course, one could argue that the domain of **3** is an unbounded polyhedron in $\mathbb{Z}^3$, where the dimensions are i, j, and n. Equation (3.1), however, makes it clear that n is a symbolic constant constraining values of i and j.

```
1   do ip = 1, 4
2      tmp1 = 1.0d+00 / tmat( ip, ip )
3      do m = ip+1, 5
4         tmp = tmp1 * tmat( m, ip )
5         do l = ip+1, 5
6            tmat(m, l) = tmat(m, l) - tmp * tmat(ip, l)
7         end do
8         v( m,i,j,k )=v(m,i,j,k )-v(ip,i,j,k)*tmp
9      end do
10  end do
```

.... *Figure 3.3. Excerpt from the* `applu` *benchmark.* ....

Now consider the nest of three loops shown in Figure 3.3. This snippet is taken from `applu.f`, a Fortran program from the SPEC CFP2000 benchmark suite—and since this is an excerpt from a well-known program, we use the original Fortran syntax rather than our pseudolanguage.

The domain of statement **2** consists of four points. We can imagine these points are four dots on a line segment, and indeed a line segment is a special case of a polytope. (It is a "flat," one-dimensional polytope.) The iteration domain of statement **4** is a triangle, because the lower bound of m is $m \geq ip + 1$ and the borderline of the corresponding half-plane, even though it is a slanted straight line. This iteration domain is depicted in Figure 3.4.

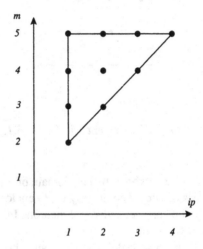

*.............. Figure 3.4. Domain of statement **4** in Figure 3.3. ....*

These nice geometrical properties can in some cases be extended to `while` loops. Figure 3.5 features a nest of two loops, with an outer `while` loop and an inner `for` loop, together with a possible iteration domain of the statement in the nest body, statement **3**. For illustration purposes, the figure assumes the `while` loop iterates three times.

It can be shown that, when there is one single and outermost `while` loop, the iteration domain is always a $\mathbb{Z}$-polyhedron. If the program is correct, that is, the `while` loop terminates, this domain is a finite $\mathbb{Z}$-polyhedron, that is, a polytope.

Conversely, the domain of a statement in the body of a nest with an inner `while` and an outer `for` is not, in general, a $\mathbb{Z}$-polyhedron. This can be seen in Figure 3.6 assuming the `while` loop iterates 4, 0, 2, and 3 times, respectively, for each of the four iterations of the outer loop. A possible iteration domain of statement **3** is also shown. We cannot draw a polyhedron that contains exactly those integer points that represent instances of statement **3**.

Symbolic Software   Several software programs provide support for symbolic manipulation of integer sets. In this book we mostly use the Omega Calculator developed by William Pugh and his team at the University of Maryland [71, 54]. For our purposes, the main benefits of this software are its intuitive text-based interface, its ability to

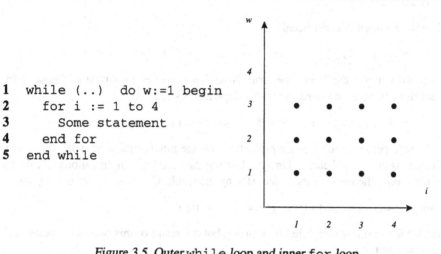

```
1    while (..)  do w:=1 begin
2       for i := 1 to 4
3          Some statement
4       end for
5    end while
```

Figure 3.5. Outer while *loop and inner* for *loop.*

```
1    for i := 1 to 4
2       while (..)  do w:=1 begin
3          Some statement
5       end while
4    end for
```

Figure 3.6. Inner while *loop and outer* for *loop.*

handle integer constants, its support for sets and relations, and the variety of functions provided in its toolbox.

A few words on syntax are in order. Throughout this book the input lines given to Omega are printed in courier font and prefixed by a pound sign, #. Omega's responses are in courier font with no prefix. This is Omega's behavior when given an input command file. Don't be misled by the fact that, in interactive sessions, the pound sign is a comment marker.

For example, the set defined in (3.1) is expressed in Omega in two steps. First, the symbolic constant n is declared:

```
# symbolic n;
```

Then the set itself is constructed:

```
# d := { [3,i,j] : 1 <= i <= n  &&  1 <= j <= n };
```

where && denotes the "and" operator. Note that variables submitted to the same in-equalities can be enumerated in comma-separated lists, as in

```
# d := { [3,i,j] : 1 <= i,j <= n  };
```

Omega performs internal simplifications on the input objects; actually, these sim-plifications are at the heart of Omega. Getting the result of simplifications is done by simply typing the name of the object storing the result. Consider the set emptyset:

```
# emptyset := { [i] : 1 <= i <= 0};
```

This set is internally simplified by Omega, but the result of this process appears only when we ask for emptyset:

```
# emptyset;
```

```
{[i]   : FALSE }
```

We have the expected result: The predicate under which i belongs to the set is always false.

Memory Accesses   We introduce storage mapping write and read mapping read in Section 2.4. We can now give them a more concrete form.

. . . .

```
1   for i := 1 to n
2     for j := 1 to n
3       B[i+j] := A[i-1,j] + A[i,j-1]
4     end for
5   end for
```

. . . . *Figure 3.7. Illustrating storage and read mappings.* . . . .

Let us consider the program in Figure 3.7. This program is very similar to the one shown in Figure 3.1, and in particular the domain of statement **3** is still given by (3.1). The store mapping for statement **3**, however, is now

$$\text{write}(3^{i,j}) = \{\text{B}[i+j]\}$$

(In contrast, this mapping was the identity on integer couples in the case of Figure 3.1.) This mapping can readily be expressed in Omega-speak:

```
# smap := {[3,i,j] -> [b] : b=i+j } ;
```

where b stands for an index to the implicit array B. Among many other possible symbolic computations, we can easily derive the set of array elements touched by statement 3. This set is defined as write($\mathcal{D}(3)$) and computed as

```
# smap(d);
```

```
{[b]: 2 <= b <= 2n}
```

which is the expected range of indices.

Expressing the Execution Order   Describing sets of integer vectors is only one issue. Another issue is to describe the order in which iteration vectors appear in the course of execution. Assuming that n equals 3, this order for the program in Figure 3.1 is $(1,1), (1,2), (1,3)$, corresponding to the first iteration of the outer loop, then $(2,1), (2,2), (2,3)$ for the second iteration. The third iteration simply changes the first value in each pair: $(3,1)$ then $(3,2)$ then $(3,3)$. This last remark leads to a formal definition of the order: If you consider these vectors are words (in the usual sense!) on the alphabet 1, 2, 3, then their order is the dictionary order, also known as lexicographic order, where the numbers 1, 2, 3 are ordered as usual. We denote this order by $\ll$, and we define it formally as follows: Two vectors a and b of the same dimension are ordered according to $\ll$ if there is an integer i such that the ith entry of a is lower than the ith entry of b, and all previous entries are equal:

$$a \ll b \iff \exists i, a_i < b_i \land (\forall i', 0 \le i' < i : a_i = b_i) \qquad (3.2)$$

One way to look at this definition is to consider each dimension in turn. Let's assume a and b are two-dimensional. Then (3.2) becomes

$$a \ll b \iff a_0 < b_0 \lor (a_0 = b_0 \land a_1 < b_1) \qquad (3.3)$$

In other words, either the first respective entries are ordered ($a_0 < b_0$, and the second conjunct in (3.2) is void), or these entries are equal but the entries for the second dimension are ordered ($a_0 = b_0 \land a_1 < b_1$). Not surprisingly, $\ll$ and $<$ denote the same order when vectors are one-dimensional.

This order is of course one more relation, as we saw in Section 2.6, and this relation can be easily expressed in Omega. Relation (3.3) is constructed as

```
orel := {[i,j]->[i',j'] : i'<i || (i'=i && j'<j)};
```

where || stands for the "or" operator.

Of course, the above applies to loops with *positive* steps that make their counters increase. Loops with negative steps, like

```
1   for i:= 10 to 1 step -1
2     ..
3   endfor
```

can be handled as well. Either they can be *normalized*, that is transformed into a loop with step 1, or we can replace $a_i < b_i$ by $a_i > b_i$ in (3.2).

So far, vectors compared with $\ll$ have had the same dimension. But what if they hadn't? What if we want to know which vector comes first among (1), $(1, 2)$, and $(1, 2, 3)$? The definition above provides the answer! If $(1) \ll (1, 2)$ was true, it would mean there is an integer i such that the ith component of one vector is strictly lower than the ith component of the other. Clearly, the first components of both (1) and $(1, 2)$ are equal. But (1) does not have a second component that could be compared to the second component of $(1, 2)$. Therefore, (1) and $(1, 2)$ are not ordered with respect to $\ll$. The same holds for (1) and $(1, 2, 3)$ and for $(1, 2)$ and $(1, 2, 3)$.

....

```
1   real x, A[N]
2   for i := 1 to N do
3     x := foo(i)
4     while ··· do
5       x := bar(x)
6     endwhile
7     A[i] := x
8   endfor
```

.... *Figure 3.8. Illustrating lexicographic ordering in imperfectly nested loops.* ....

Now imagine you want to formally define the order of instances appearing when executing the program in Figure 3.8. Possible iteration vectors for both **3** and **7** are $(1), (2)$, up to (N). As far as statement **5** is concerned, assuming an imaginary counter starting at 0 for the while loop, possible iteration vectors include $(1, 0)$, $(1, 2)$ and $(2, 0)$. Let us consider, say, instances $\mathbf{3}^1$, $\mathbf{5}^{1,2}$, and $\mathbf{7}^1$. It is obvious here that, even though their iteration vectors are not comparable by $\ll$, these instances are executed in exactly this order.[1] The simple reason is that statements **3**, **5**, and **7** appear in this top-down order in the program text. Therefore, the general definition of execution order $\prec$ on instances of loop statements can be stated as follows: Either the iteration vectors are ordered by $\ll$, or these vectors are equal on the dimensions they share and the statements themselves appear in order in the program text. Formally, this can be defined on two instances $\mathbf{S}^a$ and $\mathbf{R}^b$ of two generic statements $\mathbf{S}$ and $\mathbf{R}$ as

$$\mathbf{S}^a \prec \mathbf{R}^b \;=\; a \ll b \tag{3.4}$$
$$\lor \;\; (a = b \text{ on shared dimensions} \land \mathbf{S} \text{ appears before } \mathbf{R} \text{ in the program})$$

It was first defined by Feautrier in [31].

---

[1] This also gives an example why $(1) \ll (1, 2)$ should not be true for our purposes: (1) is the vector of both $\mathbf{3}^1$ and $\mathbf{7}^1$, which execute before and after $\mathbf{5}^{1,2}$, respectively.

3.2 Changing the Execution Order

Changing the order in which statement instances are executed is the key idea behind several optimizations and code transformations in compilers. Changing the execution order can make sure the definition of values closely precedes their uses, thus taking benefit of *temporal locality*. Loop transformations that change the execution order include loop interchange, tiling, and loop fusion.

Changing the execution order can be more radical and transform the original *total* order into a *partial order*. (An order is partial if one or more pairs of elements are not ordered. See Section 2.7.) Partial orders provide nice models for parallelism: Computations whose order is not enforced by the partial order can be done in any order, including at the same time. Typically, we may want to execute all the points on one diagonal of Figure 3.2 page 39 at the same time. Starting from the bottom left corner, each diagonal or "wave" or "front" is a group of instances we want to execute in parallel, provided enough resources are available. One such parallel front is depicted in Figure 3.9.

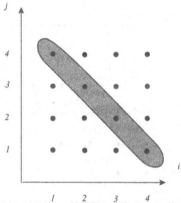

.... *Figure 3.9. An example of wavefront computations.* ....

This partial execution order on instances of statement **3** in Figure 3.1 may be defined by the following schedule:

$$3^{i,j} \prec 3^{i',j'} \iff i + j < i' + j'$$

Indeed, $i + j = k$ for some k is the equation of a diagonal.

We might want to construct the corresponding parallel program. One possible way is to build an outer loop on the logical time steps given by the schedule [17]. At each time step, a computation is performed by some computing device (a processor, a functional unit, etc.) labeled with p. Since all computations occur at the same time on different p's, the loop on p is parallel, that is, it is a `forall` loop. The transformed program appears in Figure 3.10. The value of p was chosen equal to j (more on this in a few moments).

....

```
1   for t := 2 to 2*n
2     forall p := 1 to n
3       A[t,p]:=A[t-1,p]+A[t-1,p-1]
4     end for
5   end forall
```

... *Figure 3.10. Parallelized (wavefronted) version of the program in Figure 3.1.* ...

Of course, one necessary condition for the transformed program to be correct is that each computation described in the original program be performed once and only once after transformation. Does the program in Figure 3.10 satisfy this condition? Well, we just have to draw the iteration domain of the loop body to be convinced: See Figure 3.11.

....

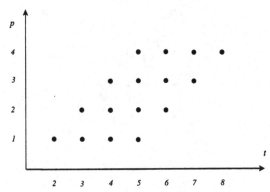

.... *Figure 3.11. Domain of statement* **3** *in Figure 3.10.* ....

We can check that all the points appearing in Figure 3.2 appear in Figure 3.11. (More precisely, there is a *one-to-one mapping* between the points in the two figures.) Geometrically, the only change is that the domain has been skewed.[2] The applied transformation mapped a polytope into another one that contains the same number of integer points.

The last step then, from a compiler's standpoint, is to generate the program that enumerates each of these points once and only once in the appropriate order. The new

---

[2]Indeed, in this particular case of schedule and processor allocation, the transformation is known as *loop skewing*.

program is a nest of loops, typically one per dimension of the transformed polytope. Each loop is a for if the dimension is laid out in time (the order is sequential) and a forall if the wave of instances is spread across processors or functional units (the instances execute in parallel along this dimension). This general problem of scanning polyhedra with loops was first investigated by Ancourt and Irigoin [3].

How can we check if a transformation is one-to-one or, equivalently, *invertible*? The transformation above corresponds to the mapping $(i, j) \mapsto (t = i + j, p = j)$, from $\mathbb{Z}^2$ to $\mathbb{Z}^2$. This mapping can be written in matrix form as

$$\begin{pmatrix} t \\ p \end{pmatrix} = \begin{pmatrix} 1 & 1 \\ 0 & 1 \end{pmatrix} \begin{pmatrix} i \\ j \end{pmatrix} \tag{3.5}$$

We then use a very general property: An affine mapping is invertible if and only if its determinant is itself *invertible in its own set*. We are familiar with real functions, and it is well known that an affine function on vectors in $\mathbb{R}$ is invertible if and only if its determinant is different from zero—because zero is the one and only real number that has no inverse. For mappings on integer sets, one-to-one mappings are those whose determinant is either 1 or -1: Indeed, the inverse of 1 is 1, which is an integer, and the inverse of -1 is -1, which is also an integer. All other integers have a noninteger inverse: The inverse of 2 is $\frac{1}{2}$. Matrices whose determinant is equal to 1 or -1 are called *unimodular*, the mappings they represent are invertible, and their inverse mappings can be represented by the inverse of the original matrix. (The reader is referred to [6] for details.) And indeed, the determinant of the matrix in (3.5) is 1, and the inverse matrix is

$$\begin{pmatrix} 1 & -1 \\ 0 & 1 \end{pmatrix}$$

whose elements, as required, are integers.

3.3 The Case of Recursive Programs

```
1   procedure P
2   do
3       v := foo(v);
4       if c1 then P() endif;
5       if c2 then P() endif
6   end
```

Figure 3.12. A simple recursive procedure.

Consider a very typical case of a recursive procedure, shown in Figure 3.12. Variable v is static and initialized before the initial call to P, which is not shown. This type of recursive procedure is said to be in *pre-order* because the job of one call is done (in statement **3**) before triggering possible new recursive calls (in statements **4** and **5**). Representing execution of this procedure, starting from the initial call can be done in a natural way by a *call tree*, a graph in which one node represents the first call to P and is called the *root*, two edges from the root lead to two nodes representing the first calls along statements **4** and **5**, respectively, etc. Drawing this call tree of course has to stop at one point, but so have real executions, too. Each node represents an instance of **3**, and each edge an instance of **4** or **5**.[3] An example of a call tree for the recursive program in Figure 3.12 appears in Figure 3.13. In this figure each node corresponds to one instance of **3**. The figure shows the call tree corresponding to the execution where the first evaluation of c1 returns true, spawning a recursive call to P where evalutations of both c1 and c2 return true. From there on, however, all evaluations of expressions c1 and c2 yield false, stopping this side of the call tree. Execution resumes at the evaluation of c2 in the very first call to P, and the call tree shows this evaluation returned true, etc.

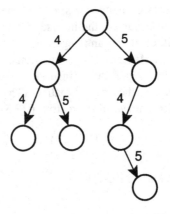

Figure 3.13. Call tree for one possible execution trace of the recursive program in Figure 3.12.

Figure 3.13 also illustrates that recursive procedures cannot always be turned into iterative ones. Simply recursive procedures (that is, recursive procedures whose bodies contain just one recursive call) can, but not higher-degree recursive procedures. For instance, there is no way to describe a doubly recursive process with a loop nest and without manipulating an explicit stack. (For an interesting discussion on iterative versus recursive processes, the book by Abelson and Sussman is a classic [1]. That discussion shows, in particular, that the time and/or space requirements of recursive

---

[3]To be consistent with what we wrote previously, any statement should correspond to an edge from a node (a state) to a node (another state). So an instance of **3** should be represented by an edge from the node of a call to P to a *leaf node* that does not itself lead to another node, that is has no outgoing edge. This representation is absolutely fine but would simply make our figures harder to read.

processes grow and shrink in the course of execution.)

You might have guessed that our next step is to label each instance of Pand, in particular, each instance of **3**. A very easy way to create such a label is to concatenate the label of each traversed statement. For example, after two recursive calls along statement **4** and then one along statement **5**, the instance of **3** that executes can be identified in a unique, unambiguous way by the word "**4453**" (the trailing **3** meaning that we consider an instance of **3**). We call this name a *control word*.

.... *Figure 3.14. Control automaton for statement 3 in Figure 3.12.* ....

All possible control words build a regular language, that is, a set of words that can be obtained by a regular automaton, which we call a *control automaton*. The control automaton of statement **3** in Figure 3.12 appears in Figure 3.14. Such a regular automaton produces a set of words, namely a language, which is the domain of statement **3** in the program of Figure 3.12:

$$\mathcal{D}(3) = (4+5)^*3$$

Indeed, after entering the automaton from the top arc, we can follow three arcs from the upper node: either the left loop, which emits a **4**, or the right one, which emits a **5**. Both can be repeated an arbitrary number of times, which is exactly what the regular expression $(4+5)^*$ means. At one point, however, the bottom arc must be followed to reach the node with a double circle. This distinguished node is a final or *accepting node*. This last step emits the trailing **3**.

Back to Iterative Programs Because a loop involves an initialization step and an iteration step, loops are given *two* labels: The first one represents the loop entry, and the second one is the loop iteration. Figure 3.15 shows a typical loop iterating over statement **2**. We contrast statement **1**, which corresponds to the loop entry or "header," from statement **b**, which captures the back edge.

The same figure also displays the control automaton associated with statement **2**. The language this automaton accepts is **1b*2**, which, indeed, includes all possible la-

....

```
1,b  for i:= 1 to 10 do
2        x := x + i
3      end for
```

.... *Figure 3.15.* for *loop and control automaton for its body.* ....

bels for all possible instances of the loop body: **12** during the first iteration of the loop, **1b2** during the second iteration, etc.

You might complain, however, that this set of labels is much more coarse than the interval of interers between 1 and 10, inclusive. Indeed, there is clearly no one-to-one mapping from $\{i \ : \ 1 \le i \le 10\}$ to **1b*2**, since the latter is not bounded. We come back to this issue in Section 5.3.1.

....

```
     int A[n];

1    void Queens (int n, int k) begin
2        if (k < n) then
3,a        for i := 0 to n-1 do
4,b          for j := 0 to k-1 do
5                ··· := ··· A[j] ···;
             end do
7            if (···) then
8              A[k] := ···;
9              Queens (n, k+1);
             end if
           end do
         end if
     end

     int main () begin
F        Queens (n, 0);
     end
```

.... *Figure 3.16. Procedure* Queens. ....

Mixing Recusion and Iteration   Consider the program example in Figure 3.16. This simple recursive procedure computes all possible solutions to the n-Queens problem, using an array A (details of the code are omitted here).

There are two statements accessing A: **8** and **5**. statements **2** and **7** are conditionals and statement **9** is the recursive call to procedure Queens. **1** is the label of the procedure, and **F** denotes the initial call in main.

Loop statements are divided into two substatements that are given distinct labels: The first one denotes the loop *entry*—e.g., **3** or **4**—and the second one denotes the loop *iteration*—e.g., **a** or **b**.

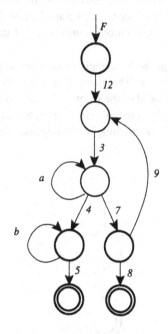

Figure 3.17. Control automaton producing the names of all possible instances of statements **5** and **8** in the Queens program.

A control automaton for the Queens program appears in Figure 3.17. This automaton produces the words labeling all possible instances of statements **8** and **5**. To use this automaton, just enter through the top incoming edge. The first output letter is **F**, which makes sense since the procedure initially has to be called from main. It then produces **1**, **2**, and **3**–the latter corresponding to entering the outermost loop. Then a nondeterministic choice takes place: Either the leftmost path is taken, producing words in the domain of **5**, that is

$$\mathcal{D}(5) = \text{F123(a)*4(b)*5} \qquad (3.6)$$

or the right path is taken, producing the domain of **8**:

$$\mathcal{D}(\mathbf{8}) = \mathbf{F1237(937)^*8} \tag{3.7}$$

Relations on Words   As we argue in Section 2.6, relations are naturally ubiquitous when reasoning about programs. We already looked at a few relations between integer tuples. But what about relations on words? Clearly the same techniques do not apply, and software like Omega is not adapted to this new task.

These relations are called *transductions*, which may sound like a frightening word but just means what we said: a relation between words. The interesting thing about transductions is that they can be expressed and manipulated using a special kind of finite automaton, called a *transducer*. Each transduction has a corresponding transducer, which provides the "computational equivalent" of the mathematical concept of transduction.

Imagine you want to express the mapping that maps any word of n letters a to the word consisting of $n - 1$ letters b. This mapping can also be seen as a relation between a word of the form a^n and a word of the form b^{n-1}, for any n greater than zero (that is, the input word consists of at least one a). By definition, this mapping is a transduction. What we want, of course, is "something" to manipulate this transduction, and this is where transducers appear.

. . . .

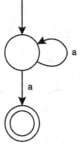

. . . *Figure 3.18. A finite automaton serving as the skeleton of our first transducer.* . . .

Let us start with input words. A finite automaton that reads words consisting of at least one a is easy to construct. For instance, the automaton can have two states, the first and entry state having a looping edge reading the letter a, and a second and "accepting" state. The edge (or "transition") from the entry state to the accepting state could be labeled a, meaning that firing this transition requires exactly one a. This finite automaton is shown in Figure 3.18. By convention, accepting states are shown as double circles.

Now let us think of the output words. The mapping we want to capture maps each a *but one* to a b. It is easy to see that if the automaton in Figure 3.18 could output one b each time it reads an a along the loop edge, and output no b while reading a along the

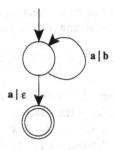

.... *Figure 3.19. A simple transducer.* ....

exit edge, then the desired mapping would be captured. For example, the word a (just one letter a) would be read by going directly from the entry state to the accepting state without looping and therefore without emitting a b. The total output word would then be the blank word, as expected. (The blank word is indeed equal to a string of zero b's, i.e., to b^0.) The word aa, then, would be mapped by reading the first a while firing the loop transition (emitting a b in the process) and by then firing the transition leading to the accepting state (then emitting no b). The total output word would then be b, as expected. Such an extended automaton is the *transducer* shown in Figure 3.19. Each edge is now labeled with input and output letters (or words) separated by a vertical bar. As you can imagine, transducers have been extended in many different ways so as to capture relations of various types. We will thus be able to leverage results from formal language theory to express precise relationships between run-time instances of program statements.

Memory Accesses We introduce storage mapping write and read mapping read in Section 2.4, and look at their concrete form, in the case of iterative programs, earlier in this chapter. We can now wonder what these mappings look like in the case of recursion.

As in the case of iterative programs, the question is not easily answered in general. One prerequisite is to be able to express the value of subscript expressions as a function of the instance labels, which may be difficult if not impossible. However, if these subscripts are simple enough and depend only on induction variables, then we can get a closed-form expression for storage and read mappings.

Consider the n-Queens program. The left-hand expression of statement **8** is A[k], and k is a parameter of procedure Queens not modified in the procedure body. The value of the actual parameter is set either by the initial call in statement **F** or by the recursive call in **9**. In other words, given an instance w of **8**, the value of k at w equals the occurrence count of the letter **9** in w. In other words, we simply have to count the **9**s. Therefore, the storage mapping for statement **8** is the function from $\mathcal{D}(\mathbf{8})$, given in (3.7) page 52, to elements of array A defined by

$$\forall w = \mathbf{F1237(937)}^q\mathbf{8}, \ q \in \mathbb{N} \ : \ \mathsf{write}(w) = \{\mathsf{A}[q]\} \tag{3.8}$$

Similarly, the subscript expression in statement **5** is j. On the other hand, words labeling an instance of **5** belong to the statement domain given in (3.6). So the value of j
equals the number of **bs**. The read mapping is therefore

$$\forall w = \mathbf{F123(a)^*4(b)^q5}, \ q \in \mathbb{N} \ : \ \mathsf{read}(w) = \{\mathtt{A}[q]\} \qquad (3.9)$$

Expressing the Execution Order The execution order can also be expressed by
transducers, more precisely by rational transducers. As an example, consider again
the program shown in Figure 3.12. Clearly, the first instance of **3** in this program is
the one at the initial call, which is labeled with ϵ**3** or simply **3**. This instance executes
before **43**, which itself comes before **443**, which in turn comes before **453**. That is,
we clearly have a relation among words in the language of the control automaton of
Figure 3.14. This relation is a (total) execution order $\prec$.

   However, it is impossible to enumerate all the elements in that relation. As before,
what we need is an expression for this order, that is, an equivalent of (3.4) for recursive
programs.

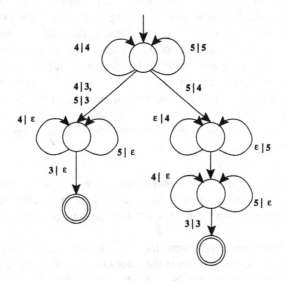

*Figure 3.20. Transducer capturing the execution order among instances of 3 in the
program in Figure 3.12.*

   A transducer for the execution order of instances of statement **3** in Figure 3.12 is
provided in Figure 3.20. You can check that, with **453** as the input word, **3**, **43** and
443 can all be emitted by the transducer, meaning they all execute before **453**. First, to
capture the pair (**453**, **3**) (i.e., **3** $\prec$ **453**), we go from the entry node directly to the left
path, consuming **4** and emitting **3**. We then take the leftmost loop arc before falling

through to the accepting node. Neither of these last two actions emits a letter, so the end result is, as expected, that the pair $(\mathbf{453}, \mathbf{3})$ belongs to the transduction. Similarly, the pair $(\mathbf{453}, \mathbf{43})$ is captured by first looping along the top left arc (consuming and emitting a $\mathbf{4}$) and then following the left path (consuming a $\mathbf{5}$ and emitting a $\mathbf{3}$). Falling though to the accepting node consumes the trailing $\mathbf{3}$. Third, the pair $(\mathbf{453}, \mathbf{443})$ is obtained by first looping along the top left arc, and then by taking the right path from the entry node. At that point, $\mathbf{45}$ is consumed and $\mathbf{44}$ is emitted. Falling through allows us to reach the rightmost accepting node after reading and emitting the final two $\mathbf{3}$s.

Finally, notice that $\mathbf{3}$ is not accepted by the transducer in Figure 3.20 because either path after the entry node consumes at least one $\mathbf{4}$ or at least one $\mathbf{5}$. This makes sense, since $\mathbf{3}$ is the executed first and therefore has no predecessors.

3.4 Further Reading

General overviews of automatic parallelization in the polytope model are given in [62, 34]. As discussed in this chapter, the polytope model was originally restricted to unimodular transformations of program fragments that can be represented by polytopes in their strict sense. However, nonunimodular transformations are studied in [78], and an extension of space-time mapping to a wider spectrum of programs has received some attention as well, including in [41, 49].

Counting the points in a polyhedron has many applications, ranging from reducing communications in compiler-generated code for multiprocessor systems to memory hierarchy optimizations [73, 15].

Concerning formal languages, surprisingly few books provide an easy introduction to transducers, either regular or pushdown. A great exception is the book by Gurari [46].

3.5 Conclusion

We saw in Chapter 2 that reasoning on instances is often useful to formally define program properties and transformations without relying on more implementation-oriented representations like control-flow graphs. However, when reasoning about a specific program, we have to be able to name these instances and to relate them to the original code (and possibly to the transformed code). Two instance-naming conventions are presented in this chapter. The first one, suitable to loop nests, is quite classical: It is based on iteration vectors. The second one, meant for recursive programs, is perhaps not so well known and is based on words from regular expressions, and therefore captured by finite-state automata. The latter convention is strictly more expressive than the former. When integer vectors label instances, relations on instances are captured by sets of vectors. When words label instances, relations are captured by transductions.

Part II

Analyses and Transformations

Chapter 4

Revisiting Some Classical Compiler Concepts

Most compiler techniques and many imperative programming concepts are described with respect to control-flow graphs. In contrast, this book defines programming language concepts using a handful of basic properties and first-order logic on these properties. To that purpose, we leverage the notations and concepts seen in Chapters 2 and 3.

We first consider alias analysis, which has a tremendous impact in parallelizing compilers. A real alias analysis has to address all the features of a real programming language, like storage location and procedure call convention. However, the key issues of possible executions and conservative approximation can be presented in a concise way, as detailed in Section 4.1. We then define reaching definition analysis in Section 4.2. Actually, reaching definition analysis is so important that two chapters, Chapters 6 and 7, are devoted to it. A key concept in reaching definition analysis is dominance, which is introduced in Section 4.4. We then define in Section 4.5 what it means for a variable to be initialized, live, or dead.

4.1 Alias Analysis

A classical problem is to check that the memory locations written by two instances are equal and, more precisely, to write a program that automatically checks this equality. The *aliasing* problem is, given two instances u and v, to decide whether there is an execution e such that both u and v execute and write in the same location:

$$e \in \mathcal{E}: \quad u \text{ Alias}_e\, v \;\equiv\; u, v \in \mathcal{I}_e \,\wedge\, \text{write}_e(u) = \text{write}_e(v) \qquad (4.1)$$

If only scalar variables were considered, checking the equality (second conjunct) would be easy since it would then boil down to comparing character strings. However, if we take arrays into account, we have to check that two array subscripts are equal. This is much more difficult, since it may require integer solving techniques.[1] And it can be even worse, since from a mathematical standpoint, testing for equality of two elements in a group is in general undecidable.

The first conjunct, which states that both u and v belong to the same execution e, can also be tricky to check. To see why, consider the program fragment below:

```
1   if foo then
2      x := 42
3   else
4      x := 43
5   endif
```

Statements **2** and **4** write in the same location, but there is no e such that both **2** and **4** execute, that is, **2** and **4** both belong to $\mathcal{I}_e$.

. . . .

```
1   if foo then
2      x := 42; y := 43
3   else
4      x := 43; y := 42
5   endif
6   a[x] := 0
7   a[y] := 1
```

. . . . *Figure 4.1. Aliasing and executions.* . . . .

The two problems are compounded, since the memory location written by an instance may depend on execution. To see why, let us slightly modify the program shown in Figure 2.6 into the program shown in Figure 4.1. During execution $e = $ **12567**, the element of a modified in **6** is $\text{write}_e(6) = $ a[42], and the element of array a modified in **7** is $\text{write}_e(7) = $ a[43]. During execution $e = $ **14567**, we have $\text{write}_e(6) = $ a[43], and $\text{write}_e(7) = $ a[42]. Therefore, statements **6** and **7** never alias.

Not surprisingly, we often have no information on individual executions e. We thus have to conservatively assume that some writes "may" alias, which is captured by the relation **Alias**:

$$\forall u, v \in W : (\exists e \in \mathcal{E} : u \text{ Alias}_e v) \implies u \text{ Alias } v \qquad (4.2)$$

Relation **Alias** proves extremely useful in Chapter 9.

Another way to look at this issue is to consider a conservative superset $\text{write}(u)$, which is characterized in (2.4) as

$$\bigcup_{e \in \mathcal{E}} \text{write}_e(u) \subseteq \text{write}(u)$$

---

[1] A related concept, dependence analysis, is discussed in Chapter 7.

Then we may be tempted to say that two instances "may" alias if

$$\text{write}(u) \cap \text{write}(v) \neq \emptyset \qquad (4.3)$$

However, (4.2) and (4.3) are *not* equivalent because, even though we do have the implication below:

$$(\exists e, \text{write}_e(u) = \text{write}_e(v)) \implies (\text{write}(u) \cap \text{write}(v) \neq \emptyset)$$

the opposite is *not* true. To see how (4.3) impacts precision, consider Figure 4.1 again. We have $\text{write}(6) = \{\text{a}[42], \text{a}[43]\}$. (The program is simple enough to have an exact superset of writes, that is, to state $\text{write}(6) = \{\text{a}[42], \text{a}[43]\}$, not $\text{write}(6) \supseteq \{\text{a}[42], \text{a}[43]\}$.) But $\text{write}(7) = \{\text{a}[42], \text{a}[43]\}$ also holds, so the intersection of $\text{write}(6)$ and $\text{write}(7)$ is not empty. An analysis based on (4.3) is easier to design than an analysis based on (4.2), but it would report a spurious alias in this case.

4.2 Reaching Definition Analysis

Another classical analysis, to which all of Chapter 5 is dedicated, is *reaching definition analysis*. Given an execution trace e, a memory location m, and an instance v in that execution (that is, $v \in \mathcal{I}_e$), the definition of m reaching v is denoted with $\text{RD}_e(\langle v, \text{m} \rangle)$ and is defined as

$$\text{RD}_e(\langle v, \text{m} \rangle) \equiv \max_{\prec} \{u \ : \ u \in \mathcal{I}_e, \ u \prec v, \ \text{write}_e(u) = \text{m}\} \qquad (4.4)$$

Intuitively, the definition of m reaching v during execution e is the last element ($\max_{\prec}$) in the set consisting of all executing instances ($u \in \mathcal{I}_e$) that precede v ($u \prec v$) and write into m in the course of the execution.[2]

Notice that $\bot$ is a valid possible solution to this equation. Indeed, $\bot$ provides some information: No instance satisfying all constraints exist in the given program or program fragment. This may mean that the reaching definition is somewhere before the program fragment under consideration or that memory location m is not initialized.

Notice also that we don't require $\text{read}_e(v) = \text{m}$, that is it makes perfect sense to consider definitions reaching a program point that does not use the definition. Furthermore, as long as the memory location is left untouched, the current last definition is unchanged. These two remarks lead to the following conclusion: The definitions reaching a given instance are the same as those reaching a preceding instance as long as there is no intervening kill of the definition:

$$\forall e \in \mathcal{E}, \forall u, v \in \mathcal{I} :$$
$$(\nexists z, u \prec z \prec v \wedge \text{write}_e(z) = \text{m})) \qquad (4.5)$$
$$\implies (\text{RD}_e(\langle v, \text{m} \rangle) = \text{RD}_e(\langle u, \text{m} \rangle))$$

This property is the basis of all analyses based on propagation, including iterative data-flow analyses.

---

[2]As an aside, notice the connection between Eq. (4.4) and temporal logic, where time is in general nonlinear. To the best of our knowledge, this connection has not been explored much (see, however, [19]).

However, memory location m is often read by the given instance v. This often makes m clear from the context, for instance when the textual statement associated with v has just one read reference. In that case, we simplify the notations above into

$$\text{RD}_e(v) \;\equiv\; \max_{\prec}\{u \,:\, u \in \mathcal{I}_e,\ u \prec v,\ \text{write}_e(u) = \text{read}_e(v)\} \qquad (4.6)$$

However, since we can seldom consider one specific execution e, we have to decide on how to approximate (4.6 when need be. Consider the program below:

```
1   if foo then x := ...
2   if bar then x := ...
3   ...   := x
```

where neither foo nor bar depends on x. We assume we have no other information on foo and bar. Let us try to find which of the two values, computed and stored into x by statements 1 and 2, respectively, is visible by or reaches statement 3. (We often say we "analyze the reaching definition of statement 3.") First, we may want the analysis to give us either all the definitions that *may* reach 3 or only the definitions that provably reach 3. In other words, we may have a *may analysis*, giving an over-approximation of the result, or a *must analysis*, which underapproximates reaching definitions by giving guaranteed definitions only.

But the program above shows why the "must" view of reaching definitions is not appealing: The read of x in statement 3 has no *guaranteed* reaching definition at all, and a "must" reaching definition analysis would report

$$\text{RD}(3) = \{\bot\}$$

which intuitively is not the result we expect.

. . . .

```
1   x := foo
2   while ··· do
3      x := x + 1
4   end while
5   y := x
```

. . . . *Figure 4.2. Illustrating conservative reaching definition.* . . . .

This issue is perhaps even more important when taking instances into account. Consider the program in Figure 4.2. Here again, knowing RD_e for every possible execution e is not possible. To see why, consider the program in Figure 4.2 and the use of x in statement 5. x is written in all iterations of the while loop, if any (indeed, it may be that the loop does not execute at all!). Let us consider "all" possible executions one by one. To begin with, let e_1 be the execution in which the loop is skipped, namely, $e_1 = \mathbf{125}$.

- In execution e_1, the while loop exits immediately, so the definition reaching statement **5** is

$$RD_{e_1}(5) = 1$$

Notice that $RD_{e_1}(5)$ clearly is shorthand for $RD_{e_1}(\langle 5, x \rangle)$.

- Let e_2 be the execution in which the while loop iterates exactly once. The definition reaching statement **5** is the first and last instance of statement **3**:

$$RD_{e_2}(5) = 3^1$$

- In execution e_3, the while loop iterates exactly twice, so the definition reaching statement **5** is the second and last instance of statement **3**:

$$RD_{e_3}(5) = 3^2$$

In other words, the use of x in statement **5** may be reached by any definition in statement **3** during any iteration of the while loop, or by statement **1**. Again, a "may" analysis makes more sense. For this reason, we only consider may reaching definition analyses in the rest of this book.

A bit more formally, we may say that a conservative approximation RD of RD_e over all possible executions is a mapping that includes all RD_e's. That is,

$$\forall u, v : \quad (\exists e \in \mathcal{E} : u, v \in \mathcal{I}_e \wedge v = RD_e(u)) \quad \Longrightarrow \quad v \in RD(u)$$

An equivalent description of a valid approximation $RD(u)$ is

$$\bigcup_{e \in \mathcal{E}} RD_e(u) \subseteq RD(u) \tag{4.7}$$

As an example, consider again the program in Figure 4.2. A valid approximation of definitions reaching x in statement **5** is

$$RD(5) = \{1\} \cup \{3^i : i \geq 1\}$$

Notice that the "theoretical" RD_e is a function: Each read has *at most one* defining write, possibly none, during one execution e. In contrast, the "practical" RD maps any given use to a *set* of possible definitions. Equivalently, it can be seen as a relation on the Cartesian product of the set of reads and the set of writes, so that[3]

$$v \in RD(u) \quad \Longleftrightarrow \quad u \; RD \; v$$

Notice also that $\{\bot\}$ is different from the empty set $\emptyset$: The definitions reaching a read that does not exist build an empty set. That is, if $u \notin \mathcal{I}$, then $RD(\langle u, m \rangle) = \emptyset$, not $\{\bot\}$.

---

[3]Note that the order in the product is important. We consider mappings from reads (uses) to writes (definitions). Therefore, when two instances u and v are in relation with respect to RD (written as $u \; RD \; v$), remember that u is a read and v is a write.

4.3   Reaching Definition Analysis and Program Transformations

The reason we put so much emphasis on reaching definition analysis is that this analysis captures a fundamental property of the *algorithm* implemented in the program: the flow of data.

To see this, contrast aliases and reaching definitions. Alias properties directly depend on the way the input program was coded. Indeed, aliases are due to the use, several times, of the same memory location. Therefore, aliasing is due to the imperative nature of the language, not to the algorithm the programmer implemented. In addition, the programmer may have viewed using the same memory location twice as a trick to save space. Aliasing therefore depends on programmers, on their skills and tastes, and on current technology! On the contrary, data flows depend on neither the programming language nor the programmer. They depend only on the underlying algorithm.

So let us try to find a more general condition for the correctness of program transformations. Our premise is that if the set of computations in both the original and transformed programs is the same, and if the values received and produced by each computation are the same for a given set of input data, then both versions of the program produce the same results.

Unfortunately, from a program analysis standpoint, this is of little help, since it is impossible in general to know the value produced by (we should say: the function implemented by) a program statement. What we can tell, however, is *where* an input value comes from. Indeed, an instancewise reaching definition analysis gives the precise relationship between producers and consumers. Therefore, we claim that preserving reaching definitions is sufficient for a program transformation to be correct, under the assumption that the transformation only changes (a) the execution order $\prec$ and/or (b) the store and read mappings write and read.

It is important to notice that the preceding claim assumes all operators and functions are unchanged. For instance, optimizations like strength-reduction are not included. Syntactical transformations like reassociation of (a + b) + c into a + (b + c) are out of scope as well. Also, the set of possible executions $\mathcal{E}$ and the set of executed instances $\mathcal{I}_e$ for any given e in $\mathcal{E}$ are assumed unchanged by the program transformation. Of course, the *name* of an instance may change, for example because statement numbering changes, but the instance itself is the same. This restriction implies that optimizations like control speculation are not covered by our correctness claim. Still, preserving reaching definitions is a sufficient condition far more general than obeying data aliasing and dependences, a punchline we hit several times throughout the book.

It is not a necessary condition though. Consider the example in Figure 4.3. The original program sets all elements of x to 0 by propagating this value from one element to the next. In the transformed version shown on the right side of Figure 4.3, statement **3** refers directly to the initial value set in statement **1**. The transformation does not change the set of computations: In the original program, there are $n + 1$ instances in both cases, the first being an initialization to 0 and the instances of **3** being copies. However, the definition reaching x[i-1] at 3^i, for $i > 1$, is 3^{i-1} in the original program, but it is **1** after the transformation. Still, the transformation is perfectly

....

```
1  x[0] := 0;                    1  x[0] := 0;
2  for i := 1 to n do            2  for i := 1 to n do
3    x[i] := x[i-1]              3    x[i] := x[0]
4  end for                       4  end for
```

(a) Original program   (b) Transformed program

...... *Figure 4.3. A correct transformation that modifies reaching definitions* ......

correct.

Some notations are in order. Transformations that comply with our restrictions change order $\prec$ into order $\overline{\prec}$ and store and read mappings into write and read. Reaching definitions in the transformed program are therefore defined in exactly the same way as (4.6) page 62:

$$\overline{\mathsf{RD}}_e(v) \;\equiv\; \max_{\overline{\prec}} \{u \;:\; u \in \mathcal{I}_e,\; u \,\overline{\prec}\, v,\; \overline{\mathsf{write}}_e(u) = \overline{\mathsf{read}}_e(v)\} \qquad (4.8)$$

Therefore, a program transformation that obeys the restrictions above is correct if

$$\forall e \in \mathcal{E},\; \forall u, v \in \mathcal{I}_e : \; u = \mathsf{RD}_e(v) \;\Rightarrow\; u = \overline{\mathsf{RD}}_e(v) \qquad (4.9)$$

that is, if it preserves all data flows during all possible executions.

4.4 Dominance

Another ubiquitous concept in compilers is *dominance*. Intuitively, an operation p dominates an operation q if q only executes if p previously executed. Usually, dominance is defined with respect to a control-flow graph: A node p dominates a node q if every possible execution path from the entry node to q includes p [68]. Notice that, in this definition, a node represents a statement or a group of statements, in general a basic block.

A typical example of dominance occurs when if statements are nested. Consider the program in Figure 4.4. Statement **2** (and statement **1**, for that matter) always executes when **4** executes, and executes *before* **4**. We say that **1** dominates statement **4**. Indeed, in a control-flow graph representation like the one shown on the right-hand side of Figure 4.4, any path from the "start" (here, **1**) to **4** would traverse **2**. What dominance says is that *if* **4** executes during one given program execution, then so does **2** in the same execution. This information can be viewed as a *relative* property between "existences" (the "existence" of one object implying the "existence" of another), not an *absolute* one (we can't guarantee that **3** or **4**, taken in isolation, executes).

. . . .

```
1  if(..)  {
2    x := 12;
3    if(..)  {
4      x:=4;
5    }
6  }
```

. . . . *Figure 4.4. Dominance.* . . . .

4.4.1   Semantic versus Syntactic Dominance

We just saw that dominance is a natural graph concept. However, graph-based definitions of dominance fail to capture interesting properties on the relative existence of executions. In other words, it is not always a natural *programming* concept. To see this, consider Figure 4.5.

. . . .

```
1  if foo then
2    x := 0
3  end if
4  if bar then
5    y := 1
6  end if
```

. . . . *Figure 4.5. Semantic dominance.* . . . .

In this example, statement **1** (the evaluation of foo) dominates **5** according to the graph-based definition. But does **2** dominate **5**? A priori, the answer is no: Since there is a path from the entry node to **5** that does not include **2**, the dominance property, in its classical definition, does not hold.

However, imagine we can independently prove that

$$([\![bar]\!]_4 = \textbf{true}) \implies ([\![foo]\!]_1 = \textbf{true}) \qquad (4.10)$$

This is the case if, for instance, bar and foo are identical expressions that do not depend on x. Or if foo equals z >= 0 and bar equals z > 0. Then we do have the property that the execution of **5** is always preceded by the execution of **2**. This shows that, from a programming point of view, Eq. (4.10) matters, not properties of the control-flow graph!

This leads to a more general definition of dominance: An instance u dominates an instance v, denoted u dom v, if and only if u can only execute before v and any program execution e containing v also contains u. In other words, the existence of v implies the execution of u before v:

$$\forall u, v \in \mathcal{I}: \quad u \text{ dom } v \equiv u \prec v \wedge (\forall e \in \mathcal{E} : v \in \mathcal{I}_e \Rightarrow u \in \mathcal{I}_e) \qquad (4.11)$$

To illustrate this definition, consider Figure 4.5 again: **2** executes each time **5** executes. If we can assert (4.10), they comply with definition (4.11):

$$\mathbf{2} \prec \mathbf{5} \wedge (\forall e, \mathbf{5} \in \mathcal{I}_e \Rightarrow \mathbf{2} \in \mathcal{I}_e)$$

so **2** dominates **5** according to definition (4.11), but not according to the classical graph-based definition. Dominance as defined above *implies* dominance in the usual sense, but the opposite is not true.

The impact of dominance on reaching definition analysis is clear when you look at (4.4) and (4.11) side by side: The read instance v is assumed to execute during a given execution e; otherwise, looking for its reaching definitions has no sense. Therefore, if u dominates v, then u executes. If in addition, for any execution e, u writes into the memory location read by v, then no definition w preceding u reaches v:

$$(\text{write}_e(u) = \text{read}_e(v) \wedge u \text{ dom } v) \implies (\forall w : w \prec u \Rightarrow w \neq \text{RD}_e(v))$$

We say that u *kills* all possible previous definitions like w during execution e.

Dominance can be extended to statements or basic blocks. Dominance then means there is a dominance relation on the instances of these statements and comes as a special case of (4.11). More precisely, a statement **p** dominates a statement **q** if, for any execution of the program and any instance of **q** in that execution, there is an instance of **p** that dominates the instance of **q**:

$$\forall \mathbf{p}, \mathbf{q} \in \mathcal{S}: \quad \mathbf{p} \text{ dom } \mathbf{q} \equiv (\forall e \in \mathcal{E}, \forall v \in \mathcal{D}_e(\mathbf{q}) : \exists u \in \mathcal{D}_e(\mathbf{p}), u \text{ dom } v) \quad (4.12)$$

Notice again that the latter definition is *stronger* than the usual definition based on control-flow graphs. Another way to look at this issue is to realize that classical dominance only captures *structural dominance*, that is, a property given syntactically by the structure of the program. Indeed, the program in Figure 4.4, if written in assembly, would probably have no dominance property according to the classical definition because the hierarchy of if nesting would probably be lost. In contrast, the more general definition of dominance given in (4.12) captures *semantic dominance*.

To top it off, because definition (4.11) works at the instance level, it also captures subtle cases of purely syntactical (nonsemantical) cases of *structural* dominance. To see this, consider the loop in Figure 4.6, where a is a scalar variable and foo some function. Assuming no knowledge of the loop exit condition, we have no way to tell whether any instance of **2** executes. But a key observation here is that *if* an instance of **2** executes, *then* so does any previous instance of **2**:

$$\forall e \in \mathcal{E}, \forall x, x' \in \mathbb{N}, 0 \leq x' < x : \quad \mathbf{2}^x \in \mathcal{I}_e \Rightarrow \mathbf{2}^{x'} \in \mathcal{I}_e$$

```
1   while (..)   do x:=0 begin
2     a := foo(a)
3   end while
```

.... *Figure 4.6. A simple* while *loop.* ....

Remember, dominance is all about what executes *assuming* execution reaches a given point. This *relative* information on "existence" can be very precise, indeed, if (a) we reason at the instance level and (b) we pay attention to the syntactic structure of the program (one more reason, indeed, to use structured programming languages that minimize the use of harmful gotos!).

```
1   while (..)   do w:=0 begin
2     while (..)   do x:=0 begin
3       a := foo(a)
4     end while
5   end while
```

.... *Figure 4.7. Extension of Figure 4.6.* ....

This observation can be leveraged in the second example shown in Figure 4.7. To really see how difficult dominance is in this example, let us draw a possible iteration domain of **3**. Clearly, this domain is in the upper right part of the plane with axes w and x. A *possible* iteration domain is shown in Figure 4.8. Black dots represent instances that do execute, gray dots instances that don't. In other words, in the particular execution represented in Figure 4.8, the innermost loop iterates four times during the first iteration of the outermost loop and does not execute at all during the second iteration of the outer loop. The outer loop iterates five times.

The dominance property we observe here is that, for any given instance of the iteration domain, if it executes, so do all preceding instances in the same iteration of the outer loop. Using our notations:

$$\forall e \in \mathcal{E}, \forall w, x \in \mathbb{N} : (\mathbf{3}^{w,x} \in \mathcal{I}_e) \Rightarrow (\forall x', 0 \leq x' < x : \mathbf{3}^{w,x'} \in \mathcal{I}_e) \quad (4.13)$$

This equation captures more information than it may look like, and indeed, it is critical in Exercise 5.10 page 110 when studying the program's data flow. The reason the equation is so important is that, contrary to what we may think and what most compilers assume, executions of while loops do follow some pattern, and this pattern can be used by later analyses.

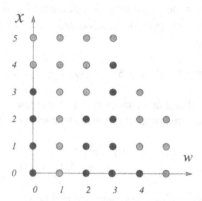

...... *Figure 4.8. One possible iteration domain for statement 3 in Figure 4.7.* ......

4.4.2 The Case of Recursive Programs

The same concepts of structural and semantical dominance apply to recursive programs. Consider the procedure in Figure 4.9, reproduced from Figure 3.12. Variable v is static and initialized before the initial call to P, but this initialization and the initial call are not shown in the figure. We hope it is now natural for you to picture instances

```
1   procedure P
2   do
3     v := foo(v);
4     if ..  then P() endif;
5     if ..  then P() endif
6   end
```

.... *Figure 4.9. A simple recursive procedure.* ....

spawned when calling this procedure and to label instances of **3** by words in alphabet **4, 5**, followed by the letter **3**. In other words, a natural set of names is the regular expression $(4 + 5)^*.3$. For the sake of clarity, we often fail to contrast an instance and the word it is labeled with.

Now consider a word w in that language. If $w = 3$, the corresponding instance of **3** is the one spawned by the very first call to P. It may or may not be followed by other calls to P (and therefore other instances of **3**) depending on the predicates of statements **4** and **5**.

But let us now consider word **43**. *If* this instance executes, then instance **3** definitely executed before, whatever the conditions in statements **4** and **5** are. In other words, **3** dominates **43**. But can this property be generalized to other instances of **3**?

First, we observe that

$$\forall e \in \mathcal{E}, \forall w, w' \in (4+5)^* : \ (w.w' \in \mathcal{I}_e) \ \Rightarrow \ (w \in \mathcal{I}_e)$$

This equation just states that if an instance of **4** or **5** executes, then any instance labeled by a prefix executes, too. This property extends to instances of **3**:

$$\forall e, \forall v \in \mathcal{I}_e, \forall w \in (4+5)^* :$$
$$(\exists w' \in (4+5)^*, v = w.w'.3) \ \Rightarrow \ (w.3 \in \mathcal{I}_e)$$

On the other hand, the execution order between $w.3$ and $w.w'.3$ is obvious if w' is not the empty word. We therefore have

$$\forall w \in (4+5)^*, \ \forall w' \in (4+5)^+ : \ w.3 \ \text{dom} \ w.w'.3$$

The property we observed on **3** and **43** can thus be generalized. What we rediscovered here is a structural dominance property that naturally appears in pre-order recursive procedures.

. . . .

```
1   Queens (int n, int k) begin
2     if (k < n) then
3,a     for i := 0 to n-1 do
4,b       for j := 0 to k-1 do
5           ··· := ··· A[j] ··· ;
          end do
7         if (···) then
8           A[k] := ··· ;
9           Queens (n, k+1);
          end if
        end do
      end if
    end

    main () begin
F     Queens (n, 0);
    end
```

. . . . *Figure 4.10. Procedure for the n-Queens problem.* . . . .

Dominance properties can be found in real-life recursive programs, too. Consider, for example, the n-Queens program in Figure 4.10, already presented in Section 3.3

page 50. In Chapter 5 page 119, we look for the definitions reaching the read in instance **F123aa7912345**. We can already discover that if **F123aa7912345** executes, then **F123aa78** executes as well before **F123aa7912345**. This dominance property is due to the fact that **F123aa78** and **F123aa79** (a prefix of **F123aa7912345**) belong to the same instance of the same basic block. This property can itself be captured in a general way. Let $\mathcal{I}$ be the set of all labels attached to instances of all statements in the procedure. We have

$$\forall w \in \mathbf{F}.(\mathbf{123a^*79})^*.\mathbf{1237}, \ \forall w' \in \mathcal{I}: \ w.\mathbf{8} \text{ dom } w.\mathbf{9}.w' \tag{4.14}$$

which states that any instance of statement **8** dominates any instance spawned by the immediately following call in statement **9**. This property can be discovered by automatic techniques presented in [16]. However, this dominance property is not captured by the usual definition based on control-flow graphs.

4.5 Initialized, Live, and Dead Variables

Let us consider a memory location m and a particular program "point." The problem of checking whether the location is initialized at that point is classically defined as the problem of checking whether there is a write to m on *all* paths from the start to the program point. In this context, a "point" refers to a specific node (or edge, depending on the representation you choose) in the control-flow graph. We can, however, have another perspective on the issue.

For a given instance u during a given execution e, checking whether memory location m is initialized can be defined as

$$\mathsf{Init}_e(u, \mathsf{m}) \equiv \exists v \in \mathcal{I}_e, \ v \prec u \wedge \mathsf{write}_e(v) = \mathsf{m} \tag{4.15}$$

In other words, we have to check that a write instance v exists during the given execution e, that this v executes before u, and that v writes into m.

The classical definition considers all executions—it's an "all-paths" or "must" definition. To be consistent with that definition, we approximate (4.15) on all executions along the lines of (2.2) page 27. The fact that m is initialized at u, written $\mathsf{Init}(u, \mathsf{m})$, is characterized as

$$\mathsf{Init}(u, \mathsf{m}) \implies \bigwedge_{e \in \mathcal{E}} \mathsf{Init}_e(u, \mathsf{m}) \tag{4.16}$$

Notice that, to strictly obey (2.2), $\mathsf{Init}(u, \mathsf{m})$ needs only to *imply* $\bigwedge_{e \in \mathcal{E}} \mathsf{Init}_e(u, \mathsf{m})$.

Obviously, if there is a definition reaching m at u, then initialization is guaranteed:

$$\mathsf{RD}_e(\langle u, \mathsf{m} \rangle) \neq \perp \implies \mathsf{Init}_e(u, \mathsf{m})$$

which itself implies

$$\mathsf{RD}(\langle u, \mathsf{m} \rangle) \not\ni \{\perp\} \implies \mathsf{Init}(u, \mathsf{m})$$

But of course, computing reaching definitions to get initialization is an overkill.

. . . .

```
1   for i := 0 to N
2     for j := 0 to N
3       a[i+j+1] := ..
4       if (P) then
5         a[i+j] := ..
6       end if
7       ..  := a[i+j]
8     end for
9   end for
```

. . . . *Figure 4.11. Is the read in* **7** *initialized?* . . . .

As an example, consider the program in Figure 4.11. We have

$$
\begin{aligned}
\mathsf{Init}(\mathbf{7}^{i,j}, \mathtt{a[i+j]}) \;=\; & (\exists\, \mathbf{3}^{i',j'} \in \mathcal{D}(\mathbf{3}): \; i' + j' + 1 = i + j \\
& \wedge\; ((i' < i) \vee (i' = i \wedge j' \le j))) \\
\vee\; & (\exists\, \mathbf{5}^{i',j'} \in \mathcal{D}(\mathbf{5}): \; i' + j' + 1 = i + j \\
& \wedge\; ((i' < i) \vee (i' = i \wedge j' \le j)) \\
& \wedge\; P(i',j') \;=\; \textbf{true})
\end{aligned}
$$

where $P(i',j')$ is shorthand for $[\![\mathrm{P}]\!]_{\mathbf{4}i',j'}$. This equation can be expressed in Omega as a relation from instances of **7** to instances of **3** or **5**. Since the execution of $\mathbf{5}^{i',j'}$ depends on the value of P, we introduce an uninterpreted function p. We come back in detail to uninterpreted functions in Section 5.2.2. For the moment, the meaning of p is pretty intuitive. Since its value may change at each iteration, this value depends on i and j. This is why we declare p to take two arguments. As in the C language, a positive value means true.

```
# symbolic n, p(2);

# init := {[i,j]->[i',j'] : 0<=i,j<=n
#    && (    (0<=i',j'<=n && i'+j'+1=i+j
#             && (i'<i || (i'=i && j'<=j)))
#         || (0<=i',j'<=n && i'+j'=i+j
#             && (i'<i || (i'=i && j'<=j))
#             && p(Out)>0)) };
```

Out is Omega shorthand for the output tuple in the relation—here, (i',j'). The domain on which this relation is defined tells which instances of **7** are initialized:

```
# domain init;
```

```
{[i,j]: 1 <= i <= n && 0 <= j <= n} union
```

```
{[i,j]: 0 <= i <= n && 1 <= j <= n} union
{[i,j]: 0 <= i <= n && 0 <= j <= n && 1 <= p(i,j)}
```

Only the first two lines do not depend on p, meaning the reference is definitely initialized only if either i or j is greater than zero. However, the last line is a set that depends on p. It does say that all reads are initialized when p evaluates to true in the current iteration, but it offers no guarantee.

As another example, let us come back to the n-Queens program in Figure 4.10. Is memory location A[j] initialized at a given instance of **5**? Since $0 \le j \le k - 1$, we know $k \ge 1$ (otherwise, statement **5** does not execute). Therefore, **5** is reached after at least one recursive call in **9**, so the word labeling the instance of **5** matches pattern $w.\mathbf{9}.w'$. Then the dominance property (4.14) we observed page 71 tells us that $w.\mathbf{8}$ always executes before $w.\mathbf{9}.w'$.

Liveness As far as *live variables* are concerned, the definition in [68] is the following: A variable is live at a particular point if there is *a* path to the exit along which its value may be used before it is redefined. It is *dead* if there is no such path.

The particular point mentioned above is, in our framework, not a vertex or an edge in a control-flow graph, but an individual incarnation of this vertex or edge: an instance. A memory location m defined by instance u during some execution e is live if

$$
\begin{aligned}
\mathsf{Live}_e(u,\mathrm{m}) \equiv \exists v \quad : \quad & v \in \mathcal{I}_e \\
\wedge \quad & u \prec v \\
\wedge \quad & \mathsf{write}_e(u) = \mathsf{read}_e(v) \\
\wedge \quad & (\not\exists w, w \in \mathcal{I}_e : u \prec w \prec v \wedge \mathsf{write}_e(u) = \mathsf{write}_e(w))
\end{aligned}
\tag{4.17}
$$

This definition is consistent with the one in [68]. It just says that there is a use v of the memory location written by u ($\mathsf{write}_e(u)$) and no intervening write w to the same location. All this should take place during the same execution e.

When comparing (4.17) with the original definition, the alert reader may have noticed the word "may" in the English definition, whereas (4.17) is more rigid: Exact equality is required to hold between the identities of memory locations being written and read. Again, this discrepancy is just due to the fact that (4.17) assumes a complete knowledge on execution. When we don't have this knowledge, liveness is approximated according to (2.1) page 27, yielding

$$
\mathsf{Live}(u,\mathrm{m}) \Longleftarrow \bigvee_e \mathsf{Live}_e(u,\mathrm{m})
\tag{4.18}
$$

Fortunately, the approximation described in (4.18) is often very precise. As it was the case for reaching definition analysis, liveness can be precisely computed when programs are affine or close to being affine. For these programs, write and read maps are reduced to singletons. They don't depend on e, nor does $\mathcal{I}$:

$$
\begin{aligned}
\mathsf{Live}(u,\mathrm{m}) \Leftrightarrow \exists v \quad : \quad & v \in \mathcal{I} \wedge u \prec v \wedge \mathsf{write}(u) = \mathsf{read}(v) \\
\wedge \quad & (\not\exists w, w \in \mathcal{I} : u \prec w \prec v \wedge \mathsf{write}(u) = \mathsf{write}(w))
\end{aligned}
\tag{4.19}
$$

This expression can then be computed directly using Omega, as illustrated in a moment.

If the memory location defined by u is not live, then u itself is useless. u is then called *dead code* in the literature. Compared to the definition in the literature, the gain here is that u is an instance. On the flip side, it might not be possible to simply discard the corresponding statement in the code. Instead, the domain of the statement might be narrowed, possibly by changing loop bounds. An example of these generalized definitions of live variables and dead code is given in [89] and shown in Figure 4.12.

....

```
1   for j := 1 to m
2      a[j] := j+1
3   end for
4   if( p ) then
5      a[m] := m
6   else
7      a[m] := 1
8   end if
9   for j := 1 to m
10     use of a[j]
11  end for
```

.... *Figure 4.12. Snippet from* ARC2D, *quoted from [89]* ....

Let us consider statement **2**. The problem is to check whether all instances of **2** produce a live value. In other words, we want to test if all array elements written by **2** are used (the reference in statement **10** being the only possible use) before they are reassigned. Intuitively, the answer is yes as long as j is different from m.

Applied to our example, (4.19) yields the following expression for $\mathsf{Live}(2^j, \mathtt{a[j]})$, for a given j:

$$
\begin{aligned}
\exists\, 2^{j'} \quad : \quad & 2^{j'} \in \mathcal{D}(10) \\
\wedge \quad & 2^j \prec 10^{j'} \\
\wedge \quad & \mathsf{write}(2^j) = \mathsf{read}(10^{j'}) \\
\wedge \quad & \left(\not\exists w \in \{5\} \cup \{7\} : 2^j \prec w \prec 10^{j'} \wedge \mathsf{write}(2^j) = \mathsf{write}(w) \right)
\end{aligned}
\tag{4.20}
$$

Figure 4.13 shows how (4.20) can readily be expressed in Omega [54]. The first line defines the symbolic constants. The third line in the expression corresponds to the first line in (4.20) since it captures the loop bounds for j', the iteration counter of $v = 10^{j'}$. The fourth line, $2 < 10$, corresponds to the second in (4.20), and indeed statement **2** always executes before statement **10**, which is reflected in their labels' order. The fifth line corresponds to subscript equality, which is the third line in (4.20). Finally, lines 6 and 7 enforce that u is live on at least one path. Since p is either greater than 0 or less than or equal to 0, there is always a w such that $j = m$. We use a trick

here to capture that both paths correspond to the same if construct: Variable w is set
to the label of the if statement (which is 4), instead of either 5 or 7.

```
# symbolic m, p;
# live :=
#   {[2,j]: exists( j' : 1<=j'<=m
#      && 2 < 10
#      && j = j'
#      && ( (not  (exists ( w : w=4 && j=m && p>0 )))
#            && (not (exists ( w : w=4 && j=m && p<=0)))))) };
```

.... Figure 4.13. Omega session to compute live instances in Figure 4.12. ....

The liveness of a[j] can be checked by requesting the simplified value of live:

```
# live;
```

{[2,j]: 1 <= j < m}

As the result points out, instance 2^j is live only if j is strictly lower than m. The last
iteration of the first loop in Figure 4.12 can thus be peeled, yielding the transformed
program in Figure 4.14.

```
1   for j := 1 to m-1
2      a[j] := j+1
3   end for
4   if( p ) then
5      a[m] := m
6   else
7      a[m] := 1
8   end if
9   for j := 1 to m
10     use of a[j]
11  end for
```

.... Figure 4.14. Figure 4.12 after peeling. ....

4.6 Conclusion

In most textbooks compiler concepts are defined with respect to control-flow graphs.
Is it mandatory? Some analyses are so complex in real life that an implementation

based on control-flow graphs is the only reasonable solution at the present time for production compilers. A good example is alias analysis, which for most imperative languages has to deal with issues like pointers, pointer arithmetic, distinct memory areas with different properties, poor typing information, procedure calls, and more.

On the other hand, compiler concepts can often be defined without the need of implementation-oriented control-flow graphs. In this chapter we see that a simplified form of the aliasing problem can be defined with first-order symbolic expressions. We also revisit reaching definition analysis, dominance, and initialized and live variables, all without the use of control-flow graphs. We even see that basing definitions on control-flow graphs can sometimes be misleading: Dominance is a good example of a property that can be expressed more generally. We additionally that definitions based on control-flow graphs fail to provide detail at the instance level: Dominance in nested while loops is again a good example. We show that the framework of Chapter 2 provides a good representation for all these concepts.

Again, keep in mind this does *not* imply that control-flow graphs are not appropriate for compiler implementation. So far, no program representation more general than control-flow graphs has been invented. However, we see here that symbolic solvers could be useful complements and can have an edge on CFG-based techniques. Also, programmers and compiler designers might want to use a formal and more abstract representation of programs when reasoning about program transformations. The main benefit is that the correctness, precision, and/or efficiency of the implementation, which is based on control-flow graphs, can then be compared against an independent, abstract specification.

Chapter 5

Reaching Definition Analysis

In Chapter 1 we give the intuition behind reaching definitions, and we give their formal definition in Chapter 2. In this chapter, we go into the details of this type of program analysis.

To better see the different issues a reaching definition analysis faces, we introduce a small program that serves as a running example and as a unit test for three key issues. The first issue is how well execution patterns, such as dominance properties, are taken into account. This issue is related to the first, but for expository reasons we discuss it last. Second, we want to assess how well a given analysis handles statement instances. Therefore, the unit test clearly has to feature a loop. And last, we want to understand how precisely arrays are manipulated, so clearly an array is the data structure of choice.

. . . .

```
0   A[1] := ..
1   for i := 1 to n
2     if i+1 < m then
3        A[i+1] := ..
4     end if
5     if i < m then
6        ..   := A[i]
7     end if
8   end for
```

. . . . Figure 5.1. Small program illustrating three comparison criteria. . . . .

With an eye on all three issues, we suggest the test program shown in Figure 5.1. The rule of the game is to find the definitions that reach a given reference A[i] in statement **6**. Clearly, some values produced by statement **3** are used by statement **6** at some point during program execution. But how specific can a reaching definition analysis be?

Statement- or Instancewise?   As you probably have guessed, this book stresses the importance of reasoning at the loop-iteration level. So the question becomes: Does a given analysis consider statements only, reporting that statement **3** is one reaching definition of statement **6**, or does it consider statement instances and report that the reaching definition RD(6^i) of the ith instance of statement **6** is 3^{i-1}, when i is greater than 1?

Classical reaching definition analyses tell us which statement defined the value read by the use site we are considering. In contrast, and as you might expect from its name, an instancewise reaching definition analysis gives not only the statement of the producer of the value, but also the appropriate instance of that statement. In other words, an instancewise reaching definition analysis computes a mapping from each read access (the use) to the statement instance or instances that may produce the value.

. . . .

```
1   for i := 0 to N
2     for j := 0 to N
3       x := ..
4       if (P) then
5          x := ..
6       end if
7       .. := x
8     end for
9   end for
```

. . . . *Figure 5.2. An example to contrast statement- and instance-based analyses.* . . . .

Another example is provided in Figure 5.2. Classical, statementwise analyses provide this:

$$\text{RD}(7) = \{3, 5\}$$

whereas instancewise analysis aims at providing something more specific:

$$\text{RD}(7^{i,j}) = \{3^{i,j}, 5^{i,j}\}$$

This confirms what we intuitively knew: Variable x is defined at the beginning of each loop iteration or, in other words, is not live on entry.

. . . .

```
1   for i := 1 to 10
2     x := x + i
3   endfor
```

. . . . *Figure 5.3. Simple loop with a recurrence, copied from Figure 2.5.* . . . .

To see why more precise means more useful, let us go back to Figure 2.5, shown again in Figure 5.3. Clearly, the definition of x reaching a given instance of **2** is the instance of **2** in the previous iteration, *provided* the read instance is not in the first iteration. In the latter case, we do not know which definition reaches x, and we have to assume the definition occurs in a missing piece of code, or does not occur at all—which then hints at a possible bug. One way to write this is

$$RD(\mathbf{2}^i) = \quad \textbf{if } 1 \leq i \leq 10 \qquad\qquad (5.1)$$
$$\textbf{then } \textbf{if } i > 1$$
$$\textbf{then } \{\mathbf{2}^{i-1}\}$$
$$\textbf{else } \{\bot\}$$
$$\textbf{else } \emptyset$$

Following up on the discussion in Section 4.2, we can also argue that the outer conditional is not required because it makes sense to assume the read instance executes in the first place. Therefore, in the sequel equations such as (5.1) are often be shorthanded into

$$RD(\mathbf{2}^i) = \quad \textbf{if } i > 1$$
$$\textbf{then } \{\mathbf{2}^{i-1}\}$$
$$\textbf{else } \{\bot\}$$

We will see in Section 5.1.2 that improving classical reaching definition analyses so as to derive similar information, like "the definition reaching x is **2** or some other previous assignment," is quite difficult. In contrast, instancewise analysis is much more precise: The loop may read a noninitialized variable during the first iteration, and only during the first iteration.[1]

How Are Arrays Handled? Does the analysis consider arrays as monolithic objects that cannot be decomposed, or is it able to contrast A[i] and A[i+1] in a program like the one shown in Figure 5.1?

Indeed, several classical analyses assume that only variables that are lexically equal refer to the same memory location. This makes sense for scalar variables, because obviously x and y are two different variables and refer to distinct memory locations (with the provision they are not declared in unions). However, it obviously does not make sense for array elements, where A[x] and A[y] may indeed refer to the same memory location. The same ambiguity applies to A[i] and A[i+1], which these analyses consider as two different variable names: the former being a string of 4 characters, the latter being another string of 6 characters. However, these two syntactically different expressions may semantically refer to the same memory location at different iterations (see [18] for details). In the best case, such analyses may provide "must" reaching definitions in the presence of arrays.

Another view is to consider arrays as *monolithic*. With monolithic arrays, an access to any element is potentially an access to *all* elements of the array. For the program shown in Figure 5.1, this implies statements **0** and **3** may write into any element of

---

[1]Indeed, when discussing the applications of instancewise reaching definitions, we see the benefit this analysis can have in debugging.

A, and statement **6** may read any element of A. A reaching definition analysis that considers monolithic arrays would then report

$$RD(6) = \{0, 3, \bot\}$$

if the analysis is statementwise, and

$$RD(6^i) = \{3^{i'} : 1 \le i' \le i\} \cup \{0, \bot\}$$

if the analysis is instancewise.

Let us now consider an analysis capable of distinguishing individual array elements. If it is statementwise analysis, then the precision of the result is still quite fuzzy:

$$RD(6) = \{0, 3, \bot\}$$

However, an instancewise analysis is able to express a more precise conclusion:

$$RD(6^i) = \quad \textbf{if } i = 1$$
$$\textbf{then } \{0\}$$
$$\textbf{else } \{3^{i-1}, \bot\}$$

Notice that we expect the analysis to prove that $\bot$ cannot reach the read of A[1] in 6^1 because statement **0** always executes. In contrast, for any read of A[i], with $1 < i \le \min(n, m-1)$, there is no guarantee that instance 3^{i-1} executes and, therefore, that there is a corresponding write of A[i].

Execution Patterns   Does the analysis take into account patterns of relative execution, like dominance, relative values of conditionals, or inference rules on logic formulas?

We have already seen the following program:

```
1   if foo then x := ...
2   if bar then x := ...
3   ...    := x
```

A naive reaching definition analysis would report

$$RD(3) = \{1, 2, \bot\}$$

Now imagine we know, perhaps thanks to a separate analysis, that foo $\Rightarrow$ bar in all program executions. Can the analysis take this knowledge into account to derive that the definition in statement **1** never reaches statement **3**? Then the result would be

$$RD(3) = \{2, \bot\}$$

In other words, how possible executions are taken into account can have a huge impact of the precision on the analysis.

Coming back to program in Figure 5.1 on page 77, we notice that, if the conditional in statement **6** is true, then so are *all* the evaluations of the conditional in statement **3** in all previous iterations. In particular, the condition i+1 < m then holds for the previous iteration (indeed, if $i < m$, then for the previous iteration $i-1$, we do have $(i-1) + 1 < m$). Without the ability to use this information, we saw that a statementwise analysis would say

$$RD(\mathbf{6}) = \{0, 3, \perp\}$$

and that an instancewise analysis would conclude to

$$RD(\mathbf{6}^i) = \quad \textbf{if } i = 1$$
$$\textbf{then } \{0\}$$
$$\textbf{else } \{3^{i-1}, \perp\}$$

In contrast, being able to plug in the implication $P(i) \Rightarrow P(i-1)$, where $P(i) = i < m$, allows each type of analysis to discover

$$RD(\mathbf{6}) = \{0, 3\}$$

and

$$RD(\mathbf{6}^i) = \quad \textbf{if } i = 1$$
$$\textbf{then } \{0\}$$
$$\textbf{else } \{3^{i-1}\}$$

respectively. Notice that in the last two results, the analysis proves that $\perp$ is not a possible reaching definition, which guarantees that all the reads refer to initialized data. This, of course, has applications to program debugging, as discussed in Chapter 6.

Iterative or Direct Techniques? In addition, we might want to contrast analyses not based on their goals, as listed above, but on their means. The main technological difference that contrasts reaching definition analyses is whether the underlying solving process is iterative (as in most classical analyses) or direct. The former type is studied in Section 5.1 and the latter in Section 5.2.

5.1 Iterative Reaching Definitions Analyses

5.1.1 The Classical Setting

The classical reaching definition problem is to compute for every statement **R** reading a variable v the set of all assignments **S** assigning to v such that there is a program path from **S** to **R** free of any modification of v.

Two remarks are in order here:

- The classical reaching definition problem is by definition statementwise: Explicitly, we are not interested here in knowing which instance of a statement **S** produces a value used by one specific instance of **R**.

- The classical reaching definition problem is defined with respect to the control-flow graph. The "path" mentioned in the definition is, indeed, a path in the control-flow graph. In other words, the definition itself is not based on the original program, but on an abstraction of the program: the control-flow graph.

Fixed-Point Computation   To see how classical reaching definition analysis works, let us study the example in Figure 5.2 using *MFP*, or *maximal fixed point*, which is probably the most widespread framework to compute solutions to the classical reaching definition problem [57].

The corresponding control-flow graph is shown in Figure 5.4. Intuitively, the fixed-point process computes, for every node S of the program, a Boolean value telling whether "there is a program path from S to 7 free of any modification of v." For all nodes, these values are initially set to "false." (For space reasons, "false" and "true" are denoted in this figure by "f" and "t," respectively.) The analysis then starts at the end, and goes backward along edges in the control-flow graph.

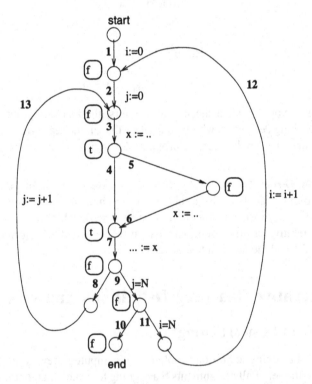

.... *Figure 5.4. Fixed-point computation on the program in Figure 5.2.* ....

We consider the read reference x in statement **7**. Starting from node end and following the control flow in the opposite direction, the value in node end is propagated to the tail of edge **10** (yielding **false** ∨ **false** = **false**) then to the tail of edge **9**. Then the read by **7** sets the Boolean value at the tail of **7** to **true**. Afterward, each assignment **S** whose left-hand side is lexically equal to x sets the propagated flag to false: Indeed, it is no longer true that there is a modification-free path from predecessors of **S** to the read. Figure 5.4 shows how assignment **5** sets the flag to **false** on the "right" path.

When several flows merge before an edge **S**, there is a modification-free path from **S** to the read if there is at least one modification-free incoming path. Therefore, the value of the flag at the confluence of paths is the logical-or of incoming paths' flags. Figure 5.4 shows that the flag at the head of edge **3** is set to **true** and, then, that the Boolean value at the tail of **3** is set to **false**.

Eventually, we have the expected result: Both definitions **3** and **6** may reach **7**, since both the head of **3** and the head of **6** are labeled "true."

The Case of Arrays   In the classical setting, reaching definition analyses consider statements only. That is, the definition point of a value, or the point this value is used, is referred to only by its statement.

However, a statement is unique, but we have seen that it can have several incarnations, or instances, when the statement is iterated by surrounding loops. Therefore, a statement may yield as many separate definition sites as it has instances. Indeed, if the left-hand side is a reference to an array, it is clear the assignment always accesses the same data structure but not necessarily the same memory location: The array element a statement writes into may depend on the values of, typically, surrounding loop counters.

5.1.2   Iterative Instancewise RD Analyses

Duesterwald et al. [26] extend the classical framework so as to capture instances of reaching definitions. They consider simple loops (or inner loops in nests) and derive, for the read in a given iteration i, the distance d such that the defining write instance occurs at iteration $i - d$. Array subscripts of both the read and the write must be affine functions of one variable only (the counter of the innermost loop). Moreover, multidimensional arrays are linearized, which requires that array bounds are known numerically at analysistime. The difference d then takes a value in the numerical lattice of integers in the interval $0..N - 1$.[2]

Consider the example in Figure 5.5, taken from Figures 1 and 3 in [26]. In this example, the definition reaching 2^i is always **3**, and the difference d always equals 1.

This analysis works even when the upper bound is a symbolic constant, such as N in Figure 5.5. However, it loses precision in many cases: To see why, let's consider a geometric interpretation of array accesses in Figure 5.6. The horizontal axis corresponds to the loop counter, and the vertical axis x corresponds to the xth element of array a. On the left, which corresponds to the program in Figure 5.5, for a given iteration i_0, the subscript of the element being read is given on the vertical axis by the intersection with line $x = i - 1$. Let $(i_0, x_0), x_0 = i_0 - 1$ be the intersection point, and let's draw

---

[2]A *lattice* is a set of elements and a partial order on this set. The set gives the possible values the analysis may return—the expressiveness of the analysis is therefore restricted to this set. The order has some nice properties allowing an iterative analysis to converge.

```
    for i := 1 to N
1       a[2*i] := ...
2       ...    := a[i-1]
3       a[i]   := ...
    end for
```

.... *Figure 5.5. Example by Duesterwald et al. [26].* ....

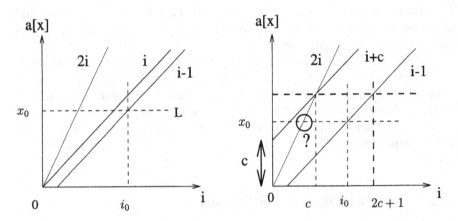

*Figure 5.6. Geometric interpretation of array accesses in programs of Figures 5.5
(left) and 5.7 (right).*

a horizontal line L that includes this point. Going to the left, the first intersected line
is $x = i$. In other words, intersecting the line segment $((0, x_0), (i_0, x_0))$ with lines
$x = 2i$ and $x = i$ gives (at most) two points, and the point with the higher abscissa
always lies on line $x = i$. Therefore, the reaching definition always comes from **3**, and
the distance between the lines of **3** and **2** is always a shift by 1.

The right-hand part of Figure 5.6, however, corresponds to the program in Figure 5.7. This program is similar to the one in Figure 5.5; the only difference is the shift
by c, $c > 0$, in the left-hand side of statement **3**. The line corresponding to the writes
by **3** is shifted upward, corresponding to the new subscript a[i+c]. Now, for a given
point $(i_0, x_0 = i_0 - 1)$, the first intersected line when walking to the left is not always
the line $x = i + c$. Actually, when thinking of integer numbers, there might not be any
intersection at all. The correct answer looks more like

If $i = 1$: $\bot$ (Nobody!)

. . . .

```
0   for i := 1 to N
1      a[2*i] := ...
2      ...   := a[i-1]
3      a[i+c] := ...
4   end for
```

. . . . *Figure 5.7. A slightly different example.* . . . .

If $i \geq 2c + 1$: 3^{i-c-1}

Otherwise: **1** or **3**, or none, depending on the oddity of i

This example is solved in detail in Exercise 5.3 page 95.

In conclusion, we see that the distance vector may not have numerical values only, but symbolic and conditional expressions, too. This makes the complete lattice very hard to construct and symbolic computations on array subscripts very limited.

Iterative Analyses and Execution Patterns   Maximal fixed point analyses work fine on the previous examples. However, one of their main drawbacks is that contextual information cannot be taken into account to detect impossible paths. To see this, let's take Figure 2.3 page 25 as an example again. A simplified version of that program appears in Figure 5.8.

. . . .

```
1   if foo then x := ...
3   if foo then x := ...
5      ...   := x
```

. . . . *Figure 5.8. A simplified version of the program in Figure 2.3.* . . . .

Just looking at the control-flow graph in Figure 2.3, we see that the four possible executions are **135**, **145**, **235**, and **245**, and there is a path from statement **1** to statement **5** free of modification of x, namely path (or execution) **145**. In other words, all four paths are considered valid, and as a result the set of definitions reaching 3 is $\{1, 3, \perp\}$. However, this is obviously more approximate than expected, since we know that either both assignments execute, or none does. What we need is a way to capture predicates of control-flow branches (such as those appearing in tests, loops, etc.) and to reason about them. This requires some form of contextual processing, which is introduced in the next section.

5.2   Direct Reaching Definition Analyses

5.2.1   The Intuition

The basic idea of direct solving techniques for the reaching definition problem is to explicitly *construct* the set (4.4):

$$\mathrm{RD}_e(\langle v, \mathrm{m} \rangle) \;\equiv\; \max_{\prec} \{u \;:\; u \in \mathcal{I}_e,\; u \prec v,\; \mathsf{write}_e(u) = \mathrm{m}\}$$

To do so, we have to find a consistent way to express that (a) the candidate write does exist (we assume the read does; otherwise looking for its reaching definition does not make sense), (b) the candidate write executes before the read, and (c) the read and the write access the same memory location.

. . . .

```
1   for i := 1 to 10
2     x := x + i
3   endfor
```

. . . . *Figure 5.9. Simple loop with a recurrence, copied from Figure 2.5.* . . . .

Consider Figure 5.9, and imagine we look for the definition reaching the read of x at 2^i for a given i. The set of all write instances can be nicely described by a set of affine inequalities on integers—a polytope, as discussed in Chapter 3:

$$\{j : 1 \le j \le 10\}$$

As discussed in Chapter 2, the execution order on integer vectors, for a sequential program, is $\ll$, which boils down to the usual inequality in the case of a single (i.e., nonnested) loop. Therefore, point (b) above is also described by an affine inequality: A write at iteration j occurs before a read at iteration i if and only if $j < i$. The last point (c) is obvious, since x and i are the only variables of the program. Solving (4.4), that is, finding the instancewise definition reaching in Figure 5.9 for a *parametric* read i is then equivalent to computing:

$$\max_{\prec} \left\{ j \;:\; \begin{array}{l} 1 \le j \\ j \le 10 \\ j < i \end{array} \right\} \tag{5.2}$$

This is why the case of *affine programs*, namely programs in which (a), (b), and (c) can be expressed by affine inequalities, has been studied extensively. In these programs, loop bounds and array subscripts are affine, and no `while` loop or `if` test is accepted. It can be shown that direct reaching definition analyses are *exact* on affine programs, which means that there is *at most* one instance u among all the write instances that reaches a given read instance v. This is because, when a piece of program is affine, there is only one execution trace e to take into account and the read and store mappings are one-to-one. In other words, there is no loss of precision when considering the "may" approximation (4.7) since $RD_e(\langle v, m \rangle)$ and $RD(\langle v, m \rangle)$ coincide. Mathematically, it means the maximum is unique and can be expressed as the maximum:

$$RD(\langle v, m \rangle) \equiv \max_{\prec} \{u \,:\, u \in \mathcal{I},\, u \prec v,\, \mathsf{write}(u) = \{m\}\} \qquad (5.3)$$

This nice property made affine programs the focus of a lot of research, and several techniques and tools have been offered to solve (5.3). Most existing techniques are based on constraint solvers or on results from operation research. More precisely, they broadly fall in two classes:

- The resolution of (5.3) using integer linear programming. This method was initiated by Feautrier [31], who crafted for this purpose a software called PIP [30, 28] to compute $\max_{\ll}$ directly. PIP stands for "parametric integer programming" and is based on a simplex algorithm.

- The use of the equivalent definition of a maximum we stress on page 33 to compute Eq.(5.3). This equivalent definition is

$$m \in \max_{\prec} S \iff m \in S \land (\not\exists y : y \in S \land m < y) \qquad (5.4)$$

This method has been pioneered by W. Pugh at the University of Maryland [76].

Using Operation Research to Compute the Maximum   To use PIP, we first construct the set of writes preceding a given (parametric) read. This set has to be expressible as a system of equalities or inequalities on integer variables. The (in)equalities must be affine with respect to free integer variables.

PIP then solves Eq. (5.3) directly, searching for the maximum using an integer version of the simplex. For the simple program of Figure 5.9, (5.3) translates into (5.2). The result PIP gives is the following *quast* (quasi-affine selection tree):

> **if** $i > 1$
> **then** $i - 1$
> **else** $\bot$

Placed in the context of the initial problem, this result is equivalent to (5.1).

This method and the associated software blazed the trail in the domain, and they are second to none in their application domain. However, the input to the PIP software is a bit too rough to be presented in an introductory book like this one. We will therefore focus on the second method and its associated software, detailed in the following section.

Using a Symbolic Equation Simplifier to Compute the Maximum   In the second method, the best-known software is Omega, developed by W. Pugh and his team [72]. Omega manipulates and simplifies formula of Presburger arithmetic, which is the first-order language on integer numbers with addition and (in)equality. Indeed, this arithmetic allows us to express reaching definition problems. For instance, (5.3), thanks to (5.4), is equivalent to

$$
\begin{aligned}
u \text{ RD } v \Leftrightarrow (u,v) \in \{(x,y) \quad : \quad & x,y \in \mathcal{I} \,\wedge\, y \prec x \\
& \wedge\; \mathsf{read}(x) = \mathsf{write}(y) \\
& \wedge\; (\not\exists z : z \in \mathcal{I} \,\wedge\, y \prec z \prec x \\
& \qquad\qquad \wedge\; \mathsf{read}(x) = \mathsf{write}(z)\,)\}
\end{aligned}
\tag{5.5}
$$

which can be expressed as a Presburger formula and can be simplified with Omega until unfeasible elements (x,y) are eliminated.[3]

. . . .

```
# rd := { [i] -> [i'] : 1 <= i,i' <= 10 && i'<i
#     && not( exists( j: 1<=j<=10 && i'<j<i )) };
```

Figure 5.10. Omega expression to compute definitions reaching x in Figure 5.3.

. . . .

To see this, first consider the reaching definition problem for the program in Figure 5.9. This boils down to simplifying the relation shown in Figure 5.10. (This figure uses the exact syntax of Omega.) Notice that this relation maps iteration i of the use to an iteration i' of a definition. That is, [i] appears first (to the left of ->), but of course the use executes after the definition in the course of program executions. Don't be misled by this point.

Omega internally simplifies this relation. To see the result, we just ask Omega to print relation rd, which is done by just calling its name (and ending with a semicolon, like all Omega commands):

```
# rd;
```

```
{[i] -> [i-1] : 2 <= i <= 10}
```

which means

$$
\mathsf{RD}(2^i) = \quad \begin{aligned} &\textbf{if } 2 \le i \le 10 \\ &\textbf{then } \{2^{i-1}\} \\ &\textbf{else } \{\bot\} \end{aligned}
\tag{5.6}
$$

Notice that, in the Omega expression of the problem, "i" refers implicitly to the ith instance of statement 2 and that we made 2 explicit in (5.6). This trick would be more difficult or even unfeasible in programs with several assignments instead of just one, as in this example. We thus have to make the statement label explicit in Omega expressions.

Consider the example shown in Figure 5.5. To derive the definitions made by statement 1 that reach statement 2, we apply (5.5). In the context of the example, u is an

---

[3]Notice that, since we are considering affine programs, there is at most one element (x,y) such that x is equal to u.

instance of **2** and v is an instance of **1**, and we are interested, for a given (input) 2^i, in computing instances $1^{i'}$ reaching 2^i. Therefore, the Omega expression for the reaching definition mapping has to start with

```
# rd21 := {[2,i]->[1,i'] :     ...
```

Tuple [2,i] stands for the ith instance of statement **2**, and [1,i'] for the i'th instance of statement **1**. That is, relation rd21 is indeed a relation from an instance 2^i to an instance $1^{i'}$ of statement **1**.

Then we have to capture the fact that both instances must exist, that is, they belong to the domains of their respective statements. This is readily obtained from loop bounds, but we have to introduce symbolic constant n:

```
# symbolic n;
# rd21 := {[2,i]->[1,i'] : 1<=i'<=i<= n ...
```

Third, we have to make sure both $1^{i'}$ and 2^i access the same memory location. Subscripts in their respective array expressions must be equal, so the reaching definition becomes

```
# symbolic n;
# rd21 := {[2,i]->[1,i'] : 1<=i'<=i<= n && 2*i'=i-1    ...
```

The last step is to denote the intervening write instance z in (5.5). This write may come from either assignment **1** or **3**. This adds two new conjuncts to rd21: one for the case $z = 1^j$ for some j, and the second for the case $z = 3^j$, again for some j.

Deriving appropriate Omega expressions is easy, except perhaps for one caveat concerning the execution order. In the first conjunct, since z and $1^{i'}$ are instances of the same statement, the counter j of z must be strictly greater than the counter i' of $1^{i'}$. In the second conjunct, since $z = 3^j$ and **3** appears after **1** in the text, it is OK that j is greater than *or equal to* i'. The same caveat applies to the relative execution order of z and the read u, which here is 2^i. A possible Omega expression for the complete mapping is

```
# symbolic n;
# rd21 := {[2,i]->[1,i'] : 1<=i'<=i<= n && 2*i'=i-1
#      && not ( exists ( j : i' < j <= i && 2*j = i-1 ))
#      && not ( exists ( j : i' <= j < i && j = i-1   ))
# };
```

Omega simplifies expression rd21 internally and prints out the result when we ask for it:

```
# rd21;
```

```
{[In_1,i] -> [Out_1,i']   : FALSE }
```

Notice that, since the first entries of both the input and output tuples are irrelevant, they are replaced by free variables called In and Out. The important fact is that the relation is false, meaning there cannot be a use-to-reaching definition mapping from **2** to **1**.

We now turn to definitions by statement **3**:

```
# rd23 := {[2,i]->[3,i'] : 1 <= i' < i <= n && i' = i-1
#     && not ( exists ( j : i' < j <= i && 2*j = i-1 ))
#     && not ( exists ( j : i' < j < i  && j = i-1 )) } ;
```

Simplifying this expression yields

```
# rd23;
```

```
{[2,i] -> [3,i-1] : 2 <= i <= n}
```

This is the expected result, as discussed earlier.

Yet Another Equivalent Formulation   Everything seems to be fine with (5.5). However, it presents a hidden challenge when there are many z's we have to eliminate. Actually, this is even a down-to-earth problem: When analyzing the reaching definitions in Figure 5.5, we saw that each of the two statements **1** and **3** writing into array a yields a "not(exists" line on the Omega command line. Imagine there are 100 statements that yield potential instances z. Then we'd have to write the second line of (5.5) 100 times! More importantly, too many exists may cause an explosion of the size of the result reported by Omega.

Fortunately, we can decompose the set in (5.5) into three subsets. Indeed, the "$\not\exists$" conjunction boils down to subtracting the set of elements satisfying the second line in (5.5) from the set of elements satisfying the first line, yielding

$$u\text{RD}v \iff (u,v) \in \ \{(x,y) : x,y \in \mathcal{I},\ y \prec x,\ \mathsf{read}(y) = \mathsf{write}(x)\} \\ \setminus \left\{ \begin{array}{l} (x,y) : \quad x,y \in \mathcal{I},\ (\exists z \in \mathcal{I} : y \prec z \prec x, \\ \qquad\quad \mathsf{read}(y) = \mathsf{write}(x) = \mathsf{write}(z)) \end{array} \right\}$$

Remember that $\setminus$ denotes set subtraction.

The latter equation gives us two subsets, which is easier to manipulate. However, we still have to face an "exists" for all possible kills. To simplify one step further, we can recognize the definition of the composition of two relations, namely

$$\mathsf{R}_1 = \mathsf{R}_2 \circ \mathsf{R}_3 \iff \forall (x,y) \in \mathsf{R}_1, \exists z : (x,z) \in \mathsf{R}_3,\ (z,y) \in \mathsf{R}_2$$

This leads to the following property: Instance v is the definition reaching instance u if and only if

$$u\text{RD}v \Leftrightarrow (u,v) \in \ \{(x,y) : x,y \in \mathcal{I},\ y \prec x,\ \mathsf{read}(x) = \mathsf{write}(y)\} \qquad (5.7) \\ \setminus \left(\circ \ \begin{array}{l} \{(z,y) : z,y \in \mathcal{I},\ y \prec z,\ \mathsf{write}(y) = \mathsf{write}(z)\} \\ \{(x,z) : x,z \in \mathcal{I},\ z \prec x,\ \mathsf{read}(x) = \mathsf{write}(z)\} \end{array} \right)$$

This expression has at least two benefits: One, all (explicit) uses of "exists" have disappeared; two, each set or relation corresponds to a dependence relation: The first set captures the "flow" dependencies from instances v to instances u.[4] Indeed, reaching definitions are a subset of flow dependencies, so it is no surprise they are obtained by subtracting from the set of flow dependencies.

We can guess what is subtracted, too: A reaching definition is a flow dependence that isn't killed by an intervening store. A killing store, by definition, writes into the same memory location as the candidate definition, which in turn is the memory location read by the use. The second set captures the output dependencies from a candidate definition to its killing store, and the third set expresses the antidependence from the kill to the use.

A nice and simple example to toy with (5.7) is the program in Figure 5.9, again. The flow dependence from a write to a read of x is expressed as

```
# f := { [2,i] -> [2,i'] : 1 <= i,i' <= 10 && i'<i };
# f;
```

```
{[2,i] -> [2,i'] : 1 <= i' < i <= 10}
```

Notice that we now make statement labels explicit, as opposed to the expression in Figure 5.10. Also, the order is $i' < i$, not the other way around, as remarked earlier, since 2^i is the read and $2^{i'}$ is the write.

The output dependence from statement **2** to itself is given by

$$\{(2^i, 2^{i'}) \;:\; 1 \leq i, i' \leq 10,\; i' < i\}$$

Well, this happens to be exactly relation f! Finally, an antidependence from **2** to itself occurs from iteration i' to iteration i if both are in the iteration domain and if i' is lower than i, which again is f! The set of kills can readily be computed by composing f with itself using the Omega command `compose`.

```
# kills := f compose f;
# kills;
```

```
{[2,i] -> [2,i'] : i'+2 <= i <= 10 && 1 <= i'}
```

To get the reaching definition mapping, we just need to subtract the `kills` from the flow dependence f:

```
# rd22 := f - kills;
# rd22;
```

```
{[2,i] -> [2,i-1] : 2 <= i <= 10}
```

which is equivalent to (5.6).

Intricate Array Subscripts   One big benefit of symbolic techniques is their robustness and precision in the presence of nontrivial affine subscripts.

---

[4]More precisely, these relations correspond to dependencies in the *opposite* direction: Notice that the bottom relation holds *from z to y*, with y executing *before* z: $y \prec z$. This unusual standpoint on dependencies is justified by the fact that reaching definition relations, which are mappings from uses to definitions, are then easily constructed. An alternative method would be to construct dependence relations with the intuitive order, and invert relations when need be.

....

```
1   for i := 1 to 2*n do
2      .. := x[2*n-i+1];
3      x[i] := ..
4   end for
```

.... *Figure 5.11. Complex subscripts.* ....

Consider the program shown in Figure 5.11, and let's find the definitions reaching x[2*n-i+1] in statement **2** during a given iteration i.

It is indeed interesting to see what reaching definitions Omega reports. Computing these reaching definitions is done, as explained earlier, in two steps. We first compose flow dependencies (rw23) after output dependencies (ww33). Second, we subtract this composition from rw23 itself. To get shorter expressions, we drop the initial statement numbers since they are clear from the context. (Actually, relation names like rw23 serve as reminders of the statements being considered.) We write rw23 as a relation from [i] to [i'], meaning indeed a relation from [2,i] to [3,i']:

```
# symbolic n;
# rw23 := {[i] -> [i'] : 2*n-i+1=i' && i'<i
#                         && 1 <= i,i' <= 2*n };
# ww33 := {[i'] -> [j] : i'=j && j<i'
#                        && 1 <= i',j <=2*n };
# rd := rw23 - (rw23 compose ww33);
```

Omega computes that

```
# rd;
```

```
{[i] -> [2n-i+1] : n < i <= 2n}
```

In the Omega session above, we compute the map from any given ith instance of statement **2** (the [i] on the left side of ->) to instance(s) of definitions in **3**. The iteration counters for these instances appear on the right side of -> in the result. Indeed, we can check that any given instance 2^i reads x[2n - i + 1], which is written by $3^{i'}$, with $i' = 2n - i + 1$. To sum it up,

$$\mathrm{RD}(\langle 2^i, \mathrm{x}[2\text{*}n\text{-}i+1]\rangle) = \begin{array}{l} \textbf{if } 1 \leq i \leq n \\ \textbf{then } \{\bot\} \\ \textbf{else } \{3^{2n-i+1}\} \end{array}$$

Another example of the robustness of symbolic techniques to complex subscripts is provided in Exercise 5.3.

Exercise 5.1 Compute the definitions reaching a[i-1] in Figure 5.5 using Eq. (5.7).

Solution To compute definitions by **1** reaching **2**, we first construct the "true" or "flow" dependencies:

```
# symbolic n;
# f21 := { [2,i] -> [1,i'] : 1 <= i' <= i <= n
#                                 && 2*i' = i-1 };
```

Notice that

$$1 <= i' <= i <= n$$

captures both the loop bounds and the execution order between the i'th instance of **1** and the ith instance of **2**, which holds as soon as $i' \leq i$.

Then we consider all possible intervening writes. These writes can occur either in **1** itself or in statement **3**. The writes by **1** are in write-after-write dependence with other instances of **1** (called ww11 below) and in read-after-write dependence with **2** (called rw21). The writes by **3** are in write-after-write dependence with **1** (ww31) and in read-after-write dependence with **2** (rw23). We first construct these dependence relations:

```
# rw21 := {[2,i]->[1,j] : 1 <= j <= i <= n && 2*j = i-1};
# rw23 := {[2,i]->[3,j] : 1 <= j < i <= n && j = i-1 };
# ww11 := {[1,j]->[1,i'] : 1 <= i'<j <= n && 2*j = 2*i'};
# ww31 := {[3,j]->[1,i'] : 1 <= i'<=j <= n && 2*i' = j };
```

These relations should be clear to you now: They capture loop bounds, execution order (the instance to the left of -> executing after the instance to the right), and subscript equality. The definitions from **1** visible by **2** are the writes not appearing in a read-after-write-after-write chain of dependencies via statement **1** or **3**. Remember that a compose b reads compose a *after* b:

```
# rd21 := f21 - (ww11 compose rw21)
#             - (ww31 compose rw23);
# rd21;
```

```
{[In_1,i] -> [Out_1,i']  : FALSE }
```

As expected from our previous study of Figure 5.5, that relation is empty. We now turn to definitions from statement **3**. Two relations are already constructed, but we still have to build the flow dependence relation from **3** to **2** and the two relations corresponding to output dependencies on **3**:

```
# f23  := {[2,i] -> [3,i'] : 1 <= i'<i <= n && i'=i-1};
# ww13 := {[1,j] -> [3,i'] : 1 <= i'<j <= n && 2*j=i'};
# ww33 := {[3,j] -> [3,i'] : 1 <= i'<j <= n && i'=j};
```

The final reaching definition relation is computed as before:

```
# rd23 := f23 - (ww13 compose rw21)
#               - (ww33 compose rw23);
# rd23;
```

```
{[2,i] -> [3,i-1] : 2 <= i <= n}
```

This is the expected result. Note that the relation correctly restricts i to be greater than or equal to 2. ∎

....

```
1   for i := 1 to N do
2     A[i] := x;
3     x := i;
4     B[i] := x;
5   endfor
```

.... *Figure 5.12. Program used in Exercise 5.2.* ....

Exercise 5.2   What are the definition instances reaching the uses of x in statements **2** and **4** in Figure 5.12?

Solution   We construct two relations, one called rd23 mapping a parametric 2^i to definitions $3^{i'}$, and the other called rd43 mapping a generic 4^i to instances of **3**. Here are Omega expressions for these relations:

```
# symbolic N;
```

```
# rd23 := {[2,i]->[3,i'] : 1<=i,i'<=N && i'<i
#     && not( exists( w: i'<w<i && 1<=w<=N )) };
```

```
# rd43 := {[4,i]->[3,i'] : 1<=i,i'<=N && i'<=i
#     && not( exists( w: i'<w<=i && 1<=w<=N )) };
```

Solving them gives

```
# rd23;
{[2,i] -> [3,i-1] : 2 <= i <= N}
```

```
# rd43;
{[4,i] -> [3,i] : 1 <= i <= N}
```

We can see that the same value of x produced in statement **3** at one iteration is used by both **4** in the same iteration and **2** in the following iteration:

$$\forall i, 1 \le i < N : \ \text{RD}(2^{i+1}) = \text{RD}(4^i) = \{3^i\}$$

At border cases, we have RD(2^1) = {$\perp$} and RD(4^N) = {3^N}. This example and this remark are leveraged on page 124. ∎

. . . .

```
0   for i := 1 to N
1     B[2*i] := ...
2     ... := B[i-1]
3     B[i+c] := ...
4   end for
```

. . . . *Figure 5.13. Program used in Exercise 5.3. We assume c > 0.* . . . .

. . . .

```
# symbolic n;
# symbolic c;
#
# rd21 := { [2,i]->[1,i'] : 1<=i'<=i<= n && 2*i' = i-1
# && not ( exists ( j : i' < j <= i && 2*j = i-1 ))
# && not ( exists ( j : i' <= j < i && j+c = i-1 ))    };
# rd21;

{ [2,i]->[1,i'] : i = 1+2i' && 1<=i'<c && 2i' < n} union
 { [2,i]->[1,i'] : i = 1+2i' && c<=-1 && 2i'< n && 1<=i'}

# rd23 := { [2,i]->[3,i'] : 1 <= i' < i <= n && i'+c=i-1
# && not ( exists ( j : i' < j <= i && 2*j = i-1 ))
# && not ( exists ( j : i' < j < i  && j+c = i-1 )) } ;
# rd23;

{ [2,i]->[3,i-c-1] : 2c, c+2 <= i <= n && 0 <= c} union
 { [2,i]->[3,i-c-1] : Exists ( alpha : 2alpha = i
                               && c+2 <= i <= 2c-2, n)}
```

. . . . *Figure 5.14. The Omega software in action on the program in Figure 5.13.* . . . .

Exercise 5.3 Find the definitions reaching B[i-1] in statement **2** in Figure 5.7, reproduced here in Figure 5.13.

Solution Intuitively, we know that the definition in **1** can reach 2^i only if i is odd. It is also clear that, when i equals 1, no definition in Figure 5.7 writes memory location

B[0] read by 2^1. Step by step, we can derive the following conditional:

$$\text{RD}(2^i) = \begin{array}{l} \textbf{if } i = 1 \\ \textbf{then } \{\bot\} \\ \textbf{else } \textbf{if } i \geq 2c + 1 \\ \qquad \textbf{then } \{3^{i-c-1}\} \\ \qquad \textbf{else } \textbf{if } i \text{ is odd} \\ \qquad\qquad \textbf{then } \{1^{(i-1)/2}\} \\ \qquad\qquad \textbf{else } \textbf{if } i \geq c+1 \\ \qquad\qquad\qquad \textbf{then } \{3^{i-c-1}\} \\ \qquad\qquad\qquad \textbf{else } \{\bot\} \end{array} \qquad (5.8)$$

An equivalent result computed using Omega is presented in Figure 5.14. Checking that the two results are equivalent is left as an exercise. (Hint: c was assumed strictly greater than 0 in the original problem, but Omega considers symbolic constant c as nonnegative.) ■

Exercise 5.4   What are the definitions reaching the right-hand side of statement **5** in Figure 5.15?

....

```
1   a[1] := 0
2   for i := 1 to n do
3     for j := 1 to n
4       a[i+j] := ...
5       a[i] := ...  a[i+j-1]
6     end for
7   end for
```

.... *Figure 5.15. Program used in Exercise 5.4.* ....

The definition reaching a[i+j-1], for any given i and j, is

$$\text{RD}(5^{i,j}) = \begin{array}{l} \textbf{if } j \geq 2 \\ \textbf{then } \{4^{i,j-1}\} \\ \textbf{else } \textbf{if } i \geq 2 \\ \qquad \textbf{then } \{4^{i-1,j}\} \\ \qquad \textbf{else } \{1\} \end{array} \qquad (5.9)$$

The program shown in Figure 5.15 has only affine loops and affine subscripts, but it takes an instancewise reaching definition analysis to see that **5** cannot reach its own right-hand expression. ■

Exercise 5.5   Figure 5.16 shows a piece of code implementing Choleski factorization. We keep the original Fortran syntax because this is exactly what was given to the

. . . .

```
        do i=1,n
1           x = a(i,i)
            do k = 1, i-1
2             x = x - a(i,k)**2
            end do
3           p(i) = 1.0/sqrt(x)
            do j = i+1, n
4             x = a(i,j)
              do k=1,i-1
5                x = x - a(j,k) * a(i,k)
              end do
6             a(j,i) = x * p(i)
            end do
        end do
```

. . . . *Figure 5.16. Fortran code for Choleski factorization.* . . . .

PAF prototype compiler developed by Prof. Feautrier at the University of Versailles in France.

Our goal here is to find the definitions reaching each use of x. The same question arises for each read of elements of array a.

Solution   We give only selected answers. The results we show were produced automatically by the PAF compiler. We first present results for scalar x:

$$1 \leq i \leq n, 1 \leq k \leq i-1: \quad \mathsf{RD}(\langle \mathbf{2}^{i,k}, x\rangle) \quad = \quad \begin{array}{l} \textbf{if } k \geq 2 \\ \textbf{then } \{\mathbf{2}^{i,k-1}\} \\ \textbf{else } \{\mathbf{1}^i\} \end{array} \qquad (5.10)$$

$$1 \leq i \leq n: \quad \mathsf{RD}(\langle \mathbf{3}^i, x\rangle) \quad = \quad \begin{array}{l} \textbf{if } i \geq 2 \\ \textbf{then } \{\mathbf{2}^{i,i-1}\} \\ \textbf{else } \{\mathbf{1}^i\} \end{array} \qquad (5.11)$$

$$1 \leq i \leq n, 1 \leq k < i < j \leq n: \quad \mathsf{RD}(\langle \mathbf{5}^{i,j,k}, x\rangle) \quad = \quad \begin{array}{l} \textbf{if } k \geq 2 \\ \textbf{then } \{\mathbf{5}^{i,j,k-1}\} \\ \textbf{else } \{\mathbf{4}^{i,j}\} \end{array} \qquad (5.12)$$

$$1 \leq i \leq n, i+1 \leq j \leq n: \quad \mathsf{RD}(\langle \mathbf{6}^{i,j}, x\rangle) \quad = \quad \begin{array}{l} \textbf{if } i \geq 2 \\ \textbf{then } \{\mathbf{5}^{i,j,i-1}\} \\ \textbf{else } \{\mathbf{4}^{i,j}\} \end{array} \qquad (5.13)$$

In (5.11) and (5.12) notice the condition on i due to the bounds of both loops on variable k: Indeed, if $i - 1 < 1$, then the k-loops do not iterate at all and neither **1** (a potential reaching definition for **3**) nor **5** (a potential reaching definition for **5**) executes. This explains the condition on i.

As far as accesses to array a are concerned, we can notice that the only assignment to a in this piece of code takes place in statement **6**. Any individual write by instance $6^{i,j}$ is thus subject to the constraints on loops surrounding **6**, that is, $1 \leq i \leq n$ and $i+1 \leq j \leq n$. The latter inequality implies that the use of a(i,i) in statement **1** has no reaching definition in this piece of code:

$$1 \leq i \leq n: \ \mathsf{RD}(\langle 1^i, \mathtt{a(i,i)} \rangle) = \{\bot\}$$

The use of a(i,j) in statement **4** has no reaching definition either, but for different reasons. A definition by an instance $6^{i',j'}$ can reach $4^{i,j}$ only if $(i' = j) \wedge (j' = i)$ (because of subscripts) and $(j' > i') \wedge (j > i)$ (because of the bounds of the loop on j), which yields to a contradiction. In conclusion, we have

$$1 \leq i < j \leq n: \ \mathsf{RD}(\langle 4^{i,j}, \mathtt{a(i,j)} \rangle) = \{\bot\}$$

However, the references to a in statements **2** and **5** do have reaching definitions:

$$1 \leq k < i \leq n: \ \mathsf{RD}(\langle 2^{i,k}, \mathtt{a(i,k)} \rangle) \ = \ \{6^{k,i}\} \tag{5.14}$$
$$1 \leq k < i < j \leq n: \ \mathsf{RD}(\langle 5^{i,j,k}, \mathtt{a(j,k)} \rangle) \ = \ \{6^{k,j}\} \tag{5.15}$$
$$1 \leq k < i < j \leq n: \ \mathsf{RD}(\langle 5^{i,j,k}, \mathtt{a(i,k)} \rangle) \ = \ \{6^{k,i}\} \tag{5.16}$$

Notice that these results are unconditional, but the correct iteration vectors of the reaching definitions are not obvious. ■

5.2.2 The Nonaffine Case

The previous method works fine on affine programs. But just add an if, and the method fails.

. . . .

```
0    for i := 1 to n do
1       if( f ) then A[i] := ...   end if
2       ...  := A[i]
3    end for
```

. . . . *Figure 5.17. Loop with conditional statement.* . . . .

Consider the program in Figure 5.17. Without the if, we would now be able to quickly solve for the reaching definitions of A[i] in statement **2**. However, assuming we know nothing about f, the previous method fails because f is not, in general, an affine function of free variables and counters of surrounding loops.

To be able to use the symbolic methods above, we need to find a way to code in an affine way the possible values predicate f may take. To that purpose, Omega supports *uninterpreted symbols*. These symbols are either constants (like symbolic constants, or free variables, as we saw earlier) or functions (the constants being, indeed, a function of arity zero, that is, a function without arguments). Adding uninterpreted functions to Presburger arithmetic makes this arithmetic nondecidable. However, as their name says, Omega does not interpret these functions but tries to make logical inferences that do help, like inferring that $f(i)$ is equal to $f(j)$ when i and j are equal—whatever function f is [77, 90].

In the Omega syntax, uninterpreted functions are declared with the keyword `symbolic` followed by the function's name and, between parentheses, the arity of the function. For instance, the following line

```
symbolic f(1);
```

declares a function of one argument.[5]

We use uninterpreted functions to code the outcome of predicates in conditionals like `if (f) then` in the program above. In contrast to languages like C, we choose the following convention (which is just a convention; we do not have to stick to the one chosen in C): The true value is coded by strictly positive values, and the false value by values less than or equal to zero.

With this coding convention in mind, to express the fact that an instance i of statement **2** has an incoming flow dependence from an instance i' of statement **1**, we write that (a) the former reads the same memory location as the latter, (b) the former executes after the latter, (c) both iteration counters are within the loop bounds, and (d) instance i' of statement **1** executes, which means $f(i')$ is true:

```
# symbolic n;
# symbolic f(1);
# f21 := {[i] -> [i'] : i=i' && i'<=i && 1<= i,i' <= n
#                             && f(i') > 0 };
```

We can then go on as before to compute the definitions in statement **1** reaching a parametric instance i of statement **2**:

```
# rw21 := {[i] -> [i'] : i=i' && i'<=i && 1<=i,i'<=n
#                             && f(i') > 0 };
# ww11 := {[i] -> [i'] : i=i' && i'<i
#                             && f(i) > 0 && f(i') > 0};
```

Notice that the execution of both write instances in ww11 must be coded by `f(i)>0` and `f(i')>0`. Relations rw21 and ww11 can be composed and subtracted from f21 to eliminate killed writes:

```
# rd21 := f21 - (ww11 compose rw21);
# rd21;

{[i] -> [i] : 1 <= i <= n && 1 <= f(i)}
```

---

[5]Omega enforces some restrictions on the way uninterpreted functions are used. In particular, the actual parameters to an uninterpreted function can only be a prefix of the tuple of variables (in a set) or, in the case of relations, a prefix of the tuple of input or output variables.

which tells us that any instance i (implicitly, of statement **2**) is reached by the ith instance of **1** if $f(i) \geq 1$. In other words,

$$\text{RD}(\mathbf{2}^i) = \quad \textbf{if } f(i) > 0 \qquad\qquad (5.17)$$
$$\textbf{then } \{\mathbf{1}^i\}$$
$$\textbf{else } \{\perp\}$$

If you have no use of the condition on f, you might prefer to simply "collapse" the two cases by taking the union of the leaf sets:

$$\text{RD}(\mathbf{2}^i) = \{\mathbf{1}^i, \perp\} \qquad\qquad (5.18)$$

Observe again that, if function f was known to be an affine function of the loop counter, the reaching definition problem would be captured by the techniques of Section 5.2.1. Say the if statement was

```
if i>4 then ..
```

We could then write

```
# f21 := {[i] -> [i'] : i=i' && i'<=i && 1<= i,i' <= n
                      && i'>4 };
# rw21 := {[i] -> [i'] : i=i' && i'<=i && 1<=i,i'<=n
                      && i'>4 };
# ww11 := {[i] -> [i'] : i=i' && i'<i
                      && i>4 && i'>4 };
```

which yield

```
# rd21 := f21 - (ww11 compose rw21);
# rd21;
```

```
{[i] -> [i] : 5 <= i <= n}
```

which is the exact result. We can take away here that, if conditional statements appear, the reaching definition problem may or may not be affine and, therefore, may or not be solved by the techniques of the previous section. If the test can be expressed as an affine function of loop counters, then this expression can be plugged into the problem's equations. These equations stay affine. Otherwise, uninterpreted functions are introduced. They merely serve as a way to code the program's behavior. Uninterpreted functions may or may not lose precision in the result—more on this point in a few moments.

Now let us consider a slightly more involved example shown in Figure 5.18. Let's find the definitions reaching statement **2**.

Symbols are declared as in the previous example. Relation f21 does not change. The other auxiliary functions are

```
# rw23 := {[i] -> [i'] : i=i'+1 && i'<i
#                     && 1 <= i,i' <= n};
```

```
0   for i := 1 to n do
1      if( f ) then A[i] := ...   end if
2      ...   := A[i]
3      A[i+1] := ...
4   end for
```

.... *Figure 5.18. Second loop with a conditional.* ....

```
# ww31 := {[i] -> [i'] : i+1=i' && i'<=i && 1<=i,i'<=n };
# rw21 := {[i] -> [i'] : i=i' && i'<=i && 1<=i,i'<=n
#                         && f(i') > 0 };
# ww11 := {[i] -> [i'] : i=i' && i'<i && f(i) > 0
#                         && f(i') > 0};
```

Definitions by **2** reaching **1** are given by

```
# rd21 := f21 - (ww31 compose rw23)
#             - (ww11 compose rw21);
# rd21;
```

```
{[i'] -> [i'] : 1 <= i' <= n && 1 <= f(i')}
```

Most of the job is already done to compute those reaching definitions coming from statement **3**:

```
# f23  := rw23;
# ww13 := {[i] -> [i'] : i=i'+1 && i'<i && 1<=i,i'<=n
#                         && f(In)>0 };
# ww33 := {[i] -> [i'] : i+1=i'+1 && i'<i
#                         && 1 <= i,i' <= n };
# rd23 := f23 - (ww13 compose rw21)
#             - (ww33 compose rw23);
# rd23;
```

```
{[i] -> [i-1] : 2 <= i <= n && f(i) <= 0}
```

This tells us that statement **3** defines a value reaching **2** only when i is greater than or equal to 2, which is quite obvious, and when the f predicate evaluates to false for the current value of i.

Depending on your tastes, you might want to collect the above results into a single expression:[6]

$$1 \le i \le n: \quad \text{RD}(2^i) = \quad \textbf{if } f(i) > 0 \qquad\qquad (5.19)$$
$$\textbf{then } \{1^i\}$$
$$\textbf{else } \textbf{if } i \ge 2$$
$$\textbf{then } \{3^{i-1}\}$$
$$\textbf{else } \{\perp\}$$

You might be interested, then, in knowing which reads in statement **2** may not read an initialized element of array A. To do so, you can ask Omega to compute all the instances of statement **2** that are not in the domain of either rd21 nor rd23. This can be done as follows:

```
# {[i] : 1<= i <= n} - domain (rd21 union rd23);

{[i]: i = 1 && f(i) <= 0 && 1 <= n}
```

As you can see, the last conjunct is a reminder that n has to be greater than or equal to 1 for the entire problem to make sense, something we might have overlooked while focusing on reaching definitions. The first conjunct does pinpoint to an iteration (the first one) that has no reaching definition if the second conjunct holds. So it is not a definite answer, but really a "may" one.

In fact, one may also want to get rid of the uninterpreted function. The reasons are twofold. First, this function is not directly related to the original program (in that program, f is a Boolean predicate that we "coded" using an integer-valued function f). Second, we or our favorite compiler might not be able to use the different cases associated with the possible values of f. If we "collapse" (5.19) to get rid of f, we get

$$\text{RD}(2^i) = \quad \textbf{if } i \ge 2 \qquad\qquad (5.20)$$
$$\textbf{then } \{1^i, 3^{i-1}\}$$
$$\textbf{else } \{1^i, \perp\}$$

which is perhaps a more intuitive result.

Exercise 5.6   What are the definitions reaching the read of a[i+j] at instance $7^{i,j}$ of statement **7** in Figure 5.19?

Solution   The definitions reaching a[i+j] at $7^{i,j}$ are given by

$$\text{RD}(7^{i,j}) = \quad \textbf{if } P(i,j) = \textbf{true} \qquad\qquad (5.21)$$
$$\textbf{then } \{5^{i,j}\}$$
$$\textbf{else } \textbf{if } i+j \ge 1$$
$$\textbf{then } \{3^{i,j}\}$$
$$\textbf{else } \{\perp\}$$

---

[6]One could argue that replacing sets by single elements in all leaves of (5.19) is correct and gives $\text{RD}_e(2^i)$ for any execution e. (Why?)

. . . .

```
1   for i := 0 to N
2     for j := 0 to N
3       a[i+j+1] := ..
4       if (P) then
5         a[i+j] := ..
6       end if
7       ..    := a[i+j]
8     end for
9   end for
```

. . . . *Figure 5.19. A program with unpredictable control flow.* . . . .

Without information on P, this may be written as

$$\text{RD}(7^{i,j}) = \begin{array}{l} \textbf{if } i+j \geq 1 \\ \textbf{then } \{5^{i,j}, 3^{i,j}\} \\ \textbf{else } \{5^{i,j}, \bot\} \end{array}$$

We can conclude that only the very first execution of **7** may read a noninitialized array element. ∎

. . . .

```
1   real x, A[N]
2   for i := 1 to N do
3     x := foo(i)
4     while (..)  do w := 1 begin
5       x := bar(x)
6     end while
7     A[i] := x
8   end for
```

. . . . *Figure 5.20. Program with a* while *loop used in Exercise 5.7.* . . . .

Exercise 5.7   Consider the program shown in Figure 5.20 (reproduced from Figure 3.8), which is a small extension of the one in Figure 4.2; This kernel appears in several convolution codes. **3** and **5** "produce" values read by **5** and **7**. However, surrounding loops produce multiple instances of **3**, **5** and **7**. Can we then be more precise on where (i.e., by which instances) values are produced and read?

Parts denoted by $\cdots$ have no side effect. Find the definitions reaching instance $5^{i,w}$.

Solution   The set of definitions reaching instance $5^{i,w}$ in Figure 5.20 is

$$\text{RD}(5^{i,w}) = \begin{array}{l} \textbf{if } w > 1 \\ \textbf{then } \{5^{i,w-1}\} \\ \textbf{else } \{3^i\} \end{array} \qquad (5.22)$$

And the set $\text{RD}(7^i)$ of definitions reaching instance 7^i is

$$\text{RD}(7^i) = \{3^i\} \cup \{5^{i,w} : w \geq 1\} \qquad (5.23)$$

∎

5.2.3 Plugging In Additional Properties

We noticed that relying on the control-flow graph has the pitfall that, when computing reaching definitions, we miss properties like "If statement **1** executes, so does statement **3**." In general, there is no provision in iterative techniques like MSP to "plug in" additional semantic information like dominance properties, which are discussed in the previous chapter. So let's explore how symbolic processing can capture such properties.

Consider again the program in Figure 5.18. Imagine that an independent analysis tells you that, in fact, f evaluates to true in statement **1** for all loop iterations. You would then want to *assert* this fact and simplify the computations we made.

In Omega one way to do this is to use the *gist* function, which simplifies (or extracts the gist of) one relation assuming a second relation holds. More formally, given two relations p and q, a gist of p given q is some relation g such that $g \wedge q = p \wedge q$ [76, 88]. Implicitly, relation g is as "small" as possible. In the case we just discussed, the definitions in statement **1** that reach a parametric instance i of statement **2** can be refined into

```
# gist rd21 given {[i] -> [i'] : f(i') > 0};

{[i] -> [i] : 1 <= i <= n}
```

which is the expected result. The definition that reaches **2** at a given iteration comes from **1** at the same iteration i, if, and *only if*, i is within the loop bounds.

Plugging in additional properties is actually a basic trick that allows for quite precise reaching definitions even in the case of nonaffine programs. Consider the following example:

```
while(..)  do i:=0 begin
    x := x + 1
    end while
```

i is the loop counter starting at 0. If the reaching definition analysis is not done carefully, its result could be something like

```
# symbolic f(1);
# r := {[i] -> [i'] : i,i'>=0 && i'<i && f(i') > 0 };
```

because we assume no information on the predicate of the loop.

But now we recall dominance properties seen in Chapter 4 and say, "Hey, if I'm iteration i and I exist, then all previous iterations i' executed too." This can be written as a relation from i to i' such as

$$i' < i \;\Rightarrow\; f(i') > 0$$

What we then want is to enhance relation r by taking this implication into account. In other words, we want to compute a gist of r given $i' < i \Rightarrow f(i') > 0$. Since

$$(A \Rightarrow B) \iff \neg(A \wedge \neg B) \iff (\neg A) \vee (B)$$

we use the following property:

$$\text{gist } p \text{ given } (q_1 \vee q_2) \;=\; (\text{gist } p \text{ given } q_1) \vee (\text{gist } p \text{ given } q_2)$$

In our case, q_1 and q_2 are $\neg A = \neg(i' < i)$ and $B = f(i') > 0$, respectively:

```
# dom1 := {[i] -> [i'] : i <= i'};
# dom2 := {[i] -> [i'] : f(i')>0};
```

Their effects on relation r can be checked as follows:

```
# gist r given dom1;

{[In_1] -> [Out_1]  : FALSE }

# gist r given dom2;

{[i] -> [i'] : 0 <= i' < i}

# r := (gist r given dom1) union (gist r given dom2);

{[i] -> [i'] : 0 <= i' < i}
```

The two intermediate relations are

```
# ww := r;
# rw := r;
# rd := r - (ww compose rw);

{[i] -> [i-1] : 1 <= i}
```

which is indeed the expected result: After the first iteration ($i \geq 1$), the definition that reaches the use of x is that done at the previous iteration.

| **Exercise 5.8** | Which definitions reach statement **6** in the program shown in Figure 5.21, assuming the value of foo is greater than zero and less than or equal to $n+1$?

. . . .

```
1   for i = 1 to n do
2     a[i] := ... ;
3     if(p) a[i+1] := ... ;
4   end for
5   a[n+1] := .. ;
6   .. := a[foo] ;
```

. . . . *Figure 5.21. Program used in Exercise 5.8.* . . . .

Solution Whatever the value of the condition in statement **3**, the corresponding write is killed in the next iteration by statement **2**. If that next iteration does not exist, that is, if n equals 1, then statement **5** kills the definition of a [n+1]. This information can easily be derived by the techniques presented above. We first construct the flow dependence relations, starting from the possible flow dependence from **2** to **6**. Remember that we use mappings from reads to definitions, however, so this first relation maps [6] (no loop counter needed) *to* [2,i]:

```
# Symbolic n, foo;
# rw62 := {[6]->[2,i] : i=foo && 1<=i<=n && 1<=foo<=n+1};
# rw62;
```

```
{[6] -> [2,foo] : 1 <= foo <= n}
```

Similarly for the dependence from **5** to **6**:

```
# rw65 := { [6] -> [5] : n+1 = foo && 1<=foo<=n+1};
# rw65;
```

```
{[6] -> [5] : 1+n = foo && 1 <= foo}
```

Capturing the similar mapping from **6** to **3** requires using a predicate function p(i) to denote possible outcomes of p in statement **3**. The fact that p is unary (i.e., it takes one argument) is declared by p(1) in the first Omega statement below.

```
# symbolic p(1);
# rw63 := {[6]->[3,i] : i+1=foo && 1<=i<=n && p(i) > 0
#                       && 1<=foo<=n+1};
# rw63;
```

```
{[6] -> [3,i] : foo = 1+i && 1 <= i <= n && 1 <= p(i)}
```

Output or "write-after-write" dependence relations are constructed in a similar fashion. There is a dependence relation from the ith instance of **2** to the i'th instance of **3** if both instances write in the same array element, if the former instance executes *after* the latter, and if both instances are valid. The last condition requires that both loop counters are within bounds and that the i'th evaluation of p returns true. The symmetrical relation from **3** to **2** is similar, but is empty:

```
# ww23 := {[2,i]->[3,i'] : i'=i-1 && i'<i
#                              && 1<=i,i'<=n && p(i')>0};
# ww23;

{[2,i'+1] -> [3,i'] : 1 <= i' < n && 1 <= p(i')}

# ww32 := {[3,i]->[2,i'] : i'=i+1 && i'<i
#                              && 1<=i,i'<=n && p(i)>0};
# ww32;

{[In_2,i] -> [Out_2,i']  : FALSE }
```

Relations for output dependencies from **2** to **2** itself, and from **3** to **3** itself, are built in a similar way:

```
# ww22 := {[2,i]->[2,i'] : i'=i && i'<i && 1<=i,i'<=n};
# ww22;

{[In_2,i] -> [Out_2,i']  : FALSE }

# ww33 := {[3,i]->[3,i'] : i'+1 = i+1 && i'<i && p(i)>0
#                              && p(i')>0 && 1<=i,i'<=n};
# ww33;

{[In_2,i] -> [Out_2,i']  : FALSE }
```

Notice in ww33 the expressiveness of p(i)>0 && p(i')>0. Since nothing is assumed about p, Omega cannot (and should not, for the sake of correctness) infer properties *except* in cases where $i = i'$ can be proven (which does not hold here).

Concerning statement **5**, we have similar conditions on array accesses and instance validity, but not on execution order: We know this order holds.

```
# ww52 := { [5] -> [2,i] : i=n+1 && 1<=i<=n };
# ww52;

{[In_1] -> [Out_2,i]  : FALSE }

# ww53 := {[5]->[3,i] : i+1=n+1 && 1<=i<=n && p(i)>0};
# ww53;

{[5] -> [3,i] : i = n && 1 <= n && 1 <= p(i)}
```

We can then construct the reaching definition relations:

```
# rd62 := rw62 - (ww22 compose rw62)
#               - (ww32 compose rw63)
#               - (ww52 compose rw65) ;
# rd62;
```

`{[6] -> [2,foo] : 1 <= foo <= n}`

The result Omega gives is clear: **3** cannot reach **6** as long as foo lies between 1 and n. More specifically, we can search for definitions from **3**:

```
# rd63 := rw63 - (ww23 compose rw62)
#               - (ww33 compose rw63)
#               - (ww53 compose rw65) ;
# rd63;
```

`{[In_1] -> [Out_2,i]   : FALSE }`

This result confirms the previous one: The definition in **3** never reaches **6**. To make the example shorter, we did not construct the relations giving definitions by statement **5** reaching statement **6**, since no kill can occur between **5** and **6**. Therefore, dependency relation `rw65` is also the reaching definition relation from **6** to **5**.

These results can be lumped into one quast:

$$RD(6) = \quad \textbf{if } 1 \le foo \le n+1$$
$$\textbf{then} \quad \textbf{if } foo = n+1$$
$$\textbf{then } \{5\}$$
$$\textbf{else } \{2^{foo}\}$$
$$\textbf{else } \{\bot\}$$

Notice we had assumed $1 \le foo \le n+1$. The above results can be simplified by plugging that information into (5.24) thanks to operator `gist`, yielding

$$RD(6) = \quad \textbf{if } foo = n+1 \qquad\qquad (5.24)$$
$$\textbf{then } \{5\}$$
$$\textbf{else } \{2^{foo}\}$$

Notice that, if no other reference to a appears in the dots of Figure 5.21, then **3** is dead code. ∎

Exercise 5.9 Consider statement **5** in Figure 5.22. In this figure statement **1** is assumed to initialize the entire array. What are the definitions reaching an instance $5^{i,j}$?

Solution Except for the first, each iteration of the j-loop reads a[i+j-1] in the preceding iteration because whatever predicate P is, the entire j-loop either doesn't execute, or execute entirely. The definition instance reaching $5^{i,j}$ is then known exactly:

$$\forall i,j, \ 1 \le i \le n, 2 \le j \le n : \ RD(5^{i,j}) = \{5^{i,j-1}\}$$

```
1   a[..]   := ...
2   for i := 1 to n do
3     if P(i) then
4       for j := 1 to n do
5         a[i+j] := 1 + a[i+j-1]
6       end for
7     end if
8   end for
```

. . . . *Figure 5.22. Example used in Exercise 5.9.* . . . .

When j equals 1, one special case stands out: If $i = 1$, then statement **5** reads a[1], which is written by no instance of **5**. Only the definition in statement **1** reaches $\mathbf{5}^{1,1}$.

In the other cases, that is, when $j = 1$ and $i > 1$, any previous definition in instance $\mathbf{5}^{i',j'}$ with $1 \leq i' < i$, $1 \leq j' \leq n$ and $i' + j' = i + j - 1$ may reach a given $\mathbf{5}^{i,j}$. It may also be the case that none of these instances executed because predicate P evaluated to false (i.e., for the i under consideration and any i' greater than 1 and less than i, we have $[\![P]\!]_{\mathbf{3}^{i'}} = \textbf{false}$). Therefore, we still have to consider statement **1** as a possible candidate.

We can sum things up with the following expression:

$$RD(\mathbf{5}^{i,j}) = \quad \textbf{if } j \geq 2$$
$$\textbf{then } \{\mathbf{5}^{i,j-1}\}$$
$$\textbf{else } \textbf{if } i = 1$$
$$\textbf{then } \{1\}$$
$$\textbf{else } \{1\} \cup \{\mathbf{5}^{i',j'} : 1 \leq i' < i, 1 \leq j' \leq n, i' + j' = i + j - 1\}$$

■

Exercise 5.10   Consider the program shown in Figure 5.23, where a is a scalar variable and foo is some function. We study this program skeleton in Chapter 4, Figure 4.7 on page 68. Find the reaching definition for a read of a.

```
1   while (..)  do w:=0 begin
2     while (..)  do x:=0 begin
3       a := foo(a)
4     end while
5   end while
```

. . . . *Figure 5.23. Program used in Exercise 5.10.* . . . .

Solution The domain of statement **3** is easy to describe using Omega. Notice we need to declare an uninterpreted function f of arity 2 to account for both w and x.

```
# symbolic f(2);
# exist := { [w,x] -> [w',x'] : w,x,w',x' >= 0
#                               && f(Out)>=0};
```

Now we can use the dominance property discovered in Eq. (4.13) on page 68:

```
# dom := { [w,x] -> [w,x'] : w,x,x'>=0 && x'<x};
# dom;
```

```
{ [w,x] -> [w,x'] : 0 <= x' < x && 0 <= w}
# exist := exist union dom;
# exist;
```

```
{ [w,x] -> [w',x'] : 0 <= w && 0 <= x && 0 <= w'
  && 0 <= x' && 0 <= f(w',x')} union
  { [w,x] -> [w,x'] : 0 <= x' < x && 0 <= w}
```

Expressing the execution order is done as usual:

```
# order := { [w,x] -> [w',x'] : w'<w || (w'=w && x'<x) };
```

Now we can compute definitions by **3** reaching **3** itself:

```
# f33  := order intersection exist;
# ww33 := f33;
# rw33 := f33;
# rd33 := f33 - (ww33 compose rw33);
# rd33;
```

```
{ [w,0] -> [w',x'] : 0 <= w' <= w-2 && 0 <= f(w',x')
                     && 0 <= x' && UNKNOWN} union
 { [w'+1,0] -> [w',x'] : 0 <= w' && 0 <= x'
                     && 0 <= f(w',x') && UNKNOWN} union
 { [w,x] -> [w,x-1] : 1 <= x && 0 <= w}
```

The key point here is the last expression. If x is greater than or equal to 1 (the first two expressions have $x = 0$), then there is a one-to-one mapping from read instances to definition instances. Dominance gave us a precise result even though both loops are while loops. ∎

Exercise 5.11 The program shown in Figure 5.24 iteratively computes the maximum among the elements of an array B. After each element is checked against the greatest current value, some function foo is applied. This program is representative of a larger class of practical algorithms such as Gaussian elimination, eigenvalue computation, integer linear programming (simplex combined with Gomory cuts), and Fourier–Motzkin elimination steps [83].

What are the definitions reaching the uses of A and B? Try to provide the best possible precision.

. . . .

```
1   for i := 1 to N
2     A[i] := ..
3     for j := 1 to N
4       if B[j]>A[i] then A[i] := B[j];
5       B[j] := foo (B[j], A[i])
6     end for
7   end for
```

. . . . *Figure 5.24. Program used in Exercise 5.11.* . . . .

Solution   When $i > 1$, it is easy to see that any value read in array B at instance $4^{i,j}$ or $5^{i,j}$ is defined by $5^{i-1,j}$. When $i = 1$, the initial value of B[j] is read: We conclude the reaching definition of $5^{1,j}$ and $4^{1,j}$ is $\perp$.

Concerning A, since **2** executes at the beginning of every iteration of the outer loop, a read access to A in instance $4^{i,j}$ may be defined only by 2^i or $4^{i,j'}$ for some j', $1 \le j' < j$. The result cannot be made more precise, however, because the value of the predicate B[j]>A[i] is unknown at compile time. The result is therefore

$$
\begin{aligned}
\text{RD}(\langle 5^{i,j}, \text{B[j]}\rangle) &= \text{RD}(\langle 4^{i,j}, \text{B[j]}\rangle) \\
&= \begin{aligned}&\textbf{if } i > 1 \\ &\textbf{then } \{5^{i-1,j}\} \\ &\textbf{else } \{\perp\}\end{aligned} \quad (5.25) \\
\text{RD}(\langle 5^{i,j}, \text{A[i]}\rangle) &= \{4^{i,j'} : 1 \le j' \le j\} \cup \{2^i\} \quad (5.26) \\
\text{RD}(\langle 4^{i,j}, \text{A[i]}\rangle) &= \{4^{i,j'} : 1 \le j' < j\} \cup \{2^i\} \quad (5.27)
\end{aligned}
$$

■

Exercise 5.12   Find the reaching definitions in the program in Figure 5.25, where foo and bar are arbitrary subscript functions.

. . . .

```
1   for i := 1 to N do
2     for j := 1 to N do
3       A[j] := ...
4     end for
5     A[foo(i)] := ...
6     ... := ... A[bar(i)]
7   end for
```

. . . . *Figure 5.25. Program used in Exercise 5.12.* . . . .

Solution   Since all array elements are assigned by **3**, the value **6** reads at the ith iteration must have been produced by **5** or **3** at the same iteration. The reaching definitions are

$$\mathrm{RD}(\mathbf{6}^i) = \left\{\mathbf{5}^i\right\} \cup \left\{\mathbf{3}^{i,j} : 1 \le j \le N\right\} \qquad (5.28)$$

■

. . . .

```
    DO 120 L = L3,L4
        CX(IJ(L)) = CX(IJ(L))+XMULT(L)*W1(L)
        CX(IJ(L)+1) = CX(IJ(L)+1)+XMULT(L)*W2(L)
        CX(IJ(L)+NX2) = CX(IJ(L)+NX2)+XMULT(L)*W3(L)
        CX(IJ(L)+NX2+1) = CX(IJ(L)+NX2+1)+XMULT(L)*W4(L)
 120 CONTINUE
```

. . . . *Figure 5.26. 146.wave5, subroutine PARMVR* . . . .

Exercise 5.13   Consider the program fragment in Figure 5.26. What are the definitions reaching each use of array CX in the right-hand expressions? In which cases can a definition reach a use during the same iteration? ■

5.2.4   Shortcomings of Direct Techniques

One shortcoming of instancewise analyses is that, because of the intricacy of parameter passing styles, handling procedure calls is still a challenge. Classical analyses, like MFPs, have an easier task because they are not meant to deal with array elements, whereas direct techniques have been explicitly designed to that end.

In addition, capturing the control flow in the presence of arbitrary procedure calls is not easy for direct techniques, whereas it comes naturally from control-flow graphs in the case of iterative techniques.

However, in the limited case of recursive procedures where parameters are passed by values, some significant results have been achieved in the design of direct reaching definition analyses. The following section presents these findings.

5.3   Recursive Programs

Instancewise dependence and reaching definition analyses for recursive control and data structures could be the topic of an entire, separate book. For details, the reader is referred to Cohen's dissertation [16].

The two main issues are, on the one hand, to label statement instances in the case of recursive programs and, on the other hand, to express relations between these instances. Labeling of statement instances using control words is introduced in Chapter 3, so let's assume instances are labeled with words in some alphabet.

Then, again, reaching definitions can be expressed as logic expressions. Indeed, there are quite a few results on the correspondence among certain classes of logic, language, and automata (for instance, monadic second-order logic [52]). So ideally, if the RD expression could fit into one of these logics, we would have for free the corresponding languages of reaching definition words and algorithms to build them. Unfortunately, reaching definition expressions do not fit exactly in any logic we know of. Perhaps one day research in that field will bring new results that compiler analysis will be able to apply.

However, existing and well-known languages and transductions, such as context-free languages and algebraic transductions, provide a more than adequate framework for our purpose. In addition, relying on these well-studied concepts allows us to benefit from a lot of known results, which we apply in the rest of this chapter.

5.3.1 Expressing Relations on Words

Let us review these concepts one at a time, taking first a simple example: the program in Figure 3.12, reproduced in Figure 5.27. Variable v is global and initialized before the initial call to P (not shown). One nice thing about this program is that **3** only reads and

```
1   procedure P
2   do
3     v := foo(v);
4     if c1 then P() endif;
5     if c2 then P() endif
6   end
```

.... *Figure 5.27. A simple recursive procedure.* ....

writes variable v (except perhaps some initialization assignment to v). Actually, every instance of **3** reads and writes variable v. In addition, we know from Section 4.4.2 of an important dominance property in this program: When an instance of **3** executes, the instance of **3** in the parent node in the call graph has *always* executed, and has executed *before*. (In other words, except perhaps at the first call of P, we can be sure variable v is initialized.)

In addition, if the instance at hand is in a *left* child, there is exactly one last write into v: the write in the parent node, because that parent node executed just before. For example, if we consider instance **4543**, we know the last instance of **3** preceding **4543** was **453**. For the same reason, instance **43** follows instance **3** — which is the incarnation of the *statement* **3** at the root node ε, hence the instance label $\varepsilon 3 = 3$. For this reason, there cannot be any write preceding instance **3** since it comes first, so there is no definition reaching that instance in the program fragment provided above.

Thanks to this dominance property, we can give perfectly precise reaching definitions for left children, like

$$RD(3) = \{\perp\} \tag{5.29}$$

$$RD(\mathbf{43}) = \{\mathbf{3}\} \tag{5.30}$$

$$RD(\mathbf{443}) = \{\mathbf{43}\} \tag{5.31}$$

$$RD(\mathbf{4543}) = \{\mathbf{453}\} \tag{5.32}$$

Except for the special case (5.29), this reaching definition pattern can be generalized as follows:

$$\forall w, w' \in (\mathbf{4+5})^* : \quad (w = w'\mathbf{43}) \Rightarrow (RD(w) = \{w'\mathbf{3}\}) \tag{5.33}$$

These results are perfect in the sense that, for each request for reaching definitions, they answer exactly one name, which is the best we can hope for since it captures what really happens at run time. We are not so lucky, however, when considering a *right* child, because even if we know that at least the parent node wrote into v, there may be an unbounded number of "cousin" nodes writing in v in the subtree rooted at the left sibling. The following two equations give two examples of reaching definition languages for two read instances:[7]

$$RD(\mathbf{53}) = \{\mathbf{3}\} \cup \mathbf{4(4+5)^*3} \tag{5.34}$$

$$RD(\mathbf{553}) = \{\mathbf{53}\} \cup \mathbf{54(4+5)^*3} \tag{5.35}$$

This can be generalized as follows:

$$\forall w, w' \in (\mathbf{4+5})^* : \quad (w = w'\mathbf{53}) \Rightarrow (RD(w) = w'(\mathbf{4}+\varepsilon)(\mathbf{4+5})^*\mathbf{3}) \tag{5.36}$$

Yes, describing reaching definitions was painstaking! First we hand-waved the description, in English. Then we used control words to refer to specific instances, without ambiguity, in Eqs. (5.29) to (5.35). However, the equations *enumerate* all cases, which would defeat the purpose of this book.

Fortunately, we have a much more convenient and still unambiguous tool to express reaching definitions: transducers. Figure 5.28 shows a transducer that exactly captures these reaching definitions.

Here is how it works. As explained in Section 3.3, each edge is labeled with at most two groups of letters separated by a vertical bar. Letters in the right-hand group are read or "accepted" from the input control word. Letters in the left-hand group are output, and concatenating them all builds the control word of a possible reaching definition.

A Quick Look Back At Loops   Let's consider Figure 5.3 again. We see in Figure 3.15 on page 50 that instances of statement **2** can be named with words. The language these words build is provided by a simple control automaton with one state.

One might wonder what an instancewise reaching definition may look like in a framework based on transductions. The reaching definition of the first read in instance

---

[7]A rational expression like $(\mathbf{4+5})^*$ defines a language, that is, a set of words. Therefore, taking the union of a set $\{...\}$ and a regular expression is correct.

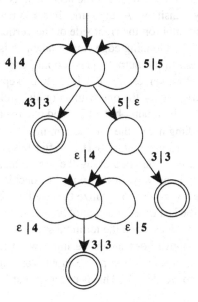

.... *Figure 5.28. Reaching definition transducer for the program in Figure 5.27.* ....

12 is the "don't-know" value. Then at instance **1b2** (that is, during the second iteration of the loop), the reaching definition is **12**. During the third iteration, instance **1b²2** reads a value defined in **1b2**, etc. One way to express this in a parametric way is to write

$$RD(x, 1b^i 2) = \{1b^{i-1}2\}, \quad i \geq 1 \tag{5.37}$$

$$RD(x, 12) = \{\bot\} \tag{5.38}$$

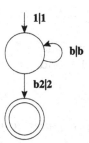

.... *Figure 5.29. Reaching definition transducer for the program in Figure 3.15.* ....

An equivalent way is offered by the transducer shown in Figure 5.29. In that transducer, the input word has to start with **1** to be accepted, as specified to the left of the vertical bar on the entry transition. At the same time **1** is read (and "erased" from the input word), the same symbol (on the right side of the vertical bar) is output. Then, if the next symbol is a "**b**,", the looping edge can be taken: **b** is absorbed from the input and immediately reprinted in the output. This looping edge may be taken as long as there are remaining **b**s. However, exactly one **b** has to be kept in the input word so that we can reach the accepting state—the one with a double circle. On that transition, two letters are consumed from the input—**b** then **2**—and one is produced: **2**.

We are explicitly making use of the "nondeterminism" of finite automata. Imagine we are looking for the word associated to **1b2**. After having passed the initial "**1|1**" transition, two paths are possible: one along the loop edge, and the other along the "fall-down" edge. There is no way, at that point, to decide which way to go. If we follow the first path, however, we soon realize that we have consumed all the **b**s from the input word and that the last transition cannot be taken. And we realize this too late! The second path, however, does reach the terminal state.

Notice also that the above does mean the input word must have at least one **b**. Otherwise, the transducer does not accept the input word, implying the transduction maps the input word to no word at all. This is exactly what (5.38) means.

5.3.2   Recursive Programs with Arrays

To introduce the general problem, let's focus on a very simple example shown in Figure 5.30. In procedure P, recursive calls appear in statements **6** and **7**. We assume the initial call to procedure P is done with arguments $(0, 0)$. The execution of this procedure can be represented by a binary call tree where the left and right children of each node, if any, can be labeled **6** and **7**, respectively, since these symbols label the statements where the recursive calls appear.

. . . .

```
1   procedure P(l, r)
2   do
3     if(l>=r) then
4        A[l-r] := A[l-r] + 1;
5     end if
6     if c1 then P(l+1, r) end if;
7     if c2 then P(l, r+1) end if
8   end
```

. . . . *Figure 5.30. A recursive procedure manipulating an array.* . . . .

First consider the following problem: Given an integer n, what instances of **4** access array element A[n]? For $n = 0$, the values of l and r in expression l - r in **4** must clearly be equal. Since both l and r are initially equal to zero, and since these variables are incremented in calls **6** and **7**, respectively, the number of times we go through statement **6** must equal the number of calls in statement **7**. Therefore, the very first instance of **4** accesses A[0]. So do **674**, **764**, **67674**, among others. In general, for any n, values l and r are such that $l = r + n$, and l and r give the number of occurrences of letters **6** and **7** in words labeling instances of **4**.

How can we capture these sets of instances? In the case of A[0], we know the occurrence counts of **6** and **7** must be equal, but a finite automaton cannot recognize languages of words in which letters appear the same number of times. A solution is to add a counter to an automaton and let it output a letter only if a specific condition holds and/or a specific action is taken. In our example this counter is initialized to n. Then each time an 1 is output, the counter is decremented, and each time an r is printed out, the counter is incremented. We then enforce that the accepted state can be reached only if the counter equals zero. This is realized by the special kind of automaton shown in Figure 5.31.

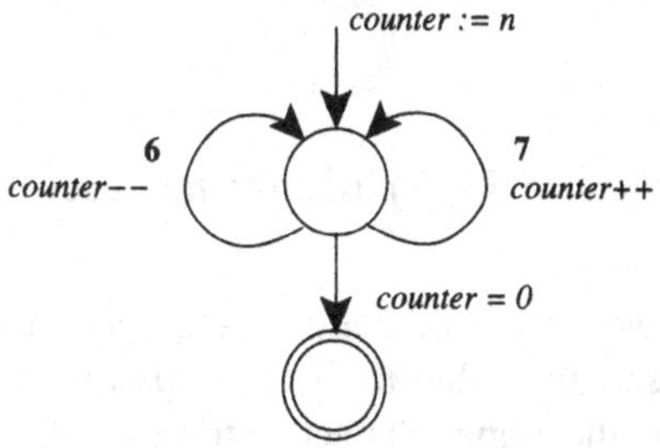

Figure 5.31. A pushdown automaton

The counter of this automaton is initialized to n on the entry arc. Then, from the first node, three arcs can be taken. Taking the leftmost loop arc outputs a **6** and decrements the counter. Following the rightmost one emits a **7** and increments the same counter. Finally, the bottom arc leads to the exit or accepting state. It outputs no symbol but requires the counter to be equal to zero. Therefore, for a given initialization n, this automaton prints out the identities of all accesses to array element A[n].

This automaton is a special case of a *pushdown automaton*. Pushdown automata are finite automata with stacks and stack elementary operations. In our case, we are not even interested in the content of the stack but in its height, because it is enough to implement a counter.[8]

However, this pushdown automaton still has shortcomings. It recognizes or produces a language of words but does not represent a *relation* between two languages. This kind of relation, however, soon becomes necessary, because we might want to map an instance of the read in statement **4** to all instances of **4** writing into the same element of array A. For example, given **676** (which identifies an instance of **4** that reads A[1]), we want an "apparatus" that automatically generates **6**, **667**, **676**, **67676**, etc., which all label instances of **4** writing into A[1].

---

[8]We refer to the content of the stack only to distinguish between positive and negative values. See details in [16].

In other words, given a parametric instance of **4**, we want to capture all instances accessing that same element. We then need both the mapping capabilities of transducers and the counting capabilities of pushdown automata. We need a *pushdown transducer*, also known as an *algebraic transducer*, like the one shown in Figure 5.32.

.... *Figure 5.32. A pushdown transducer.* ....

This transducer has two parts: the bottom part, which is similar to Figure 5.31, and the top part, which sets the value n. The top part reads **6**s and **7**s and outputs no symbol, as indicated by the empty-character-string symbol ϵ on the right-hand side of the vertical bars. Each time a **6** or a **7** is consumed from the input, however, the counter is incremented or decremented. Then the middle arc is taken and the bottom part of the transducer starts. No symbol is read from the input (as indicated by ϵ at the *left-hand* side of the vertical bar), but a **6** or a **7** is output depending on which loop arc is taken. The counter is updated accordingly. We can reach the accepting state only if the counter is zero and if the input character string is empty (the former condition being explicit, the latter implicit). Therefore, when the accepting state is reached, all the letters labeling a given read instance have been taken into account.

This transducer captures all possible writes into the same array element because of the nondeterministic choice of arcs in the bottom part. Consider again the read instance labeled **676**. This character string is the input string, and the counter equals 1 when exiting the top part of the transducer.[9] In the bottom part, following the left arc once and exiting satisfy all the termination criteria, and indeed the instance (of **4**) labeled **6** writes into A[1]. Alternatively, the left arc may be taken a second time and followed by one traversal of the right arc, which eventually resets the counter to zero and produces a correct label, **676**.

Procedure Queens   Let's now study a more involved and more realistic example: procedure Queens, presented in Section 3.3 page 50 and shown here again in Figure 5.33.

---

[9] All input letters must be consumed in the top part since the bottom part does not read any.

....

```
1   Queens (int n, int k) begin
2     if (k < n) then
3,a     for i := 0 to n-1 do
4,b       for j := 0 to k-1 do
5           ··· := ··· A[j] ···;
          end do
7         if (···) then
8           A[k] := ···;
9           Queens (n, k+1);
          end if
        end do
      end if
    end


    main () begin
F     Queens (n, 0);
    end
```

.... *Figure 5.33. Procedure* Queens. ....

Studying accesses to array A, our purpose is to find dependencies between run-time instances of program statements. Let's study instance **F123aa7912345** of statement **5**, depicted as a black circle in Figure 5.34. In order to find some dependencies, we would like to know which memory location is accessed. Since j is initialized to 0 in statement **4** and incremented by 1 in statement **b**, we know that the value of variable j at **F123aa7912345** is 0, so **F123aa7912345** reads A[0]. In fact, the straightforward way to get this information is to apply the store mapping given in (3.9) page 54.

We now consider instances of *s*. Since statement *s* writes into A[k], we are interested in the value of variable k: It is initialized to 0 in main by the first call Queens(n, 0) and incremented at each recursive call to procedure Queens in statement **9**. Thus, instances such as **F12378**, **F123a78**, or **F123aa78**, depicted as squares in Figure 5.34, write into A[0], and are therefore in dependence with **F123aa7912345**.

Let us now derive which of these definitions *reaches* **F123aa7912345**. Looking again at Figure 5.34, we notice that instance **F123aa78**, denoted by a black square, is the last to execute among the three possible reaching definitions shown. And it does execute: Chapter 4 shows that **F123aa78** dominates **F123aa7912345**: Since we assume that **F123aa7912345** executes, then **F123aa78** has to execute. Therefore, other instances writing in the same array element, such as **F12378** and **F123a78**, cannot reach the read instance, since their value is always overwritten by **F123aa78**. Noticing that no other instance of *s* could execute after **F123aa78**, we can ensure that **F123aa78** is the definition reaching **F123aa7912345**. In other words, if an imaginary oracle could give us the most precise set of definitions reaching **F123aa7912345**, it would give us

$$RD(\textbf{F123aa7912345}) = \{\textbf{F123aa78}\}$$

which is a singleton. Ideally, an analysis should be able to derive this property.

. . . .

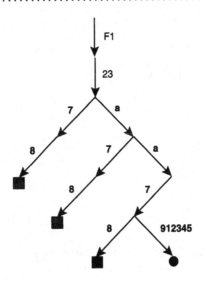

. . . . *Figure 5.34. A possible call tree for procedure* Queens. . . . .

This leads us to our second point. Enumerating reaching definitions is interesting for human understanding but is not practical in a compiler. As advocated throughout this book, we are looking for a compact, parametric representation of a relation that may have an unbounded number of elements. Fortunately, formal language theory provides such a tool: pushdown transducers.

A transducer that describes the reaching definitions in program Queens appears in Figure 5.35. Let's see how it works on read instance **F123aaa7912345**. On entering the transducer, the counter is assumed equal to zero. The first arc reads *FPIA*. It also outputs **F123** (right-hand side of the vertical bar), which is a suffix of **F12378**, **F123a78**, and **F123aa78** – which we know write in A[0]. At the first node, we can't proceed directly to the second node because two *as* have to appear now before *J*. For the same reason, we can't go along the top right loop arc.[10] We thus loop twice along the top left arc and then proceed to the middle node. What remains of the input word is now just **45**, and **F123aa78** has been output. The counter is still zero. Falling through the last two downward arcs leads us to the accepting state after reading the remaining **4** and **5** while keeping the counter equal to zero.

Not only does the transducer produce **F123aa78**, as expected, but more importantly it cannot output any other word with input **F123aa7912345**. You can check that

---

[10]In addition, following that arc would increment the counter, which we know can only be decremented back to zero in the bottom left arc. This arc, however, requires a *b* in the input word, which **F123aaa7912345** does not contain. Again, we take advantage here of the nondeterministic behavior of automata.

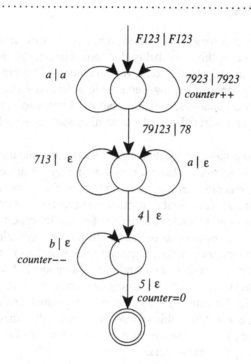

...... *Figure 5.35. Transducer of reaching definitions in procedure* Queens. ......

F12378 and **F123a78**, which labels writes into A[0] preceding **F123aa7912345**, are both discarded by the transducer. In other words, the transducer in Figure 5.35 gives the *exact* analysis result we were hoping for.

5.4 Further Reading

An overview of the work by Bill Pugh and his team on array dependence analysis is given in [77]. The case of nonaffine programs is studied in depth in [90, 88]. Other related work includes a paper by Maydan et al. [66]. The precise analysis of reaching definitions in loop programs with arrays is often called *array data-flow analysis* in the literature [31, 66]. Symbolic array data-flow analysis for array privatization and program parallelization appears in [44, 45]. Creusillet and Irigoin [22, 21] also developed a very precise analysis of array accesses. How to leverage predicates in array data-flow analysis is investigated in [67].

Regarding recursive programs, the first instancewise dependence analysis was presented in [35]. Parallelizing programs with recursive data structures is an interesting related work detailed in [48].

5.5 Conclusion

Reaching definitions have long been limited implicitly to statement-to-statement information. The reason for this is probably that most classical underlying techniques for reaching definition analyses rely on a representation of programs—control-flow graphs—that basically captures step-by-step execution from one statement to another.

Instead, instancewise analyses, including but not limited to reaching definitions, capture properties at a finer granularity: the dynamic instances of each statement in the source code.

Each reference to a memory location has at most one reaching definition in the course of *one given execution*. Therefore, still assuming we are considering a certain execution trace, reaching definitions are functions from one instance (of some statement) to one instance (of possibly another statement). However, because compiler analyses don't have an accurate knowledge of dynamic properties of input codes, conservative approximations have to be made. In practice, reaching definitions are therefore *relations* on instances, that is, mappings from instances to sets of instances.

We saw that control words offer a general means to uniquely label any instance of any statement in a structured program (i.e., without gotos). However, in the case of loop nests, iteration vectors offer an equivalent but more usual labeling scheme. A lot of research has been conducted in this special case (especially when loop bounds are affine), and reaching definitions can then be expressed by closed-form expressions and manipulated using integer linear solvers.

In the more general case of (control) words, relations happen to be called *transduction* by language theorists. Results in that field include classifications of the respective expressive powers of language, corresponding automata that "accept" or "produce" these languages, and properties when applying classical operators (like union, intersection, etc.).

Chapter 6

Applications of Reaching Definition Analysis

Reaching definitions provide a description of the successive definitions and uses of variables, but they do not say what the values of these variables are. However, data flow and value flow are tightly related, and this relation is leveraged in this chapter. We first examine when values are provably equal, in Section 6.1. We then show that this piece of information can be useful to program verification (Section 6.3) or even to a second iteration of reaching definition analysis (Section 6.2).

6.1 Value Sharing

Consider a simple piece of straight-line code:

```
1   x := i;
2   y := x;
3   z := x
```

Obviously, the definition of x reaching both **2** and **3** is the one in statement **1**. Therefore, the *value* of x is always the same in both statements. In other words, we have the following implication: If there exists a unique statement s such that

$$RD(\langle 2, x \rangle) = RD(\langle 3, x \rangle) = \{s\}$$

(here, **s** obviously equals **1**), then we can conclude that

$$[x]_2 = [x]_3 \tag{6.1}$$

which means that the values of x at **2** and **3** are equal, as detailed in Chapter 2. In other words, we can state that **in straight-line code, sharing a reaching definition is sharing a value.**

This property may still hold in some simple cases of more complex programs. Suppose we now wrap a loop around the previous piece of program:

```
0   for i := 1 to N do
1     x := i;
2     y := x;
3     z := x
4   end for
```

Because statements **1**, **2** and **3** still build a straight-line piece of code (a basic block), we can still conclude that the value of x is *always* the same in both statements *during the same iteration*. With this assumption, a statementwise analysis could then report that:

$$\text{RD}(\langle 2, x \rangle) = \text{RD}(\langle 3, x \rangle) = \{1\} \implies [\![x]\!]_2 = [\![x]\!]_3 \qquad (6.2)$$

Remember that only the singleton matters; what the singleton contains (here, **1**) does not.

This observation justifies SSA and explains its tremendous popularity in compilers (see Chapter 8). However, remember: Both (6.1) and (6.2) are correct *only because* we are considering straight-line pieces of code. Even in the second case, where a loop does appear, we consider one fixed iteration of the loop. We come back to this point in a moment.

As soon as we remove this assumption, sharing a reaching definition, in its classical sense, *does not imply* sharing a value. To see this, consider the loop from Exercise 5.2 page 95, shown here again in Figure 6.1.

. . . .

```
1   for i := 1 to N do
2     A[i] := x;
3     x := i;
4     B[i] := x
5   end for
```

. . . . *Figure 6.1. Sharing a statementwise definition is not sharing a value.* . . . .

Even if the definition of x in statement **3** reaches both statements **2** and **4**, we cannot say that x has the same value in statements **2** and **4**. The nice "sharing a definition is sharing a value" property of reaching definitions can only extend to general programs, whether iterative or recursive, if reaching definitions are at the instance level.

We claim that if two variables have the exact same and unique instancewise reaching definition, then they have the *same* value, even if we might not be able to tell what this value is. To sum it up:

Sharing an instancewise reaching definition is *always* sharing a value.

The rest of this book shows multiple applications of this property.

To be more formal, we claim that, for any execution e and any references r1 and r2, if the definition reaching r1 at instance u is the same as the definition reaching r2 at instance v, then the value of $r1$ at u equals the value of $r2$ at v:

$$\begin{aligned}\forall e \in \mathcal{E}, \forall u, v \in \mathcal{I}_e : \\ (\; \exists\, w \in \mathcal{I}_e, w \neq \bot, RD_e(\langle u, r1\rangle) = RD_e(\langle v, r2\rangle) = w\;) \\ \Longrightarrow \quad (\; [\![r1]\!]_u = [\![r2]\!]_v\;)\end{aligned} \qquad (6.3)$$

Notice that w, if it exists, is unique by construction in expression (6.3).

If the "may" approximation RD is precise, that is, if u and v are mapped to exactly one write different from $\bot$, then the result above applies, too:

$$\begin{aligned}\forall u, v \in \mathcal{I} : \\ \exists\, w \in \mathcal{I}, w \neq \bot, RD(\langle u, r1\rangle) = RD(\langle v, r2\rangle) = \{w\} \\ \Longrightarrow \quad [\![r1]\!]_u = [\![r2]\!]_v\end{aligned} \qquad (6.4)$$

Observe that, as in (6.3), w, if it exists, is unique. In other words, $RD(\langle u, r1\rangle)$ and $RD(\langle v, r2\rangle)$ have to be singletons. However, (6.3) and (6.4) differ in subscript e. Therefore, reaching definitions are instances in the first case and *sets* of instances in the second. Hence the braces in (6.4) around w.

Coming back to our code sample with a loop, making instances explicit forces us to make explicit our assumption that statements **1**, **2**, and **3** were considered in isolation from the rest of the world, that is, for one given iteration i,

$$\forall i \in \mathbb{N}, 1 \leq i \leq N : \\ \left(\exists u \in \mathcal{I}, RD(\langle 2^i, x\rangle) = RD(\langle 3^i, x\rangle) = \{u\}\right) \Longrightarrow \left([\![x]\!]_{2^i} = [\![x]\!]_{3^i}\right) \qquad (6.5)$$

Take a few moments to contrast (6.2) and (6.5).

This property also gives symbolic names to *values*, at no additional cost. Indeed, equal values can be named after their defining instances. The problem of giving arbitrary names to values is called *value numbering* [81], but names need not be limited to numbers. If two variables are mapped to the same value number, it means they are equal—but here again, we don't know *what* they are equal to.

This result has lots of useful applications. For instance, if (6.4) holds for two expressions $r1$ and $r2$ subscripting some array A, then $A[r1]$ at u and $A[r2]$ at v refer to the same array element.

As another example of an application, consider again the program in Figure 6.1 page 124. We found in Exercise 5.2 page 95 that reaching definitions, for any i less than N, were

$$RD(\langle 2^{i+1}, x\rangle) = RD(\langle 4^i, x\rangle) = \{3^i\} \qquad (6.6)$$

Therefore, the value x is equal at both execution points 2^{i+1} and 4^i, and 3^i is a valid "value number" for both.

Remember that (6.3) is more general than (6.4). The example in Figure 6.2 should help you keep this in mind. We clearly have, for any execution e,

$$RD_e(\langle 6, x\rangle) = RD_e(\langle 7, x\rangle) \qquad (6.7)$$

However, the "may" approximation is

$$RD(\langle 6, x\rangle) = RD(\langle 7, x\rangle) = \{2, 4\} \qquad (6.8)$$

. . . .

```
1   if( p )
2     x := 0
3   else
4     x := 1
5   end if
6   y := x;
7   z := x
```

. . . . Figure 6.2. Reaching definition approximation and value sharing. . . . .

which is not a singleton. Therefore, (6.8) does not imply that the values of x at **6** and **7** are equal, but (6.7) does.[1] This apparent contradiction is just due to the fact that the latter expression is the contraction of

$$RD(\langle 6, x \rangle) = RD(\langle 7, x \rangle) = \quad \textbf{if } p \\ \textbf{then } \{2\} \\ \textbf{else } \{4\}$$

where p is the value of p in **1** of Figure 6.2. The leaves of the conditional are all singletons, and the conditional is the same for both **6** and **7**. The value of x at **6** therefore equals the value of x at **7**. To sum it up, when two conditional reaching definition expressions have the same conditions and their leaves are identical singletons, the variables are equal.

Notice, however, that the above properties are fragile in the sense that there must be exactly one non-$\perp$ definition. Otherwise, it means the analysis does not know for sure which definition reaches the read at runtime (there is more than one reaching definition) and/or that there might be *no* reaching definition ($\perp$ appears among reaching definitions). Equation (6.6) can be asserted only because there is exactly one definition reaching each read. Change the program in Figure 6.1 just slightly and this property disappears:

```
1   for i := 1 to N do
2     A[i] := x;
3     if(..)  x := i;
4     B[i] := x
5   endfor
```

The instancewise definitions reaching x become

$$\forall i \in \mathbb{N}, 1 \leq i < N : \quad RD(2^{i+1}) = RD(4^i) = \{3^{i'} : 1 \leq i' \leq i\} \cup \{\perp\}$$

There are two reasons why no property on values of x can be derived any longer. First, the result is a nonsingleton set. And second, it contains a $\perp$.[2]

---

[1] We had a similar issue when contrasting (4.2) and (4.3) page 61.

[2] The case of $\perp$ must be considered with care. One may argue that, in a program snippet like

However, as we point out earlier, when the instancewise reaching definition is exact (that is, it returns exactly one instance different from $\perp$), knowledge on values can prove to be very useful in two ways. First, if two variable references are proved to read the same value, then only one access to memory is necessary, not two as a conservative compilation would do, potentially yielding big performance improvements. Second, closed-form, symbolic expressions of values can be provided to another analysis and improve the precision of the latter. In fact, the first analysis that may benefit from reaching definition analysis is reaching definition analysis itself.

6.2 Successive Reaching Definition Analyses

As suggested in Barthou's dissertation [7], the result of an instancewise reaching definition analysis can itself be usefully reinjected in a second pass of the analysis. As an application, even if we can't guess the values of variables and even in the presence of complex functions, we can sometimes prove that two values are equal.

....

```
1   x := 0 ;
2   for i := 1 to n
3     A[x] := ... ;
4     x := foo(x) ;
5     A[x] := ...
6   end for
7   .. := a[bar]
```

.... *Figure 6.3. Deriving value equality.* ....

The program in Figure 6.3 will now serve as a running example. This program looks like the one in Figure 6.1, but observe that x is now the subscript of array A in both statements **3** and **5**.

Consider the reads of variable x. Even without information on foo, we can derive value equality on x. Indeed, we have

$$\forall i \in \mathbb{N}, 1 \leq i < n : \mathrm{RD}(\langle \mathbf{5}, x \rangle) = \mathrm{RD}(\langle 3^{i+1}, x \rangle) = \{\mathbf{4}^i\}.$$

```
1   y := x;
2   z := x
```

the definition reaching x in both **1** and **2** is exactly $\perp$ and, therefore, the read of x is upward exposed and reads the same value. However, consider this program snippet:

```
1   y := A[1];
2   z := A[2]
```

Since there is no definition to A at all, the reaching definition for both **1** and **2** is also exactly $\perp$. However, we cannot conclude that both right-hand expressions read the same value! There is no "type" in $\perp$.

The x read in **5** obviously comes from the definition in **4** in the same iteration. That same instancewise definition by **4** also provides the value, in the subsequent iteration, read by the reference to x in **3**. Of course, we have no clue about the value of x at any iteration. However, we can build on the equation above because it does tells us that, because the ith instance of statement **5** and the $(i+1)$th instance of statement **3** share this definition, *therefore* they read the same value:

$$\forall i \in \mathbb{N}, 1 \leq i < n : \quad [\![x]\!]_{\mathbf{5}^i} = [\![x]\!]_{\mathbf{3}^{i+1}} \tag{6.9}$$

Now consider the analysis of definitions reaching a [bar] in statement **7**. Because of the complex function "foo," we cannot do any better than saying that all instances of both statements **3** and **5** may reach statement **7**, that is,

$$RD(7) = \{\mathbf{3}^i : 1 \leq i \leq n\} \cup \{\mathbf{5}^i : 1 \leq i \leq n\} \cup \{\bot\} \tag{6.10}$$

(Notice that $\bot$ is needed.) This looks like a dead end. However, (6.9) implies that $\mathbf{5}^i$ and $\mathbf{3}^{i+1}$ write into the same memory location. In addition, $\mathbf{3}^{i+1}$ always executes after $\mathbf{5}^i$. Therefore, the former kills the latter, so we can safely conclude that $\mathbf{5}^i$, for all $i < n$, *can never reach any use of array* A *after the loop.*

To sum things up, using a first reaching definition analysis (on x), we were able to derive that definitions in $\mathbf{5}^i$, for all $i < n$, never reach **7**. We can therefore make (6.10) more precise:

$$RD(7) = \{\mathbf{3}^i : 1 \leq i \leq n\} \cup \{\mathbf{5}^n\} \cup \{\bot\}$$

In fact, instances $\mathbf{5}^i$, $1 \leq i < n$, reach no read reference.

Using Values   In the previous case, we strictly limit ourselves to using equality of instancewise reaching definitions. The *value* this definition gives to the memory location was not taken into account. However, in quite a few cases in real programs, this value is simple — typically a constant.

A case in point is the program in Figure 6.4. Consider finding the definitions reaching some use of array A later in the code. Looking at the definitions of elements of A in the program snippet above, this sounds like a difficult question because the bounds of the loop in statement **6** depend themselves on nonconstant variables lmin and lmax.

However, we can look for the definitions reaching lmin and lmax themselves. Instancewise, the definition of lmin reaching $\mathbf{6}^{i,j,k}$ is

$$RD(\langle \mathbf{6}^{i,j,k}, \text{lmin} \rangle) = \quad \begin{aligned} &\textbf{if } k = i \\ &\textbf{then } \{\mathbf{3}^{i,j}\} \\ &\textbf{else } \{\mathbf{9}^{i,j,k-1}\} \end{aligned}$$

Since there is exactly one non-$\bot$ definition in all cases, we know that the *value* of lmin at $\mathbf{6}^{i,j,k}$ is the value of the right-hand expression at that point in time. This value is

$$[\![\text{lmin}]\!]_{\mathbf{6}^{i,j,k}} = \quad \begin{aligned} &\textbf{if } k = i \\ &\textbf{then } [\![j]\!]_{\mathbf{3}^{i,j}} \\ &\textbf{else } [\![1]\!]_{\mathbf{9}^{i,j,k-1}} \end{aligned} \tag{6.11}$$

. . . .

```
1   for i := 1 to m do
2     for j := 1 to i do
3       lmin := j;
4       lmax := i
5       for k:= i to m do
6         for l := lmin to lmax do
7           A[l] := ...
8         end for
9         lmin := 1;
10        lmax := k + 1
11      end for
12    end for
13  end for
```

. . . . *Figure 6.4. Fragment of procedure OLDA.* . . . .

Notice it would be incorrect to infer

$$[\![\text{lmin}]\!]_{6^{i,j,k}} = \begin{array}{l} \textbf{if } k = i \\ \textbf{then } [\![\text{lmin}]\!]_{3^{i,j}} \\ \textbf{else } [\![\text{lmin}]\!]_{9^{i,j,k-1}} \end{array}$$

since $[\![\text{lmin}]\!]_{3^{i,j}}$ and $[\![\text{lmin}]\!]_{9^{i,j,k-1}}$ denote the values of lmin just before assignments $3^{i,j}$ and $9^{i,j,k-1}$ execute, respectively. The values of the right-hand expressions must be considered instead. Eq. (6.11) equals

$$[\![\text{lmin}]\!]_{6^{i,j,k}} = \begin{array}{l} \textbf{if } k = i \\ \textbf{then } j \\ \textbf{else } 1 \end{array}$$

In a similar fashion, the instancewise definition of lmax in statement 6 is unambiguous:

$$RD(\langle 6^{i,j,k}, \text{lmax}\rangle) = \begin{array}{l} \textbf{if } k = i \\ \textbf{then } \{4^{i,j}\} \\ \textbf{else } \{10^{i,j,k-1}\} \end{array}$$

and, therefore,

$$[\![\text{lmax}]\!]_{6^{i,j,k}} = \begin{array}{ll} \textbf{if } k = i \\ \textbf{then } i & \quad (6.12) \\ \textbf{else } k \end{array}$$

Don't forget that the last step above, which consists of deriving symbolic values from instancewise reaching definitions, is not as easy as it looks. Indeed, the value reported in (6.12) in the case $k > i$ is k, not $k + 1$, because the right-hand expression of statement **10** must be evaluated in the context of the reaching definition $(\mathbf{10}^{i,j,k-1})$, yielding $(k-1)+1 = k$.

These results turn out to provide a better understanding of the loop on 1 in statement **6**. The values of the lower and upper bounds of 1 happen to be affine with respect to counters of surrounding loops, depending on certain conditions (here, on k). In addition, these conditions have a nice property: They themselves are affine.[3] The bounds on j (and therefore the domain of **7**) are *piecewise affine*, that is, are affine on subsets that can be defined themselves by affine inequalities.

$$k = i \quad \Rightarrow \quad j \le l \le i$$
$$i < k \le m \quad \Rightarrow \quad 1 \le l \le k$$

The domain of statement **7** is then

$$\{(i,j,k,l) \in \mathbb{N}^4 \ : \ 1 \le j \le l \le i \le m \wedge k = i\}$$
$$\bigcup \ \{(i,j,k,l) \in \mathbb{N}^4 \ : \ 1 \le j \le i < k \le m \wedge 1 \le l \le k\}$$

Let us now come back to the original problem of understanding which elements of array A are modified by which instance of statement **7**. The fact that the domain of statement **7** is piecewise affine allows us to splinter the analysis depending on whether k is greater than or equal to i. In addition, the bounds on l are, in both cases, affine with respect to the current set of free variables (constants and the counters i, j, and k of surrounding loops). Therefore, loop **6** can be considered as a piece of affine program, and computing the definitions reaching a use of A later in the code can now be done using methods presented earlier in this book.

Exercise 6.1   Consider the following program:

```
1    for := 0 to 2*n
2       b[i] := ...
3    end for
4    for := 0 to n
5       a[b[i]] := ...
6    end for
7    for := n to 2*n
8       a[b[2*n-i]] := ...
9    end for
10   for := 0 to 2*n
11      ... := a[b[i]]
12   end for
```

What are the definitions reaching the use of a[b[i]] at some instance i of statement **11**? Consider the same problem by first analyzing the definitions of b[i] reaching statements **5** and **8**.

---

[3]These conditions could have been "if $k = foo(i)$," with foo a complicated function, which would not have helped us much because we don't know, in general, how to manipulate such an expression. Instead, $k = i$ can be written as $k \le i$ and $k \ge i$, which is a system of affine inequalities.

Solution   A brute-force reaching definition analysis would say that

$$\forall i \in \mathbb{N}, 0 \leq i \leq 2n \;:\; RD(\mathbf{11}^i) = \{\mathbf{5}^{i'} : 0 \leq i' \leq n\} \cup \{\mathbf{8}^{i'} : n \leq i' \leq 2n\}$$

However, if we first consider the read accesses to b in statements **5** and **8**, we have

$$\forall i \in \mathbb{N}, 0 \leq i \leq n \;:\; RD(\mathbf{5}^i) = RD(\mathbf{8}^{2n-i}) = \{\mathbf{2}^i\}$$

and, therefore, the values read by the two corresponding references are equal. Plugging this information into the analysis of definitions reaching statement **11**, we derive that the values produced in statement **5** cannot reach statement **11**, that is,

$$\forall i \in \mathbb{N}, 0 \leq i \leq 2n \;:\; RD(\mathbf{11}^i) = \{\mathbf{8}^{i'} : n \leq i' \leq 2n\}$$

■

A Good Strategy   When applying an instancewise analysis on a nonaffine program, there is no simple way to know where to start—that is, knowing which reference should be analyzed first. Analyses of each variable can be iterated until none of their results can mutually be improved, or we can apply a "demand-driven" strategy, as outlined below.

Indeed, a good strategy is to try and get properties on variables appearing in the equation we want to solve. In the case of reaching definition analysis, this equation typically is (5.5):

$$
\begin{aligned}
u \text{ RD } v \Leftrightarrow (u, v) \in \{(x, y) \;\;:\;\; & x, y \in \mathcal{I} \;\wedge\; y \prec x \\
\wedge\;\; & \mathsf{read}(x) = \mathsf{write}(y) \\
\wedge\;\; & (\not\exists z : z \in \mathcal{I} \;\wedge\; y \prec z \prec x \\
& \wedge\; \mathsf{read}(x) = \mathsf{write}(z))\}
\end{aligned}
$$

In the case of Figure 6.4, the subscript expression i.e., $\mathsf{read}(x) = \mathsf{write}(y)$ is not an issue: 1 is a counter of a surrounding loop. As we saw earlier, the hard part lies in the bound of this loop (i.e., $x, y \in \mathcal{I}$), so it makes sense to postpone the reaching definition analysis for array A, trigger a reaching definition analysis for lmin and lmax, and try to use that result when resuming the analysis on A.

In a similar fashion, analyzing the reaching definitions for A in Figure 6.3 is immediately hampered by the lack of information on x. More precisely, we face two hurdles: On the one hand, we can't move on because the value of x at either **3** or **5** is not an affine function, so we don't have a satisfying symbolic expression for $\mathsf{read}(x) = \mathsf{write}(y)$. On the other hand, we have no information on kills, so we have no information to prove or disprove the existence of intermediate writes z. Fortunately, (6.10) provides the second kind of information: Definitions in $\mathbf{5}^i$, for all $i < n$, never reach **7**.

6.3   Reaching Definition Analyses and Verification

We see in Section 6.2 that a first pass of reaching definition analysis can make a second pass more precise. But clearly enough, the result of many other analyses could be "injected" into reaching definition analysis, or vice versa, to improve the precision of the result.

The interplay between static analyses and verification is still the subject of active research. For instance, Heintze et al. have recently shown [47] how verification and static analysis can complement each other to gather more precise properties on the variables of a program. In this book, Section 6.3.1 presents how assertions can help reaching definition analysis. Then, Section 6.3.2 details the interaction between reaching definitions and weakest preconditions. For the sake of completeness, let's first explain these concepts.

Assertions   Verification relies on predicates on the relative values of variables, called *assertions*. Assertions hold after one statement and before the next statement, since they assert properties on variable values after side effects occur. An example of such an assertion is $\{i \leq 11\}$, to indicate that the value of variable i is less than or equal to 11. Another example that is handy in Section 6.3.2 is assertion $\{b[i] = i\}$, which asserts that the value of array element b[i] equals the value of i where the assertion appears.

Notice also that assertions may be stated by the user or derived by an analysis, or a mixture of both. Very often, assertions can be plugged directly in a symbolic reaching definition analysis, exactly in the way discussed in Section 5.2.3.

In the landmark book cited above, Gries [42] demonstrates how inserting appropriate assertions can help debug a program. Here is one of the examples of his book, which intends to compute the integer division of x by y:

```
r := x; q :=0;
while r > y do
    r := r-y;
    q := q+1
end
print q, r
```

The quotient is q. We can expect, assuming that (a) x is positive, (b) y is *strictly* positive, and (c) the program halts, that $x = q \times y + r$, with remainder r smaller than y. Such properties can be made explicit in the program text by assertions, as illustrated below.[4]

```
{0 ≤ x ∧ 0 < y}
r := x; q :=0;
while r > y do
    r := r-y;
    q := q+1
end
print q, r
{0 ≤ r ≤ y ∧ x = q × y + r}
```

Semantic analyses can derive sophisticated assertions. Consider, for instance, the program in Figure 6.5 taken from [39]. We are interested in finding properties on i, j,

---

[4]Some languages, like Eiffel, actually feature assertions as first-class elements of the language.

. . . .

```
1   i := 0; j := 0; k := 0;
2   while ...  do
3      i := i+4;
4      if ...
5         then j := j+4
6         else j := j+12
7      end
8      k := k+4;
9      print i, j, k;
10  end
11  print i
```

. . . . *Figure 6.5. Illustrating linear and congruence relations.* . . . .

and k, that is, on the values of memory locations i, j, and k , respectively, just before statement **9**. Several semantic analyses have been proposed to derive such results, with, of course, more and more precise information.

The simplest result is just that $i, j, k \geq 4$. Cousot and Halbwachs [20] present techniques to derive more general linear predicates, such as

$$i \leq j \leq 3i \land i \geq 4 \land i = k$$

Later research [39, 40] shows we can derive *congruence relations*, such as

$$i \equiv j \bmod 8 \land i \equiv 0 \bmod 4 \land i = k$$

Weakest Preconditions   For a given statement **S** and a given predicate P, the *weakest precondition* is a set of states. Execution of **S** begun in any of these states is guaranteed to terminate in a finite amount of time in a state satisfying P [42]. Coming back to the first predicate above, in a program fragment like

```
1   i := i+1 ;
2   print i
```

the weakest precondition for $i \leq 11$ to hold *after* statement **1** is

$$wp(\mathbf{1}, i \leq 11) = i \leq 10$$

Notice that in this traditional notation, expressions should be evaluated in their corresponding "local" states. This implies that ambiguities may arise: The symbol i stands for two different values, which are the value stored in i just before statement **2** (in expression $i \leq 11$) and the value stored in i just before statement **1** (in $i \leq 10$). It would be nonstandard but more precise to write that the weakest precondition for $[i]_2$ to be less than or equal to 11 is $[i]_1 \leq 10$.

With predicate $b[i] = i$ and statement

3   `b[b[i]] := i`

the weakest precondition is

$$wp(\mathbf{3}, b[i] = i) \ = \ (b[i] = i)$$

implying that the execution of statement **3** has no effect on predicate $b[i] = i$.

Again, let us stress that variables in assertions are implicitly evaluated in the current program state. Indeed, in the above examples, we didn't know the context surrounding, say, variable i. Perhaps statement **1** was executed 100 times. Asserting $i \leq 11$ just after statement **1** should then be understood as

$$\forall u \in \mathcal{D}(\mathbf{1}): \ [\![i]\!]_u \leq 11$$

that is, execution of any instance of **1** leaves the value of i less than or equal to 11.

6.3.1   Reaching Definitions and Assertions

. . . .

```
1   while ((ito >= 1)
        && (heap[ifrom]->cost < heap[ito]->cost)) {
2       temp = heap[ito];
3       heap[ito] = heap[ifrom];
4       heap[ifrom] = temp;
5       ifrom = ito;
6       ito = ifrom/2;
7   }
```

. . . . . . *Figure 6.6. Excerpt from the SPEC CINT2000 benchmark* `175.vpr`. . . . . . .

Consider the loop in Figure 6.6, which is a key loop in the `175.vpr` benchmark of the SPEC CINT2000 suite. It really *looks* like `heap[ifrom]` (and therefore `heap[ifrom]->cost`) is loop-invariant. If we could be sure this observation is true, we could load these values only once and hoist the memory references out of the loop, as shown in Figure 6.7.

But first, let's run this loop by hand to convince ourselves that this property indeed holds. Let's start with, say, `ifrom` equal to 12 and `ito` equal to 42.

During the first iteration ($i = 0$), `temp` receives the value stored in `heap[42]`, say 5. The second instruction sets `heap[42]` to the value of `heap[12]`, say 8, and after the third statement `heap[12]` contains 5, the original value in `heap[42]`. Eventually, `ifrom` is equal to 42 and `ito` to 21.

During the second iteration ($i = 1$), the first instruction sets `temp` to the value stored in `heap[21]`, whatever this value is. The second instruction then reads the value of `heap[42]`, which is 8 again, and assigns it to `heap[21]`. The third instruction assigns the value of `temp` to `heap[42]`. At the end of the second iteration,

```
temp = heap[ifrom];
ifrom_cost = temp->cost;

while ((ito >= 1) && (ifrom_cost < heap[ito]->cost)) {
  heap[ifrom] = heap[ito];
  heap[ito] = temp;
  ifrom = ito;
  ito = ifrom/2;
}
```

.... *Figure 6.7. Potential optimization of the loop in Figure 6.6.* ....

ifrom is equal to 21 and ito to 10. Clearly, during the third iteration, the second instruction will read heap[21], which is once again 8!

This simulation by hand may not have convinced you, and you would be right to be skeptical. *Proving* that heap[ifrom] is constant is of course more difficult. But instancewise reaching definition analysis can help do it.[5] The trick is to apply the analysis to the read of heap[ifrom] in statement **3** for a parametric instance i.

Clearly enough, a candidate reaching definition is statement **4** at the previous iteration, *provided* the old index of heap, which was the old value of ifrom, is equal to the current index, which is the current value of ifrom. If this equality does not hold, then the next candidate (next in reverse execution order) is statement **3** during the previous iteration, provided again that the values of indexes are equal. These different cases are summed up in the formula below.

$$i \geq 1 : \qquad \mathrm{RD}(3^i) = \begin{array}{l} \mathbf{if}\ [\![\mathtt{ifrom}]\!]_{3^i} = [\![\mathtt{ifrom}]\!]_{4^{i-1}} \\ \mathbf{then}\ \{4^{i-1}\} \\ \mathbf{else}\ \ \mathbf{if}\ [\![\mathtt{ifrom}]\!]_{3^i} = [\![\mathtt{ito}]\!]_{3^{i-1}} \\ \qquad \mathbf{then}\ \{3^{i-1}\} \\ \mathbf{else}\ \dots \end{array} \qquad (6.13)$$

The key to proving the constant value of heap[ifrom] lies in the equalities. The first one

$$[\![\mathtt{ifrom}]\!]_{3^i} = [\![\mathtt{ifrom}]\!]_{4^{i-1}} \qquad (6.14)$$

cannot be true because, on the other hand,

$$[\![\mathtt{ifrom}]\!]_{3^i} = [\![\mathtt{ito}]\!]_{5^{i-1}} = [\![\mathtt{ito}]\!]_{1^{i-1}} \qquad (6.15)$$

Equations (6.14) and (6.15) imply $[\![\mathtt{ifrom}]\!]_{4^{i-1}} = [\![\mathtt{ito}]\!]_{1^{i-1}}$, which contradicts the second condition of the while loop. In other words, that second condition should be

---

[5] At least on paper! Implementing it is another issue, which we address later. However, notice that checking these properties is not easy for humans, so instancewise RD analysis has a value in itself as a framework to reason about programs and their transformations!

considered as assertion

$$\{heap[ifrom] \neq heap[ito]\}$$

or even

$$\{ifrom \neq ito\}$$

inserted at the beginning of the loop body, that is, before statement **2**.

To sum it up, we can now simplify (6.13) into

$$i \geq 1: \qquad \text{RD}(3^i) = \quad \textbf{if } [\![\texttt{ifrom}]\!]_{3^i} = [\![\texttt{ito}]\!]_{3^{i-1}} \qquad (6.16)$$
$$\textbf{then } \{3^{i-1}\}$$
$$\textbf{else } ...$$

But we know that $[\![\texttt{ifrom}]\!]_{3^i} = [\![\texttt{ito}]\!]_{3^{i-1}}$. So the one and only reaching definition is 3^{i-1}. What this proves is that statement **3** propagates the very same value it has stored in the previous iteration. Notice that an instancewise reaching definition would not have been conclusive if any another instance, including the "don't-know" instance $\perp$, had been a possible reaching definition.

Exercise 6.2   Consider the program in Figure 6.8, discussed in [64, 65].   What are

. . . .

```
1   i1 := 1
2   IP[1] = X
3   for k := 1 to N do
4     i2 := 3 - i1
5     IP[i2] := IP[i1]
6     i1 := i2
7   end for
```

. . . . *Figure 6.8. Fragment of program CFFT2D1.* . . . .

the definitions reaching i1 and i2 in statements **4** and **6**, respectively, during a given iteration of the loop? (Clearly, the same definition of i1 reaches both statements **4** and **5** for a given iteration k.) What then is the value of i1 at statement **5** for a given iteration k of the loop?

Solution   It is easy to see that the definition of i1 reaching the kth instance of **4** is **1** the first time and **6** for all remaining iterations:

$$\forall k \in \mathbb{N}, 1 \leq k \leq N: \quad \text{RD}(\langle 4^k, \texttt{i1} \rangle) = \quad \textbf{if } k = 1 \qquad (6.17)$$
$$\textbf{then } \{1\}$$
$$\textbf{else } \{6^{k-1}\}$$

Since the leaves of this conditional are singletons, we can propagate values. In this example, the right-hand sides of statements appearing in this reaching definition are very simple: One is a constant; the other is a variable, i2, whose value at instance 6^{k-1} is denoted $[\![i2]\!]_{6^{k-1}}$. We can therefore conclude that the value $[\![i1]\!]_{4^k}$ of i1 at 4^k is

$$\forall k \in \mathbb{N}, 1 \le k \le N : \quad [\![i1]\!]_{4^k} = \textbf{if } k = 1 \qquad (6.18)$$
$$\textbf{then } 1$$
$$\textbf{else } [\![i2]\!]_{6^{k-1}}$$

Notice that the "**1**" appearing in the first leaf of the conditional in (6.17) is different from the "1" appearing in the first leaf of the conditional in (6.18). The former is a statement label, the second a value. It so happens that the right-hand side of the assignment in statement **1** is the constant 1.

Naturally, we now look for the definition reaching i2 at 6^k, for a given k:

$$\forall k \in \mathbb{N}, 1 \le k \le N : \quad \text{RD}(\langle 6^k, i2 \rangle) = \{4^k\}$$

Again, this information readily gives an expression of the value of i2 at that instance:

$$\forall k \in \mathbb{N}, 1 \le k \le N : \quad [\![i2]\!]_{6^k} = 3 - [\![i1]\!]_{4^k} \qquad (6.19)$$

Plugging (6.19) into (6.18) yields

$$\forall k \in \mathbb{N}, 1 \le k \le N : \quad [\![i1]\!]_{4^k} = \textbf{if } k = 1 \qquad (6.20)$$
$$\textbf{then } 1$$
$$\textbf{else } 3 - [\![i1]\!]_{4^{k-1}}$$

Plugging (6.20) into itself gives

$$\forall k \in \mathbb{N}, 1 \le k \le N : \quad [\![i1]\!]_{4^k} = \textbf{if } k = 1$$
$$\textbf{then } 1$$
$$\textbf{else } 3 - \left(\begin{array}{l} \textbf{if } k - 1 = 1 \\ \textbf{then } 1 \\ \textbf{else } 3 - [\![i1]\!]_{4^{k-2}} \end{array} \right)$$

that is

$$\forall k \in \mathbb{N}, 1 \le k \le N : \quad [\![i1]\!]_{4^k} = \textbf{if } k = 1 \qquad (6.21)$$
$$\textbf{then } 1$$
$$\textbf{else if } k = 2$$
$$\textbf{then } 2$$
$$\textbf{else } [\![i1]\!]_{4^{k-2}}$$

The value of i1 is therefore a uniform recurrent equation on k. We can easily conclude from this recurrence that

$$
\begin{array}{rll}
[\![i1]\!]_{4^k} & = & 1 \quad \text{if } k \ge 1 \text{ and } k \text{ is odd} \\
[\![i1]\!]_{4^k} & = & 2 \quad \text{if } k \ge 1 \text{ and } k \text{ is even}
\end{array} \qquad (6.22)
$$

As you might imagine, having a compiler automatically derive this property is difficult. Deriving the reaching definitions and the symbolic values in (6.18) and (6.19) is the easy part. However, plugging (6.20) into itself is a trick to solve recurrences that we can hardly teach a computer. ∎

6.3.2   Reaching Definitions and Weakest Preconditions

We have seen that weakest preconditions are a special kind of predicates asserted in programs. We will see how they can interact with reaching definition information on a very concrete example: using the program in Exercise 2.1 page 21. This program is shown again below:

```
1   x[0] := 0;
2   x[1] := 0;
3   x[x[0]] := 1;
4   if (x[x[0]] = 1)
5   then b := true
6   else b := false
```

First, let's use reaching definition analysis only. The key to determining the final value of b is the subscript x[0] in statement **4**. The value stored in x[0] at that point depends on what definition reaches **4**. Clearly, the reaching definition might be statement **3**, provided it does write into x[0] —that is, provided x[0] inside expression x[x[0]] in the left-hand side of **3** evaluates to 0. Otherwise, the reaching definition is the last previous write to x[0], which is statement **1**:

$$RD(\langle 4, x[0]\rangle) = \quad \textbf{if } [\![x[0]]\!]_3 = 0 \qquad\qquad (6.23)$$
$$\textbf{then } \{3\}$$
$$\textbf{else } \{1\}$$

In this result the condition depends on the value of x[0] at **3**. Its reaching definition gives a hint on what this value is:

$$RD(\langle 3, x[0]\rangle) = \{1\}$$

Since **1** is the only possible reaching definition, the value of x[0] at **1** equals the value of the right-hand side of **1**, which is zero. Therefore

$$[\![x[0]]\!]_3 = 0 \qquad\qquad (6.24)$$

In turn, plugging (6.24) into (6.23) implies

$$RD(\langle 4, x[0]\rangle) = \{3\}$$

Again, since **3** is the only possible reaching definition, the value of x[0] at **4** equals the value of the right-hand side of **3**:

$$[\![x[0]]\!]_4 = 1$$

which implies that the element of x read by **4** is

$$x[[\![x[0]]\!]_4] = \quad x[1]$$

This implies two things. First, since references x[x[0]] and x[1] refer to the same location in **4**, their values are equal:

$$[\![x[x[0]]]\!]_4 = [\![x[1]]\!]_4 \qquad\qquad (6.25)$$

Second, their reaching definitions are the same:

$$RD(\langle 4, x[x[0]]\rangle) = RD(\langle 4, x[1]\rangle)$$

This leads us to looking at the definitions reaching x[1] in 4:

$$RD(\langle 4, x[1]\rangle) = \textbf{if } [\![x[0]]\!]_3 = 1$$
$$\textbf{then } \{3\}$$
$$\textbf{else } \{2\}$$

In fact, we already know from (6.24) that $[\![x[0]]\!]_3 = 0$, therefore:

$$RD(\langle 4, x[1]\rangle) = \{2\}$$

This single reaching definition has a constant right-hand-side value, and in turn indicates that $[\![x[1]]\!]_4 = 0$. Thanks to (6.25), $[\![x[x[0]]]\!]_4 = 0$. We have thus *proven* that the conditional is *always* false and therefore that b is always assigned false.

When Weakest Preconditions Kick In   It is interesting to compare the method above with weakest preconditions. To guess which branch the if statement takes, we can consider two cases: Either 4 checks whether x[0] equals 1, or it checks whether x[1] equals 1. We are therefore interested in, on the one hand, the weakest precondition for the value of x[0] at 4 to equal 1 and, on the other hand, the weakest precondition for the value of x[1] at 4 to equal 1.

The first case depends on what 3 does. Either the left-hand side of 3 is x[0], meaning the subscript x[0] contains 0, so we know the value in x[0] is then set to 1; or the left-hand side is x[1], meaning the subscript x[0] contains 1, in which case statement 3 does nothing as far as x[0] is concerned and the value stored in x[0] must already be 1. The first case is

$$wp(4, x[0] = 1) = ([\![x[0]]\!]_3 = 0) \vee ([\![x[0]]\!]_3 = 1)$$

which is always true (it is a tautology) since the value of x[0] is either 0 or 1.

However, things are not so easy in the second case:

$$wp([\![x[1]]\!]_4 = 1) = ([\![x[0]]\!]_3 = 1) \vee ([\![x[1]]\!]_3 = 1) \qquad (6.26)$$

At this point, a pure logic reasoning is not enough. However, reaching definition analysis can now help. We already know from (6.24) that $[\![x[0]]\!]_3 = 0$, so (6.26) becomes

$$wp([\![x[1]]\!]_4 = 1) = [\![x[1]]\!]_3 = 1$$

However,

$$RD(\langle 3, x[1]\rangle) = \{4\} \implies [\![x[1]]\!]_3 = 0$$

which implies that weakest precondition $wp([\![x[1]]\!]_4 = 1)$ is false.

We can now turn to our original problem, which is computing $wp([\![x[x[0]]]\!]_4 = 1)$. Since $wp([\![x[0]]\!]_4 = 1)$ equals true, we have

$$wp([\![x[x[0]]]\!]_4 = 1) = wp([\![x[1]]\!]_4 = 1)$$

which we know is false. In conclusion, the expression x[x[0]] *cannot* evaluate to 1 in statement 4, implying statement 6 is executed and b is eventually false.

. . . .

```
1   a := ...
2   b := ...
3   if a = 2 then
4     a := 0
5   end if
6   if b = 2 then
7     b := 0
8   end if
9   if a != b then
10    ...
11  end if
```

. . . . *Figure 6.9. Program used in Exercise 6.3.* . . . .

Exercise 6.3   Consider the program shown in Figure 6.9. The challenge is to understand under which conditions statement **10** can be reached, that is, under which conditions the values of a and b differ at statement **9**. To do so, use weakest preconditions first, then reaching definitions plus substitution.

Solution   Using weakest preconditions, we first derive the largest set of possibilities before statement **6** for $a \neq b$ to hold after the if, that is, just before statement **9**:

$$wp(6, a \neq b) \; = \; (b = 2 \wedge a \neq 0) \; \vee \; (b \neq 2 \wedge a \neq b) \qquad (6.27)$$

This precondition can be found as follows: Either the side effect in statement **7** does not execute, implying the condition in **6** does not hold ($b \neq 2$). In this case, since neither a nor b is modified, $a \neq b$ must hold before statement **6**, yielding the second disjunct in (6.27). Or the assignment b := 0 does execute, which first requires that b equals 2 on entry in **6**, and second implies that a must be different from the new value of b, which is 0.

Notice again that an equivalent notation for (6.27) is

$$wp(6, [a]_9 \neq [b]_9) \; = \; ([b]_6 = 2 \wedge [a]_6 \neq 0) \; \vee \; ([b]_6 \neq 2 \wedge [a]_6 \neq [b]_6)$$

Let's go up one step in the chain of weakest preconditions:

$$
\begin{aligned}
wp(3, (b = 2 \wedge a \neq 0) \vee (b \neq 2 \wedge a \neq b)) \; &= \; (b = 2 \wedge a \neq 2 \wedge a \neq 0) \; (6.28) \\
&\vee \; (b \neq 2 \wedge a = 2 \wedge b \neq 0) \\
&\vee \; (b \neq 2 \wedge a \neq 2 \wedge a \neq b)
\end{aligned}
$$

This expression gives the three cases that exercise statement **10**.

Alternatively, we can formulate the problem in terms of reaching definitions. The definition reaching a in statement **9** is

$$RD(\langle \mathbf{9}, a \rangle) = \begin{array}{l} \textbf{if } [a]_{\mathbf{3}} = 2 \\ \textbf{then } \{4\} \\ \textbf{else } \{1\} \end{array}$$

and similarly for b:

$$RD(\langle \mathbf{9}, b \rangle) = \begin{array}{l} \textbf{if } [b]_{\mathbf{3}} = 2 \\ \textbf{then } \{7\} \\ \textbf{else } \{2\} \end{array}$$

Since there is no assignment to a between statements **1** and **4**, the value of a at statement **3** is the same as the value of a at statement **1**. Let us denote this value by a. A similar remark can be pointed out for the values of b, the initial value being denoted by b, that is, $b = [b]_{\mathbf{2}}$. Then, substituting the right-hand-side constants yields possible values of a and b:

$$[a]_{\mathbf{9}} = \begin{array}{l} \textbf{if } a = 2 \\ \textbf{then } 0 \\ \textbf{else } a \end{array}$$

and

$$[b]_{\mathbf{9}} = \begin{array}{l} \textbf{if } b = 2 \\ \textbf{then } 0 \\ \textbf{else } b \end{array}$$

The inequality statement **9** checks for is then equivalent to

$$[a]_{\mathbf{9}} \neq [b]_{\mathbf{9}} = \begin{array}{l} \textbf{if } a = 2 \\ \quad \textbf{then } \textbf{if } b = 2 \\ \qquad \textbf{then } 0 \neq 0 \\ \qquad \textbf{else } b \neq 0 \\ \quad \textbf{else } \textbf{if } b = 2 \\ \qquad \textbf{then } 0 \neq a \\ \qquad \textbf{else } b \neq a \end{array}$$

which is readily simplified into

$$[a]_{\mathbf{9}} \neq [b]_{\mathbf{9}} = \begin{array}{l} \textbf{if } a = 2 \\ \quad \textbf{then } \textbf{if } b = 2 \\ \qquad \textbf{then } false \\ \qquad \textbf{else } b \neq 0 \\ \quad \textbf{else } \textbf{if } b = 2 \\ \qquad \textbf{then } 0 \neq a \\ \qquad \textbf{else } b \neq a \end{array} \qquad (6.29)$$

The first leaf can be dropped, and the conditional expression is equivalent to the logic formula:

$$\begin{array}{lll} [a]_{\mathbf{9}} \neq [b]_{\mathbf{9}} &=& (a = 2 \wedge b \neq 2 \wedge b \neq 0) \quad \text{second leaf in (6.29)} \\ &\vee& (a \neq 2 \wedge b = 2 \wedge 0 \neq a) \quad \text{third leaf in (6.29)} \\ &\vee& (a \neq 2 \wedge b \neq 2 \wedge b \neq a) \quad \text{last leaf} \end{array}$$

which is indeed equal to (6.28).   ∎

6.4 Conclusion

The main advantage of instancewise reaching definition analysis is that, for any program and any control or data structures, sharing a single reaching definition is *always* sharing a value. "Single" is the important word here, and a natural consequence is that the result of reaching definition analysis must be a singleton set for this property to hold. The difficult part, of course, is to design an analysis precise enough to provide singleton results for a significant number of programs.

Thanks to this property, instancewise reaching definition analysis blends nicely with programming language concepts like value numbering, assertions, and weakest precondition. We saw that each concept complements the others, resulting in the precise understanding of data flow in fragments of kernels found in benchmarks or in the literature. The result of an instancewise reaching definition analysis can also be re-injected into a second iteration of the same analysis, yielding even more precise data-flow information.

Chapter 7

Some Classical Compiler Concepts, Part II

Chapter 4 introduces selected compiler and programming language concepts. One is reaching definition analysis, which is detailed in Chapter 5 and whose applications are presented in Chapter 6.

This chapter now revisits two related analysis we did not want to present earlier. The first analysis, dependence analysis, is often presented in textbooks before reaching definition analysis because it is usually simpler. However, we prefer to discuss reaching definitions first because it shows what the root of the issue is: A program transformation must preserve the data flow. As discussed in Section 7.1, checking that there is no dependence is a *sufficient* condition, not a necessary one.

The goal of the second analysis is to find cases where values can be reused or "copy-propagated" in a program. Reusing a value instead of loading it from memory is possible if the memory location is not written since it was last accessed. Sounds familiar? Indeed, it boils down to looking for def-use *or* use-use chains, which makes it an extension of def-use chains captured by reaching definitions. We elaborate on this in Section 7.2.

7.1 Dependence Analysis

Consider the definition of instancewise reaching definition (4.6) page 62:

$$\text{RD}_e(v) = \max_{\prec} \{u \ : \ u \in \mathcal{I}_e, \ u \prec v, \ \text{write}_e(u) = \text{read}_e(v)\} \qquad (7.1)$$

Now imagine you want to optimize the program by changing the execution order in the program, using, for instance, your favorite loop transformation or code scheduling. Such a transformation satisfies the assumptions of Section 4.3, so we know the transformation has to preserve reaching definitions, that is, to obey (4.9) page 65. However, assume that for some reason applying an instancewise reaching definition analysis is

143

too complicated — perhaps because it might exceed your compile-time budget. What can you do?

One solution is to find a *sufficient* condition for reaching definitions to be preserved after transformation. One easy sufficient condition is to make sure that, given any pair of instances, the memory location(s) written by one instance is not written or read by the other.

We saw on page 90 that (7.1) could be rephrased as[1]

$$
\begin{aligned}
\mathrm{RD}_e(v) = \quad & u : u \in \mathcal{I}_e \wedge u \prec v \wedge \mathsf{write}_e(u) = \mathsf{read}_e(v) \\
& \wedge \, (\not\exists z \in \mathcal{I}_e : \quad z \prec v \wedge \mathsf{read}_e(v) = \mathsf{write}_e(z) \\
& \qquad\qquad\quad\; \wedge \quad u \prec z \wedge \mathsf{write}_e(u) = \mathsf{write}_e(z))
\end{aligned}
\tag{7.2}
$$

This is actually of no surprise: The relationship from definitions to reached uses consists of all write-to-read relations *less* those whose write is killed by an intervening write z. We observe that Eq. (7.1) can be decomposed into three simpler expressions, one for each line of (7.2). Each expression corresponds to what is known as *dependencies*.

Dependencies come in three flavors, each corresponding to one of the three conditions defined by Bernstein [9]. Dependencies of the first kind are called *flow dependence*. They capture the relationship between a write to a later read of the same memory location. To be formal, we have to make explicit something implied in the sentence above: Both accesses to the memory location have to actually exist, that is, to execute in the *same* program run. To wrap this up in one mathematical sentence, two instances u and v are in flow dependence in some execution e if and only if

$$
u, v \in \mathcal{I}_e \wedge u \prec v \wedge \mathsf{write}_e(u) = \mathsf{read}_e(v)
\tag{7.3}
$$

So in retrospect, a definition and a use it reaches are in flow dependence. We recognize in (7.3) the first line in (7.2).

The two other dependencies are *output dependencies*, between two writes to the same memory location, and *antidependencies* from a read of a memory location to a later write to the same location. The former can be formally written as

$$
u, v \in \mathcal{I}_e \wedge u \prec v \wedge \mathsf{write}_e(u) = \mathsf{write}_e(v)
\tag{7.4}
$$

and the latter as:

$$
u, v \in \mathcal{I}_e \wedge u \prec v \wedge \mathsf{read}_e(u) = \mathsf{write}_e(v)
\tag{7.5}
$$

In retrospect, the intervening write z in (7.2) is, one the one hand, in output dependence with the reaching definition and, on the other hand, in flow dependence with the use.

Because the equation for reaching definition can be broken down into three simpler equations, we have found the sufficient condition we were looking for. Imagine you want to apply a program transformation that will change the execution order $\prec$ into $\preceq$. To preserve the program semantics, you have to make sure that, for any pair of

---

[1] The expression in (7.1) only differs in its use of relations.

instances a and b, swapping them does not impact the reaching definitions given by (7.2). In other words, you want to make sure that executing b before a ($b \precsim a$) instead of $a \prec b$ does not modify (7.2) for *any tuple* (u, v, z). We therefore have to consider three cases. First, $a = u$ and $b = v$ correspond to the first line of (7.2) and to (7.3). Second, $a = u$ and $b = z$ corresponds to the third line of (7.2) and (7.4). Also, you need to check that b, if executed before a, does not kill the definition reaching a. To that purpose, it is *sufficient* to test that a and b do not satisfy (7.5).

In other words, if any of the three dependencies (7.3) or (7.4) and (7.5) holds, enforcing $u \precsim v$ in the transformed program is a *sufficient* but *not necessary* condition for data flow to be preserved, as formalized in (4.9) page 65.

Did we win something? Isn't checking three dependence conditions more complicated than computing just one reaching definition equation? Computing reaching definitions is definitely more difficult because we have to consider, for a given use, all possible definitions *and* all possible intervening writes. Dependencies are therefore much easier to compute. The price to pay, of course, is that dependencies are more conservative.

Simple Symbolic Manipulations   In the case of loop nests, the natural expression of dependencies are relations on integer vectors. Sets of integer vectors can easily be described and manipulated using Omega, as we said earlier. Many other techniques for dependence analysis on arrays have been published, and the reader is referred to [5, 6].

For our purposes, we focus only on special cases that reach the limits of existing dependence analysis. The first case, discussed in this section, shows how we could leverage existing symbolic manipulation techniques. The second illustrates the use of assertions, whether provided by the user or by other analyses, in dependence testing. The third and last shows how existing symbolic solvers go beyond affine equalities and can be applied to polynomial equations.

Consider the program snippet in Figure 7.1, taken from the SPEC CFP2000 benchmark 301.apsi. At the entry of the outer loop, we know that

$$2 \leq L \leq IPPH = \frac{IP + 1}{2} \tag{7.6}$$

or, equivalently,

$$-\frac{IP + 1}{2} \leq -L \leq -2 \tag{7.7}$$

From statement **2**, we get $IPP2 = IP + 2$. After statement **5**, we know that $LC = IPP2 - L$, that is

$$LC = IP + 2 - L$$

Substituting in the latter equations the inequalities on $-L$ from (7.7), we get

$$IP + 2 - \frac{IP + 1}{2} \leq LC \leq IP + 2 - 2$$

$$\frac{IP + 3}{2} \leq LC \leq IP \tag{7.8}$$

From (7.6) and (7.8), we can reach the conclusion that L is strictly less than LC.

. . . .

```
1    IX_C2(I,J) = (J-1)*IDL1+I
2    IPP2 = IP+2
3    IPPH = (IP+1)/2
4    DO 120 L=2,IPPH
5      LC = IPP2-L
6      DO 117 IK=1,IDL1
7        CC(IX_C2(IK,L)) = CH(IK,1)+AR1*CH(IK,2)
8        CC(IX_C2(IK,LC)) = AI1*CH(IK,IP)
9      117 CONTINUE
10     DO 119 J=3,IPPH
11       JC = IPP2-J
12       DO 118 IK=1,IDL1
13         CC(IX_C2(IK,L)) = CC(IX_C2(IK,L))+AR2*CH(IK,J)
14         CC(IX_C2(IK,LC)) = CC(IX_C2(IK,LC))+AI2*CH(IK,JC)
15       118 CONTINUE
16     119 CONTINUE
17   120 CONTINUE
```

. . . . *Figure 7.1. Excerpt from routine* RADGC *in benchmark* 301.apsi. . . . .

So what? Now turn to the inner loops 117 and 118 on IK. Can there be output dependence from $7^{L,IK}$ to $8^{L,IK}$? Is there a flow dependence from **13** to **14** in the same iteration, or in other words, can it be that CC(IX_C2(IK,LC)) in $14^{L,J,IK}$ is modified by $13^{L,J,IK}$?

The stakes are quite high. For instance, if the answer to the last question is no, then the value of CC(IX_C2(IK,LC)) in $13^{L,J,IK}$ can be loaded at the entry of the basic block of loop 118, hiding part of its latency by the computation in statement **13**.

Now we just have to look at the index function IX_C2. We know that $IDL1$ is different from zero, because the bounds on loops 117 and 118 say that either $IDL1 \geq 1$ or the loops exit immediately. So for a fixed value of IK, $L < LC$ implies that the value of IX_C2(IK,L) is different from the value of IX_C2(IK,LC) in the same iteration of either loop 117 or loop 118. This does mean there is no output dependence from **7** to **8** in the same iteration of loop 117 and no flow dependence from **13** to **14** in the same iteration of loop 118.

Uninterpreted Symbols and Assertions   Consider the example in Figure 7.2, taken from [88]. Omega cannot directly handle expression m*i. It can be handled using an uninterpreted symbol, though. For instance, the loop-carried output dependence would be captured by

```
symbolic f(1);
dep := {[i] -> [i'] : i < i'  &&  f(i) = f(i')};
```

. . . .

```
for i := 1 to n do
  A[m*i] := ..
  .. := A[i]
end for
```

. . . . *Figure 7.2. Plugging in information on a non-affine subscript.* . . . .

but this would boil down to throwing in the towel and accepting the dependence, because we know nothing of f. However, we know that if m is different from zero, then
this dependence does not exist. We can hope that a separate analysis or a user assertion
provides this information. However, providing $m \neq 0$ cannot be used directly, because
m does not appear in the expression above for dependence dep. However, providing
information such as $i < i' \Rightarrow f(i) < f(i')$ is easy to use[2] since it can be plugged in
using the gist function.

Polynomial Equations   However, the trick seen above cannot save affine solvers in
all cases. Consider the program shown in Figure 7.3.   There is a read-after-write

. . . .

```
1  for i = 1 to N do
2     A[b+m*n*i*i*i] = ...
3  end for
4  ... = A[0]
```

. . . . *Figure 7.3. A polynomial array subscript.* . . . .

dependence from **2** to **4** if and only if there is an i, $i \in \mathbb{N}$ and $1 \leq i \leq N$, such that
$b + mni^3 = 0$.

   To check if a dependence exists, we can use a more powerful symbolic solver such
as REDLOG from the University of Passau in Germany [25]. This solver applies classical math to derive that a necessary condition for a solution to exist is that $b = 0$ or
$ab < 0$. REDLOG stands for REDuce LOGic system and is a piece of software for
computing with first-order formulas. Contrary to PIP or Omega, REDLOG handles
real numbers only, so it cannot prove that an integer solution exists. Nevertheless, it
can prove that a real (and therefore, integer) solution does *not* exist.

   The user interface of REDLOG is self-explanatory. Here is a snippet of a RED-
LOG session for the dependence problem above. The user prompt is a colon. We ask
REDLOG if there is an i satisfying $b + mni^3 = 0$:

```
: a := ex({i}, b + m*n*i*i*i = 0);
```

---

[2]Even though it is stronger than $m \neq 0$, since it corresponds to $m > 0$.

Exponents, like i^3, are printed by REDLOG using a top row to mimic standard math notation:

```
                        3
a := ex i (b + m*n*i  = 0)
```

Solving a is requested by the operator `rlqea`. The output is a list, starting and ending with braces and whose elements are separated by commas. Each element is itself a list of two elements, the second giving the solution and the first being the condition for the solution to be valid.

```
: rlqea a;

{{b = 0 and (m = 0 or n = 0),{i = infinity1}},

 {m <> 0 and n <> 0,

              b    1/3
    {i =  - (-----)    }}}
             m*n
```

Interestingly, we have not only the conditions for a solution to exist, but also an expression of the solution. Notice, however, two traps when reading this result. First, concerning the first answer, the reserved keyword `infinity1` does not stand for infinity alone, but for any real value *or* infinity. Therefore, we cannot conclude from this answer that there is no solution (that is, that there is no integer solution within the loop bounds). Indeed, any integer *is* a solution when b equals 0 and either m or n equals 0. Second, when both m and n are different from zero (second answer), we need more work to prove that no dependence exists because we also have to make sure the solution is an integer (the condition only checks for *real* solutions) and that this integer solutions is in the loop range, that is, greater than or equal to 1 and less than or equal to N. But of course, a tool like REDLOG can be very useful to *disprove* dependencies.

Exercise 7.1   Consider the loop nest shown in Figure 7.4. Are there output dependencies between instances of the nest's body? What kind of symbolic solver would be able to check that? ∎

7.2   Previous References

With modern processors and memory hierarchies, memory access time is a huge cost compared to processor cycle time. Therefore, reducing the count of memory accesses is a top priority in optimizing compilers. It then makes sense, when a value is needed, to first check whether this value is already available and therefore does not need to be reloaded.

Consider the program in Figure 7.5, where lines are intentionally numbered starting with **2**. Clearly, each value of element A[i] used during one iteration is also needed

. . . .

```
Do IL=1,NX
   Do JL=1,NY
      Do i=1,NKX
         Do j=1,NKY
            POP( NKY*(i-1)+j, NY*(IL-1)+JL ) = ...
         End Do
      End Do
   End Do
End Do
```

Figure 7.4. Excerpt from benchmark program syshtn.f *used in Exercise 7.1.*

. . . .

. . . .

```
2   for i := 1 to n do
3      B[i] := A[i] + A[i-1]
4   end for
```

. . . . . *Figure 7.5. Reducing the number of loads at each iteration: an easy case.* . . . . .

(to serve as A[i-1]) in the following iteration. And indeed, most compilers see this opportunity and issue just one load per iteration. To do so, one classical technique is *scalar replacement*: Reference A[i-1] is replaced by a reference to a temporary variable, call it t. This variable is initialized before the loop and set to the value of A[i] at the end of each iteration.

. . . .

```
1   t := A[0]
2   for i := 1 to n do
3      B[i] := A[i] + t;
4      t := A[i]
5   end for
```

. . . . *Figure 7.6. Scalar replacement in the program shown in Figure 7.5.* . . . .

The result of scalar replacement is given in Figure 7.6. The nice thing about scalar replacement is that it makes it easy for the compiler to place t in a register. However, a small change in the program makes some compilers fail, even at decent optimization levels, to identify a similar opportunity.

. . . .

```
1  for i := 1 to n do
2    for j := 1 to n do
3      B[i,j] := A[i+j] + A[i+j-1]
4    end for
5  end for
```

. . . . *Figure 7.7. Reducing loads count: a more difficult case.* . . . .

Consider the program shown in Figure 7.7. Compiling the inner loop just boils down to compiling the loop shown in Figure 7.5 for a fixed value of the outer loop's counter. Nevertheless, some compilers issue two loads per iteration, meaning a total of $2n^2$ requests to memory.

We can generalize the phenomenon described above. Given a read reference, we are looking for the last previous read or write of the *same* memory location. Notice that this last previous access may not have the same syntactical form. Notice also that this reference may be a write, because it is then possible to avoid fetching this value from memory, and that it may also be a read, because the value is then already at hand in a register. So for an execution e and an instance u reading a memory location m, we define the *previous reference* $\text{PrevRef}_e(\langle u, m \rangle)$ as the last executed access (and therefore, the maximum element with respect to order $\prec$) that came before u *and* read the memory location referred to by m.

$$
\text{PrevRef}_e(\langle u, m \rangle) \equiv
\max_{\prec} \left\{ \langle v, c \rangle : \begin{pmatrix} v \in \mathcal{I}_e,\ v \prec u, \\ \text{write}_e(\langle v, c \rangle) = \text{read}_e(\langle u, m \rangle) \\ \vee\ \text{read}_e(\langle v, c \rangle) = \text{read}_e(\langle u, m \rangle) \end{pmatrix} \right\} \qquad (7.9)
$$

Note how close definition (7.9) is to (4.4) page 61. Finding the reaching definition is the problem of finding the last previous write to the memory location accessed by a read. When tracking accesses to memory locations for "registerization" purposes, whether previous accesses are writes or reads is no longer relevant (of course, in the motivating example, we wanted to avoid reloading A[min], so this reference had implicitly to be a read). However, the underlying phenomenon is the same as in the case of reaching definitions: We are looking for the maximum instance, according to execution order, of the set of instances accessing a given memory location.

Notice also that, by construction, $\text{PrevRef}_e(\langle u, m \rangle)$ is a single instance, possibly $\bot$.

Properties of Previous References   If syntactic reference 1, evaluated at v, is the previous reference for $\langle u, m \rangle$, then the two have to evaluate to the same value. Formally,

$$
\text{PrevRef}_e(\langle u, m \rangle) = \langle v, 1 \rangle \implies [\![m]\!]_u = [\![1]\!]_v \qquad (7.10)
$$

As usual, this information holds for a given e only. Along the lines described in Chapter 2, a conservative approximation $\mathsf{PrevRef}(\langle u, m \rangle)$ is characterized by

$$\bigcup_{e \in \mathcal{E}} \mathsf{PrevRef}_e(\langle u, m \rangle) \subseteq \mathsf{PrevRef}(\langle u, m \rangle)$$

We saw that the value of reference m at u is the same as at $\mathsf{PrevRef}_e(\langle u, m \rangle)$. When taking all possible executions into account, we can also have the same property if the previous reference is a singleton set containing exactly one non-$\perp$ element. In that case we have

$$\forall u, v \in \mathcal{I} : \mathsf{PrevRef}(\langle u, m \rangle) = \{\langle v, 1 \rangle\} \implies [\![m]\!]_u = [\![1]\!]_v$$

Observe that, for this property to hold, $\mathsf{PrevRef}(\langle u, m \rangle)$ must be a singleton set.

Coming back to the program in Figure 7.7, we can compute previous references as follows. First, we declare n and an auxiliary relation that captures loop bounds and the lexicographic order:

```
# symbolic n;
# rel := {[i,j] -> [i',j'] : 1<=i,j,i',j'<=n
                        && (i'<i || (i=i' && j'<j))};
```

The two syntactic references to A in statement **3** may mutually be the previous reference for both of them. This yields four possible combinations, and therefore four relations. To make notations systematic, "r" will stand for A[i+j-1] and "s" for A[i+j]. No trick here, it just makes it easier to remember what each relation stands for: "rr" for the relation from "r" to "s," "rs" for the relation from "r" to "s," etc.:

```
# rr:= {[i,j]->[i',j'] : i'+j'-1=i+j-1} intersection rel;
# ss:= {[i,j]->[i',j'] : i+j=i'+j'} intersection rel;
# rs:= {[i,j]->[i',j'] : i+j-1=i'+j'} intersection rel;
# sr:= {[i,j]->[i',j'] : i+j=i'+j'-1} intersection rel;
```

Notice that each relation boils down to intersecting tuples that refer to the same array element with tuples that satisfy both the conditions on loop bounds and the lexicographic order.

Then, given an input tuple (i, j), instances of syntactic reference A[i+j-1] (which we nicknamed "r") that are previous references are obtained by subtracting transitive compositions from rr. The intuition is very simple: If we can go from one "r" to an "s" (relation rs) and then from that "s" to another "r" (relation sr, composed after rs), then the former "r" cannot be a previous reference (because at least the interleaving "s" beats it). The same intuition is valid using an intervening third "r." To get previous references from "r" to "r" (relation rtor below), we can thus compute

```
# rtor := rr - (sr compose rs) - (rr compose rr)
# rtor;

{[i,1] -> [i-1,2] : 2 <= i <= n}
```

```
# stor := rs - (rs compose ss) - (rr compose rs) ;
# stor;
```

```
{[i,j] -> [i,j-1] : 1 <= i <= n && 2 <= j <= n}
```

These results can be summarized in a single conditional expression:

$$\text{PrevRef}(\langle 3^{i,j}, \text{A[j+i-1]}\rangle) = \quad \textbf{if } j \geq 2$$
$$\textbf{then } \{\langle 3^{i,j-1}, \text{A[i+j]}\rangle\}$$
$$\textbf{else } \textbf{if } i \geq 2$$
$$\textbf{then } \{\langle 3^{i,j-1}, \text{A[i+j]}\rangle\}$$
$$\textbf{else } \{\bot\}$$

This tells us exactly what we are looking for. First, during the very first execution of the loop body (i.e., when both i and j equal 1) there is no way to avoid loading the value of A[i+j-1] (i.e., A[1]) because it is the first time this loop nest refers to that array element. When j is greater than 1, however, we are sure array element A[i+j-1] was syntactically referenced as A[i+j] in the previous iteration of the j-loop and the same iteration of the i-loop. This is precisely what we need for easy scalar replacement and registerization. The remaining case corresponds to the very first iteration of the j-loop for each iteration except the first of the i-loop. In that case, the loop nest has loaded the value, but $n - 1$ iterations earlier—probably too long ago to hope keeping the value in a register.

. . . .

```
1   min := 0;
2   for i := 1 to N do
3     if( A[i]<A[min] ) then
4       min := i
5     endif
6   end for
```

. . . . *Figure 7.8. Motivating example of [10].* . . . .

The previous example is too simple to be realistic. Consider the program snippet in Figure 7.8, given in [10]. The property we would like to discover (and prove) is that the value of A[min], at any given iteration, was read no later than during the previous iteration. If the compiler knows this property, then the corresponding load, together with the computation of the address of A[min], can be eliminated.

In terms of scalar replacement, we would like to detect that the reference to A[min] in statement **3** can be replaced by a reference to some temporary t. This requires adding an assignment t:=A[0] before the loop and an assignment t:=A[i] between statements **4** and **5**. The resulting optimized program is shown in Figure 7.9. The bottom line is that the previous reference to A[min] in statement **3**, regardless of the value of min, was done in the previous iteration. That previous reference occurred when evaluating either the same syntactical reference A[min] or A[i].

. . . .

```
1   min := 0;
1b  t := A[0];
2   for i := 1 to N do
3     if( A[i] < t ) then
4        min := i;
4b       t := A[i]
5     endif
6   end for
```

. . . . *Figure 7.9. Optimized version of Figure 7.8.* . . . .

To detect this property, let's first consider the definition reaching `min` at statement **3**. This definition is

$$RD(\langle 3^i, \texttt{min}\rangle) = \quad \textbf{if } [\![\texttt{A[i]<A[min]}]\!]_{3^{i-1}} \qquad (7.11)$$
$$\textbf{then } \{4^{i-1}\}$$
$$\textbf{else } RD(\langle 3^{i-1}, \texttt{min}\rangle)$$

Notice that (7.11) explicitly uses property (4.5) page 61. Furthermore, (7.11) implies that the value of `min` either was set by statement **4** or is the same as at the beginning of the previous iteration:

$$(7.11) \Rightarrow [\![\texttt{min}]\!]_{3^i} = \quad \textbf{if } [\![\texttt{A[i]<A[min]}]\!]_{3^{i-1}} \qquad (7.12)$$
$$\textbf{then } [\![\texttt{i}]\!]_{4^{i-1}}$$
$$\textbf{else } [\![\texttt{min}]\!]_{3^{i-1}}$$

Notice that $[\![\texttt{i}]\!]_{4^{i-1}} = i - 1$.

We now look for the previous reference to `A[min]`:

$$PrevRef(\langle 4^i, \texttt{A[min]}\rangle) =$$
$$\max_{\prec} \left\{ \langle 3^j, m\rangle \; : \; j < i \wedge \left(\begin{array}{l} (m = \texttt{A[i]} \wedge [\![\texttt{min}]\!]_{3^i} = [\![\texttt{i}]\!]_{3^j}) \\ \vee \;\; (m = \texttt{A[min]} \wedge [\![\texttt{min}]\!]_{3^i} = [\![\texttt{min}]\!]_{3^j}) \end{array} \right) \right\}$$

Thanks to (7.12), we know this maximum is reached with either disjunct when $j = i - 1$:

$$PrevRef(\langle 4^i, \texttt{A[min]}\rangle) = \quad \textbf{if } [\![\texttt{A[i]<A[min]}]\!]_{3^{i-1}}$$
$$\textbf{then } \{\langle 3^{i-1}, \texttt{A[i]}\rangle\}$$
$$\textbf{else } \{\langle 3^{i-1}, \texttt{A[min]}\rangle\}$$

This gives us the expected information: The value of `A[min]` does not have to be reloaded at each iteration. Instead, it might simply be copy-propagated from either `A[i]` or `A[min]` at the previous iteration.

Exercise 7.2 Consider the fragment of bubble sort program `bubble03` shown in Figure 7.10, taken from the benchmark suite `ltstsC`. How can this loop be compiled with only one load per iteration?

```
1      for i:= 0 to last-1 do
2        if( tab[i]>tab[i+1] ) then
3          temp := tab[i];
4          tab[i] := tab[i+1];
5          tab[i+1] := temp;
6        end if
7      end for
```

.... *Figure 7.10. Fragment of bubble sort program* bubble03. ....

Solution   The key is to notice that tab[i] was referred to as tab[i+1] in the previous iteration, possibly in statement **5** (which is then the previous reference) and definitely in statement **2**. In other words,

$$\text{PrevRef}(\langle 2^i, \texttt{tab[i]} \rangle) = \begin{array}{l} \textbf{if } i > 0 \\ \quad \textbf{then if } [\texttt{tab[i]>tab[i+1]}]_{2^{i-1}} = \textbf{true} \\ \quad\quad\quad \textbf{then } \{5^{i-1}\} \\ \quad\quad\quad \textbf{else } \{2^{i-1}\} \\ \quad \textbf{else } \{\bot\} \end{array}$$

Let's emphasize that expression $[\texttt{tab[i]>tab[i+1]}]_{2^{i-1}} = \textbf{true}$ in the innermost conditional is not relevant. What matters is that, whether or not this condition holds, the previous reference comes from either 5^{i-1} or 2^{i-1}, that is, from some instance at iteration $i - 1$.

```
a      s1 := tab[0];
1      for i:= 0 to last-1 do
b        s2 := tab[i+1];
2        if( s1>s2 ) then
3          temp := s1;
4          tab[i] := s2;
5          tab[i+1] := temp;
c          s1 := temp;
d        else
e          s1 := s2;
6        end if
7      end for
```

.... *Figure 7.11. Optimized version of* bubble03. ....

This result leads to the optimized program shown in Figure 7.11. Statements **a** through **e** were inserted. Since the value of s1 is not modified in the "then" part of the conditional, statement **c** is, in fact, useless. ∎

7.3 Last References

In the previous section, we focus on the last previous dynamic reference to a given memory location. We see that, to compute this previous dynamic reference, we cannot simply rely on the syntactic equality of references as they appear in the program text. One immediate application of previous reference information is in value reuse, which avoids spurious expensive loads from memory.

In contrast to looking at past accesses, this section studies what happens to a memory location "in the future." More specifically, the first question we might ask is where and when is the result of a given computation used for the last time. In other words, given a write access, what is the last read instance for which the read is a possible reaching definition? Formally, for an execution e and an instance u in $\mathcal{I}_e$,

$$\mathsf{LastUse}_e(u) \; = \; \{v \; : \; v \in \mathcal{I}_e, \; u \in \mathsf{RD}(v)\} \tag{7.13}$$

Answering this "where" question has one main application: Once all instances in $\mathsf{LastUse}_e(u)$ have executed, the value u produces can be discarded. The memory location used to store this value can be reused.

A second related question is, given a memory location, where and when is this memory location accessed for the last time? Answering the "where" question boils down to computing

$$\mathsf{LastRef}_e(\mathtt{m}) \; = \max_{\prec} \{v \; : \; v \in \mathcal{I}_e, \; \mathsf{read}_e(v) = \mathtt{m}\} \tag{7.14}$$

The application is again related to memory usage: After $\mathsf{LastRef}_e(\mathtt{m})$ executes in a given program run e, we can safely deallocate the storage at memory location m.

As you probably noticed, we did not tell *when*, on the one hand, a value can be discarded and, on the other hand, a *memory location* can be discarded. In a transformed program, the question can be answered analytically if a schedule θ is provided. Corresponding to (7.13), a value is last used at time step $\theta(\mathsf{LastUse}_e(u))$ and the associated storage can be overwritten at the following time step. Similarly, deallocation of location m can safely occur at time step $\theta(\mathsf{LastRef}_e(\mathtt{m})) + 1$, assuming the schedule yields values in $\mathbb{N}$.

7.4 Iteration-based Slicing

7.4.1 A Few Words on Transitive Closure

Relations are a very general concept that we manipulate every day, without even knowing it or thinking of it. When reasoning about programs and their transformations, relation properties are ubiquitous. This book focuses on one type of relation, from the set of value definitions to the set of value uses.

Relations naturally lend themselves to composition. Indeed, each time some property holds between points x and y (for any property and for any values of x and y) and another property holds between y and some z, we might wonder what can be said about x and z. We say we take the *composition* of the latter property after the former.

The two properties may be the same. In fact, this is our case of interest in this section. In mathematical words, our problem can be stated as follows: For a given relation R, we are looking for pairs of elements x and z such that there is an "intermediate" y serving to "carry along" relation R between x and z: x R y and y R z. If this is the case, x and z are linked by a new relation, which is the composition of R with itself, denoted by R $\circ$ R.

Composing relation R with itself can of course be repeated. Not surprisingly, we denote by R^k the relation obtained by composing R with itself k times:

$$R^k = \underbrace{R \circ R \circ \ldots \circ R}_{k \text{ times}}$$

The *positive transitive closure* is defined as the *union* of all possible compositions of R with itself.[3] Formally,

$$R^+ = \bigcup_k R^k, \quad k \in \mathbb{N}, \quad k \geq 1$$

The *transitive closure* just adds the case where k is equal to zero. Composing a relation zero times with itself amounts to not considering that relation at all. What is left is just the identity, the simplest relation that maps any element to itself. The transitive closure is defined as

$$R^* = R^+ \cup \text{Identity} \tag{7.15}$$

Using the Omega calculator is a great way to play with relations and their closures [55]. For instance, the session excerpt below defines the relation between an integer and the value immediately preceding, in the interval $[0, n]$, for some n:

```
# symbolic n;
# R := {[i] -> [i-1] : 1 <= i <= n};
```

Its transitive closure is computed using the star operator:

```
# R* ;
{[i] -> [i]} union
    {[i] -> [Out_1] : 0 <= Out_1 < i <= n }
```

Omega generated variable `Out_1`. Variables like this one serve as "wildcard" variables when Omega needs to introduce bounded variables–in this case, to denote a variable less than i and greater than or equal to zero.[4]

---

[3]Remember that a relation between two sets can also be seen as a subset of the Cartesian product of these sets. Therefore, talking about the union of two relations makes sense. Formally, for any sets A and B, any elements a and b in A and B, respectively, and any relation R, writing a R b is equivalent to writing $R \subseteq A \times B \wedge (x, y) \in R$.

[4]Notice that Omega makes no claim to produce the syntactically minimal result. Clearly, the result above could be simplified into

$$\{[i] -> [Out\_1] : 0 <= Out\_1 <= i <= n\}$$

Transitive closure has several applications. One application is *iteration space slicing* [74, 75], which consists of extracting (a superset of) the chain of instances that have been necessary, at one point or another in the course of program execution, in producing a given value. This application is detailed in Section 7.4.2. Another application is the subject of Chapter 9.

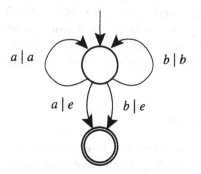

Figure 7.12. A simple transducer.

Of course, transitive closure also applies to relations described by transduction. As an example, consider the transduction that maps a word on alphabet $\{a, b\}$ to the same word with the last letter stripped. This transduction is implemented by the transducer shown in Figure 7.12.

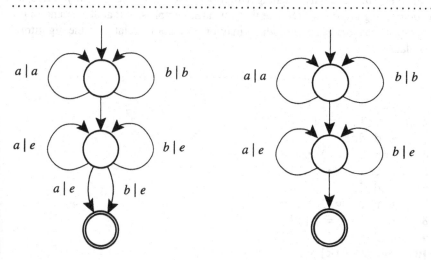

Figure 7.13. Positive closure (left) and transitive closure (right) of Figure 7.12.

A closure of this mapping would repeatedly strip the last character of the output string and would repeat this process an arbitrary number of times. This can be captured by another transducer, as shown on both sides of Figure 7.13.

In both "closed" transducers in Figure 7.13, a (possibly empty) prefix of the input string is picked in the top part. The length of this prefix is chosen nondeterministically.

The bottom parts of the closure transducers then differ. For positive closure, the initial relation has to be applied at least once. Therefore, at least one trailing letter has to be removed. To make sure the suffix contains at least one letter, the bottom part iterates the two loop arcs in a nondeterministic way. However, at least one of the two transitions leading to the accepting state must be feasible. This requires having either a or b in the input string. In contrast, in the transitive closure transducer on the right side of Figure 7.13, a (possibly empty) suffix of the string is read and no character is output. In compliance with the definition of transitive closure (7.15), the suffix can be empty.

7.4.2 Program Slicing

Dependencies give the set of *memory accesses* that need to be performed before a given computation. In contrast, reaching definitions give the set of *values* that need to be produced before a given computation. Both relations, however, can be repeated. We might want to know the dependencies of a dependence, or the definitions reaching a reaching definition. In other words, dependencies on the one hand or reaching definitions on the other can be linked to one another, forming a chain of events. (Notice that chaining dependencies and reaching definitions does not have an obvious meaning.)

For a given computation, forming the chain of preceding events is called program *slicing*. As you can guess, program slicing based on dependencies is not what this book studies most, since many dependencies can be removed (using techniques presented in Chapter 8) and because only reaching definitions, not dependencies, really correspond to the underlying algorithm. (Notice that we earlier emphasize that dependencies give the history of *memory accesses*, which may or may not be related to the algorithm's flow of data.)

. . . .

```
1     for i := 1 to n
2       a[i] := 1
3     end for
4     for i := 1 to n
5       b[i] := a[i]
6     end for
7     for i := 1 to n
8       c[i] := b[i]
9     end for
10    print c[k]
```

. . . . *Figure 7.14. Illustrating instance-based slices.* . . . .

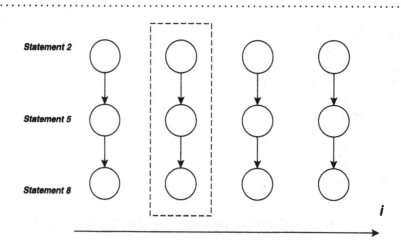

The idea behind slicing is best illustrated by an example, shown in Figure 7.14. The original slicing [87], trying to find out which statements are needed to eventually print the value of c[k] in **10**, would reply **2**, **5**, and **8**. However, it is pretty clear here that the answer is overly approximate. The value needed in the right-hand expression of **8** to compute one specific element c[k] is $[\![b[i]]\!]_{8^k}$. Therefore, 5^k is the only computation instance needed by 8^k. In turn, we can clearly see the definition reaching the right-hand side of 5^k is 2^k. The bottom line is that, for any k greater than or equal to 1 and less than or equal to n, the chain of computations to produce value $[\![c[k]]\!]_{10}$ is exactly $2^k, 5^k, 8^k$. This *iteration space slicing* [74, 75] or *instance-based slicing* is depicted in Figure 7.15. In this figure, one instance-based slice is emphasized in the dotted box. This slicing could be implemented by the following sequence of instructions:

```
a[k] := 1 ; b[k] := a[k] ; c[k] := b[k]
```

which is of course parametrized with k.

Applications of instance-based slicing obviously include parallelization. Since each slice contains all the input data and all the intermediate computations to produce a value, it is self-contained. Since it does not depend on other slices, it is standalone. Therefore, each slice can be computed independently of and simultaneously with other slices. Indeed, it is pretty clear that any slice to compute value $[\![c[k]]\!]_{10}$, for any k, in Figure 7.15 can execute independently of others.

However, a glitch appears when two different slices use the same value. Then the two slices are no longer stand-alone, independent chains of computations. To illustrate the matter, Figure 7.16 shows a variation of Figure 7.14. (Lines **8** and **10** changed.) Both values $[\![b[i]]\!]_{5^i}$ and $[\![b[i]]\!]_{5^{i-1}}$ are needed to eventually produce $[\![c[i]]\!]_{10}$. Since 5^i and 5^{i-1} need values $[\![a[i]]\!]_{2^i}$ and $[\![a[i]]\!]_{2^{i-1}}$, respectively, instances 2^i

. . . .

```
1    for i := 1 to n
2      a[i] := 1
3    end for
4    for i := 1 to n
5      b[i] := a[i]
6    end for
7    for i := 2 to n
8      c[i] := b[i]+b[i-1]
9    end for
10   print all c[i]'s
```

. . . . *Figure 7.16. Illustrating instance-based slices that share values.* . . . .

. . . .

. . . . *Figure 7.17. Instance-based slices for the program in Figure 7.16.* . . . .

and 2^{i-1} should also be included in the slice. Corresponding instance-based slices, together with their overlaps, are shown in Figure 7.17.

One option to fix this is merging the two slices into one that produces two values. But merging slices would contradict the intuition: Some values produced by one slice may be needed by the other, but some would *not*. Furthermore, it would also often defeat the purpose of slicing, since many (if not all) slices could end up being lumped together.

Another solution is to follow the intuition more closely. Since the slices to compute $[\![c[i]]\!]_{10}$ and $[\![c[i+1]]\!]_{10}$ both need $[\![b[i]]\!]_{5^i}$, we can copy or *clone* instance 5^i in both slices. This cloning allows for nonoverlapping slices, as shown in Figure 7.18. The code corresponding to one slice ends up being shown in Figure 7.19.

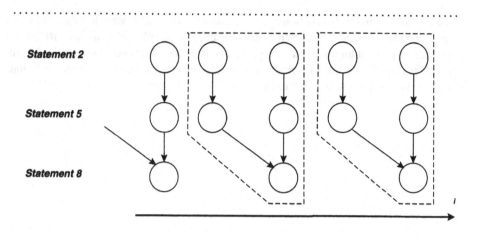

.... *Figure 7.18. Nonoverlapping slices, after cloning.* ....

```
2     a[i] := 1
2b    a[i-1] := 1
5     b[i] := a[i]
5b    b[i-1] := a[i-1]
8     c[i] := b[i]+b[i-1]
10    print c[i]
```

.... *Figure 7.19. Code for slice i, $i > 1$, with cloning.* ....

7.5 Conclusion

This chapter presents two concepts related to reaching definitions: dependencies and previous reference computation. Dependencies are memory-based, whereas reaching definitions are value-based. We saw that the reaching definition relation can be decomposed into dependence relations, and therefore computing dependencies is easier than computing reaching definitions. Another consequence is that, if a program transformation satisfies dependencies, then it does not change reaching definitions. In other words, dependence checking is a sufficient (but not necessary) condition for a transformation to keep the data flow untouched.

Computing the previous reference to a variable, on the other hand, happens to be an extension of reaching definitions: The problem definition just adds a disjunction to the formal description of reaching definitions. Its main application is to avoid redundant loads of values.

Another point to take away from this chapter is that symbolic solvers are of various types and power but always provide some useful hindsight on a program. A simple integer constraint solver eliminates dependencies in a key loop of the SPEC benchmark

301.apsi. The Omega software, a simplifier of first-order integer formulas, can also help disprove dependencies even in the presence of simple polynomials. REDLOG provides a general tool to handle polynomials. This tool, however, works on real numbers. It can still be used to disprove dependencies, since the lack of real solutions implies that no integer solution exists either.

Part III

Data Flow and Expansion

Chapter 8

Single-Assignment Forms

Imperative programming encourages programmers to use and reuse memory locations over and over again to store different values. Clearly, this "history" of values implements the data-flow graph, but not in a clear fashion. One way to expose the data flow is to transform the data structures of the program so that memory locations are less often reused, or perhaps even used only once. This clearly implies that data structures contain more elements.

Transforming a data structure to make it larger, whether conceptually (in an intermediate representation) or in the actual generated code, is called *expansion*. Formally, expansion (we should rather say: expansion of a data structure) means that there are two writes w_1 and w_2 such that, on the one hand,

$$\text{write}(w_1) \cap \text{write}(w_2) \neq \emptyset \tag{8.1}$$

meaning that both writes access overlapping memory locations in the original program, and, on the other hand, these same two writes access different locations in the transformed program:

$$\overline{\text{write}}(w_1) \cap \overline{\text{write}}(w_2) = \emptyset \tag{8.2}$$

Notice that both conditions are required: The first means there was a need for expansion in the first place, and the second means that expansion indeed took place.

8.1 Single-Assignment Form

If expansion is pushed to the extreme, all elements of all data structures are written at most once. The program is then said to have the *single-assignment* property, or to be in single-assignment form. Single-assignment form has been ubiquitous, in various flavors, not only in functional languages but in imperative programming as well. It appears in widespread languages, such as SISAL [12], and, in a restricted form, in a very popular intermediate representation called static single assignment, or SSA, which we study later in this chapter.

8.1.1   The Intuition: Straight-Line Codes

To see the purpose of single assignment, and how it works, it is best to start with an
example without branches or calls, that is, a piece of straight-line code. Consider the
simple example shown in Figure 8.1.

. . . .

```
1   if (foo) then              1   if (foo) then
2     x := 0                    2     x2 := 0
3   else                       3   else
4     x := 1                    4     x4 := 1
5   end if                     5   end if
6   y := x+1;                  6   y6 := ?;
7   x := 11                    7   x7 := 11
8   if .. then                 8   if .. then
9     x := x + 1               9     x9 := ? + 1
10  else                      10  else
11    x := 3                  11    x11 := 3
12  end if                    12  end if
13  z := x                    13  z13 := ?
```

  (a) Original program   (b) Program after renaming left-hand sides

. . . . *Figure 8.1. Straight-line code being put in single-assignment form.* . . . .

Converting to single-assignment form is conceptually done in two steps. The first
step consists of giving a new and unique name to each variable appearing in all left-
hand-side expressions of all statements, as shown in Figure 8.1.(b). That way, each
variable is assigned to at most once.[1] Hence the name "single assignment."

However, since variable names in left-hand sides have changed, we have to modify
all right-hand expressions accordingly. Each time an x appears in a right-hand expression, we have to decide to which "new" x it now corresponds. For the moment, we
have no idea how to do it, and so we just fill in with question marks.

The second step is to replace the question marks. A question mark means we don't
know which memory location to read from because it corresponds to a use that had
several possible reaching definitions. However, when only one definition reaches a use
(the reaching definitions set consists of a nonbottom singleton), then the ambiguity is
lifted. In addition, thanks to the first step, each definition has its own memory location.
Therefore, in the case of singleton reaching definitions, replacing the question mark by
the correct reference is straightforward. As an example, the definitions reaching the
use of x in statement **9** is the singleton {**7**}. As a consequence, we are sure that reading
this memory location provides the right value: This memory location is not polluted
by other definitions. The question mark can safely be replaced by the name of this
memory location. In the case of statement **9**, x can be replaced by the "x" of statement
7, that is, x7.

---

[1]A variable may not be written, depending on the outcome of the conditionals.

. . . .

```
1   if (foo) then
2      x2 := 0
3   else
4      x4 := 1
5   end if
6   y6 := φ(x2,x4)+1;
7   x7 := 11
8   if .. then
9      x9 := x7 + 1
10  else
11     x11 := 3
12  end if
13  z13 := φ(x9,x11)
```

. . . . *Figure 8.2. Complete single-assignment form.* . . . .

In other cases, solving the "question mark" problem is not so easy, because we have at least two definitions to choose from. If we pick the wrong one, the program transformation is incorrect. Indeed, x in **6** has two possible reaching definitions:

$$RD(6) = \{2, 4\}$$

Similarly, x in statement **13** also has two reaching definitions:

$$RD(13) = \{9, 11\}$$

In either case, we have no direct means to guess which version of x should be read.

We solve the problem by using an oracle function called a ϕ or ϕ-*function*. A ϕ selects which of its arguments is the correct x. Thanks to this oracle, we can say in statement **6** that y6 receives the sum of 1 and the value of whichever variable x2 or x4 is adequate. We also insert a ϕ-function where an x appeared in statement **13** (see Figure 8.2).

It is important to notice here that a ϕ-function is not a function at all in the mathematical sense. Indeed, expression $\phi(x2,x4)$ returns either the value of x2 *or* the value of x4—no decent function would return two possible results depending on its mood. Clearly, there are additional hidden arguments to ϕ, such as the memory state and guards for each explicit argument. Detailing all these hidden arguments would be tedious, so writing expressions like $\phi(x2,x4)$ is appealing shorthand.

For the moment, adding ϕ-functions may look like cheating. We just hand-waved their definition, and we did not say a word on how they work, let alone on how to implement them. For the moment, what matters is to realize two key properties of the program in Figure 8.2. First, each memory location defined in the program is never written twice. Second, the flow of data is clear and, in a sense, explicit: From the program in Figure 8.2, we could easily draw a graph like those on the first pages of this book. Input values in x2 and x4 would be passed along edges to an "operator" (not a multiply, like in Figure 1.1, but here a ϕ), creating a new value called y_6 (stored in y6). In addition, the program in Figure 8.2 is a very compact way of representing the flow of values in the program in Figure 8.1(a). In contrast, drawing a similar graph from the program in Figure 8.1(a) would be much more difficult and would require some program understanding that boils down to reaching definition analysis.

Notice also that x2 and x4 do not appear as arguments of the second ϕ in statement **13**. At this point in this book, the profound reason is probably clear: The definitions of x in statements **2** and **4** cannot reach statement **13** (and therefore, statement **13**). The reason is that the write of x in statement **7** kills all previous definitions of x that could otherwise be seen by statement **13**. In turn, the reason **7** kills all previous definitions of x possibly reaching statement **13** is that statement **7** *dominates* statement **13**. But the definition in statement **7** is itself killed by either statement **9** or statement **11**, so x7 is not a possible argument of the ϕ-function.

Left-Hand Sides   Let us take one step back and look in retrospect at the example above. In the transformed program, we made sure that all writes access different memory locations. In that particular program, each write corresponds to one statement, but of course, in general, one write corresponds to one statement instance. A formal definition of a single-assignment form is

$$\forall u, v \in W : (u \neq v) \;\Rightarrow\; (\overline{\text{write}}(u) \cap \overline{\text{write}}(v) = \emptyset) \tag{8.3}$$

which says that two distinct writes do not access overlapping memory locations. Notice that this equation holds for *all* write pairs, whereas (8.2) was meant for a given pair of writes only. In other words, an expansion is not necessarily a conversion to single-assignment form.

Enforcing the single-assignment rule boils down to changing the left-hand expressions of assignments to make sure each assignment instance writes in its own private memory location. We saw that, when the source code is straight-line, instances and statements are equivalent. Therefore, a sufficient condition for this piece of code to be in single assignment is that each left-hand side writes to a separate structure name. This works for all data structures, scalars, arrays, and more complex ones.

When the code includes (structured) loops, the obvious and typical case of loop nests in single-assignment form appears when all statements in the nest body write to a separate array, and all arrays are subscripted by the iteration vector. For instance, the loop nest below is in single-assignment form:

```
1  for i := 1 to n do
2    for j := 1 to n do
3      a[i,j] := ..
4    end for
5  end for
```

Indeed, (8.3) holds because there are no pairs of instances of **3** that write to the same memory location:

$$\forall 3^{i,j}, 3^{i',j'} \in \mathcal{D}(3) : \left(3^{i,j} \neq 3^{i',j'}\right) \;\Rightarrow\; \left(\text{write}(3^{i,j}) \cap \text{write}(3^{i',j'}) = \emptyset\right)$$

which is even more obvious in the following equivalent expression:

$$\forall i, j, i', j' \in \mathbb{N} : ((i \neq i') \lor (j \neq j')) \implies ((i, j) \neq (i', j'))$$

However, remember that the above gave only a *sufficient* condition. Data structures in a loop nest do not need to be indexed by the counters of surrounding loops for the nest to be in single-assignment form. Figure 8.3 shows an excerpt of the SPEC benchmark 176.gcc that illustrates this. Variables offset, i, bit, and sometimes_max serve as counters. The relevant modified data structures are arrays reg_basic_block and regs_sometimes_live and, indeed, we can check that two iterations of the body never write into the same array element. Indeed, variable sometimes_max is incremented each time regs_sometimes_live is accessed, making sure the next access will refer to another element of the array.

```
for (offset = 0, i = 0; offset < regset_size; offset++)
  for (bit = 1; bit; bit <<= 1, i++)
  {
    if (i == max_regno)
      break;
    if (old[offset] & bit)
    {
      reg_basic_block[i] = REG_BLOCK_GLOBAL;
      regs_sometimes_live[sometimes_max].offset = offset;
      regs_sometimes_live[sometimes_max].bit = i % REGSET;
      sometimes_max++;
    }
  }
```

Figure 8.3. Excerpt from 176.gcc.

The reason reg_basic_block is in single-assignment form is more subtle. Variable i is initialized in the initialization phase of the outer loop and is incremented at each iteration of the inner loop. Therefore, the index of reg_basic_block never has the same value twice while executing the loop nest.

Right-Hand Sides Situations where a ϕ-function is needed can be defined formally without the help (or should we say the additional complexity?) of the control-flow graph. A ϕ-function must be substituted to a reference m in the right-hand side of a statement **S** if there is an instance r of **S** that has more than one instancewise reaching definition:

$$\exists u, v \in \mathcal{W}, \ u \neq v \land u \in \mathsf{RD}(\langle r, m \rangle) \land v \in \mathsf{RD}(\langle r, m \rangle) \qquad (8.4)$$

In such cases, the arguments of the ϕ-function are exactly the memory locations written by the us and vs satisfying (8.4). Formally, if (8.4) holds, then m should be replaced by

$$\phi(\overline{\mathsf{write}}(\mathsf{RD}(\langle r, x \rangle))) \tag{8.5}$$

For instance, in Figure 8.1, the definitions reaching statement **6** are $\mathsf{RD}(\mathbf{6}) = \{\mathbf{2}, \mathbf{4}\}$, so the reference to x in the right-hand expression of **6** should be replaced by

$$\phi(\overline{\mathsf{write}}(\overline{\mathsf{RD}}(\mathbf{6}))) = \phi(\overline{\mathsf{write}}(\{\mathbf{2}, \mathbf{4}\})) = \phi(x2, x4) \tag{8.6}$$

It is important to notice that conditionals commute with

$$\phi \circ \overline{\mathsf{write}}$$

In other words, **if-then-else** expressions that may appear in $\mathsf{RD}(\langle r, x \rangle)$ in (8.5) can be pulled out of expression $\phi(\overline{\mathsf{write}}(\mathsf{RD}(\langle r, x \rangle)))$. For instance, another valid expression for the definitions reaching x in Figure 8.1 could have been

$$\mathsf{RD}(\langle r, x \rangle) = \textbf{if } foo \textbf{ then } \{\mathbf{2}\} \textbf{ else } \{\mathbf{4}\}$$

The occurrence of x in the right-hand expression of **6** could then be replaced by

$$
\begin{aligned}
\phi(\overline{\mathsf{write}}(\overline{\mathsf{RD}}(\mathbf{6}))) &= \phi(\overline{\mathsf{write}}(\textbf{if } foo \textbf{ then } \{\mathbf{2}\} \textbf{ else } \{\mathbf{4}\})) \\
&= \textbf{if } foo \textbf{ then } \phi(\overline{\mathsf{write}}(\{\mathbf{2}\})) \textbf{ else } \phi(\overline{\mathsf{write}}(\{\mathbf{4}\})) \\
&= \textbf{if } foo \textbf{ then } x2 \textbf{ else } x4 \tag{8.7}
\end{aligned}
$$

When no compile-time information of foo is available, (8.7) is just another way of saying (8.6). More precisely, it provides a possible *implementation* of (8.6) since it tells what ϕ should test to deliver the right value: foo in (8.7) gates the use of x2 and x4. This idea is the key to *gated SSA* [86]. Moreover, when the conditional depends on the iteration vector and its leaves are singleton sets, ϕ can be eliminated completely. We come back to this point in a few moments.

8.1.2 The Case of Loops

. . . .

```
0   x := 0
1   for i := 1 to 10 do
2       x := x + i
3   end for
```

. . . . *Figure 8.4. Simple loop with a recurrence.* . . . .

Consider Figure 2.5, shown again here in Figure 8.4. The first step of conversion to single-assignment form consists, as before, of giving one private memory location

. . . .

```
0   x0 := 0
1   for i := 1 to 10 do
2      x2[i] := ?  + i
3   end for
```

. . . . . *Figure 8.5. First step in converting Figure 8.4 to single-assignment form.* . . . . .

to each individual write—in this example, to each of the 10 individual instances of
statement **2**.

The solution is probably obvious: Give statement **2** its own entire array, and give
each instance of **2** an element of the newly defined array. In other words, construct
a data structure that has the same shape as (which is isomorphic to) the domain of
statement **2**. The result of step 1 is shown in Figure 8.5. Array x2 is statement **2**'s own
private array, and we suppose it is declared as an array of 10 elements.

. . . .

```
0   x0 := 0
1   for i := 1 to 10 do
2      x2[i] := φ(write(RD(2ⁱ))) + i
3   end for
```

Here the line 2 reads: $x2[i] := \phi(\overline{\text{write}}(\overline{\text{RD}}(2^i))) + i$

. . . . *Figure 8.6. Second step in converting Figure 8.4 to single-assignment form.* . . . .

As before, the second step consists of replacing all occurrences of x in right-hand
sides. A memory reference like x is replaced by a ϕ-function if there are multiple
reaching definitions. This replacement is done according to (8.5). The resulting program appears in Figure 8.6.

We can go one step further. We saw in (5.1) page 79 that the definitions reaching x
in **2** are

$$RD(2^i) = \text{if } i > 1 \qquad\qquad (8.8)$$
$$\text{then } \{2^{i-1}\}$$
$$\text{else } \{0\}$$

We now commute the conditional in (8.8) and $\phi \circ \overline{\text{write}}$ in **2** in Figure 8.6, yielding
the program shown in Figure 8.7. The whole process boils down to plugging in the
conditional expression returned by the instancewise reaching definition analysis.

You may argue that the if construct in Figure 8.7 *is* a ϕ-function. This is wrong,
however, because both parts of the if contain a single array element. ϕ-functions
serve as syntactic sugar for a lack of compile-time knowledge on the flow of data.
They are fancy forms of "don't-know" answers, any argument to a ϕ-function being
a valid candidate. In contrast, the if construct in Figure 8.7 makes explicit the exact
compile-time knowledge on the pattern of the data flow. This can be used in turn in

....

```
0   x0 := 0
1   for i := 1 to 10 do
2     x2[i] := (if i=1 then x0 else x2[i-1]) + i
3   end for
```

...... *Figure 8.7. Simple loop with a recurrence, in single-assignment form.* ......

additional optimizations, like loop peeling. As shown in Figure 8.8, the first iteration is removed from the iteration domain of statement **2**, so the initial value of i becomes 2. The corresponding instance $\mathbf{2}^1$ of statement **2** is inserted back in as a full statement line.

....

```
0    x0 := 0
2¹   x2[1] := x0 + 1
1    for i := 2 to 10 do
2      x2[i] := x2[i-1] + i
3    end for
```

.... *Figure 8.8. Figure 8.7 after loop peeling.* ....

The point we would like to make is that there is no way the loop-peeled version could be obtained from Figure 8.6. Contrasting Figures 8.6 and 8.7 shows that there is an intrinsic difference between a ϕ-function and a reaching definition expression with singleton leaves.

Let us also stress that the single-assignment form in Figure 8.7 is interesting not only as a sketch for the code actually generated, but also as an intermediate program representation. It provides, indeed, most of the information we know on the program's data flow, including the actual behavior of ϕ-functions.

This process is very general and extends to more complex programs. Consider the code for Choleski factorization studied in Exercise 5.5 and reproduced here in Figure 8.9. Applying the first step of single-assignment conversion yields left-hand sides x2[i], x4[i,k], p6[i], x8[i,j], x10[i,j,k], and a12[i,j] for statements **2**, **4**, **6**, **8**, **10**, and **12**, respectively. Notice that the left-hand side of statement **6** is just renamed. The modification for statement **12** is both subtle and brute-force: Strictly obeying the rules for the first step, the array in the left-hand side must be indexed by the iteration vector, which is (i,j), not (j,i). This leads to subscript [i,j] in the left-hand side, in contrast with [j,i] in the original program.

We now apply step 2 of conversion to single-assignment form. In particular, statement **4** is transformed into

```
x4[i,k] := (write(RD(⟨4^{i,k},x⟩))) - (write(RD(⟨4^{i,k},a[i,k]⟩)))^2;
```

. . . .

```
1   for i :=1 to n do
2     x := a[i,i];
3     for k := 1 to i-1 do
4       x:= x - a[i,k]^2;
5     end for
6     p := 1.0/sqrt( x );
7     for j := i+1 to n do
8       x := a[i,j];
9       for k := 1 to i-1 do
10        x := x - a[j,k] * a[i,k] ;
11      end for
12      a[j,i] := x * p[i];
13    end for
14  end for
```

. . . . Figure 8.9. Choleski factorization. . . . .

. . . .

```
1   for i := 1 to n do
2     x2[i] := a[i,i];
3     for k := 1 to i-1 do
4       x4[i,k]:=(if k>=2 then x4[i,k-1] else x2[i] endif)
                  - a12[k,i]^2;
5     end for
6     p6[i]:=1.0/sqrt(if i>=2 then x4[i,i-1] else x2[i]);
7     for j := i+1 to n do
8       x8[i,j] := a[i,j];
9       for k := 1 to i-1 do
10        x10[i,j,k]:=
              (if k>=2 then x10[i,j,k-1] else x8[i,j] endif)
              - a12[k,j] * a12[k,i];
11      end for
12      a12[i,j] :=
              (if i>=2 then x10[i,j,i-1] else x8[i,j] endif)
              * p6[i];
13    end for
14  end for
```

. . . . Figure 8.10. Single-assignment form for Choleski. . . . .

We can leverage the result of reaching definition analysis provided in Eq. (5.10) through (5.16) page 97. In particular, Eq. (5.10) and (5.14) are:

$$RD(\langle \mathbf{4}^{i,k}, \mathbf{x} \rangle) \; = \quad \begin{array}{l} \textbf{if } k \geq 2 \\ \textbf{then } \{\mathbf{4}^{i,k-1}\} \\ \textbf{else } \{\mathbf{2}^i\} \end{array} \qquad (8.9)$$

$$RD(\langle \mathbf{4}^{i,k}, \mathtt{a[i,k]} \rangle) \; = \quad \{\mathbf{12}^{k,i}\} \qquad\qquad\qquad (8.10)$$

Plugging (8.9) and (8.10) in statement **4**, and using the commutativity property, we get

```
x4[i,k]:= (if k>=2 then write(4^{i,k-1}) else write(2^i) endif)
        - write(12^{k,i})^2;
```

that is,

```
x4[i,k]:= (if k>=2 then x4[i,k-1] else x2[i] endif)
        - a12[k,i]^2;
```

Indeed, thanks to step 1, there is a one-to-one mapping between definition instances and memory locations. In addition, this mapping is just syntactical. Therefore, accesses to x and a in right-hand sides are just replaced by references to the array of the defining statement. Subscripts are given by the iteration vector of the defining instance.

The final program is shown in Figure 8.10. Observe that the right-hand side of statement **8** is not a typo. Page 98 shows that there are no definitions in this kernel reaching reference a[i,j]. We therefore consider that some previous statement outside the kernel provides the input values for a.

The code in Figure 8.10 was produced automatically (in a syntactically different but semantically equivalent form) by the PAF compiler developed by Prof. Feautrier and his team at the University of Versailles.

Other Data Structures Appropriate for Single Assignment   Consider again the program in Figure 8.4. It is simple enough to tell us array x2 needs exactly 10 elements. When the lower or upper bound is not so clear, or when the loop is a while, single assignment stays conceptually identical.

There are cases, however, where single assignment cannot serve "as is" to generate the actual code. Consider the program in Figure 5.20 page 103, shown again in Figure 8.11. The while .. do construct is just a counted while loop and is introduced page 12.

Each instance $\mathbf{3}^i$ assigns variable x. In turn, statement **5** assigns x an undefined number of times (possibly zero). The value read in x by statement **7** is thus defined *either* by **3** *or* by some instance of **5** in *the same iteration* of the for loop (the same i). Therefore, if the expansion assigns distinct memory locations to $\mathbf{3}^i$ and to instances of $\mathbf{5}^{i,w}$, how can instance $\mathbf{7}^i$ "know" which memory location to read from?

As before, to solve this problem, we use the result of an instancewise reaching definition analysis. This result is given in (5.22) and (5.23) page 104:

$$(5.22) \; \Leftrightarrow \; RD(\mathbf{5}^{i,w}) = \quad \begin{array}{l} \textbf{if } w > 1 \\ \textbf{then } \{\mathbf{5}^{i,w-1}\} \\ \textbf{else } \{\mathbf{3}^i\} \end{array}$$

. . . .

```
1   real x, A[N]
2   for i := 1 to N do
3     x := foo(i)
4     while (..)  do w := 1 begin
5       x := bar(x)
6     end while
7     A[i] := x
8   end for
```

. . . . *Figure 8.11. Program with a* while *loop introduced in Exercise 5.7.* . . . .

and

$$(5.23) \Leftrightarrow \mathsf{RD}(\mathbf{7}^i) = \{\mathbf{3}^i\} \cup \{\mathbf{5}^{i,w} : w \geq 1\}$$

Now let us convert the program to single-assignment form, making **3** write into x3 [i] and **5** into x5 [i, w]. Then each memory location is assigned to at most once, complying with the definition of single assignment. To transform right-hand sides, we use (5.22) and (5.23). This yields the program in Figure 8.12. The right-hand side of **5** depends only on w. The right-hand side of **7** depends on the control flow, thus needing a ϕ-function.

. . . .

```
2   for i := 1 to N do
3     x3[i] := foo(i)
4     while (..)  do w := 1 begin
5       x5[i,w] := if w>1 then bar(x5[i,w-1])
                          else bar(x3[i])
                   end if
6     end while
7     A7[i] := φ({x3[i]} ∪ {x5[i,w] : w ≥ 1})
8   end for
```

. . . . *Figure 8.12. Program in Figure 8.11 put in single-assignment form.* . . . .

The program in Figure 8.12 has the property that any reference to, say, x5 [3,2] refers to the same value. However, that program cannot be compiled as is, because we have no upper bound on the second dimension of x5. (We face the same issue when addressing recursive programs in a few moments.)

Another solution, therefore, is to use data structures that can be extended dynamically. Indeed, to implement single-assignment form, these structures have to manage as many elements as the instance count. In addition, these data structures should have the same shape as the iteration domains to simplify the mapping of instances to data elements. (We say the domain of a statement and its new associated data structure are isomorphic.) In this example, each instance 5^w of **5** pushes the produced value on a stack. (A list would do the trick as well.) The assignment in **5** then has the following form:

```
mystack := push(mystack, newvalue);
```

In Section 1.8, we agree on the convention that the counters of "counted" while loops are set to 0 if the loop does not iterate at all. The ϕ-function therefore has a natural implementation: If w equals 0 at statement **7**, then the value defined by **3** can be used. Otherwise, statement **7** simply has to pop the value from the appropriate stack. The transformed program can be summarized as shown in Figure 8.13.

. . . .

```
1   Declare N stacks x5[1]..x5[N];
2   for i := 1 to N do
3     x3[i] := foo(i)
4     while (..)  do w := 1 begin
5       x5[i] := push(x5[i],
                      (if w>1 then bar(pop(x5[i]))
                              else bar(x3[i])
                      end if));
6     end while
7     A7[i] := if w=0 then x3[i] else pop(x5[i]);
8   end for
```

. . . . *Figure 8.13. Single assignment for Figure 8.11, using stacks.* . . . .

Notice that the use of dynamic data structures can be generalized: For example, in theory two nested while loops can be converted to single assignment using a list of lists. We see later that single assignment for a binary (or n-ary, with $n > 1$) recursive procedure can be supported by a tree of appropriate degree.

8.1.3   Recursive Procedures

Conversion of recursive programs to single-assignment form has been much less studied in the literature. However, the conversion guidelines given above still apply.

For one, the new data structure a recursive procedure writes into has the same shape as the procedure's domain. For instance, if the procedure is doubly recursive, then the a tree of degree 2 is enough to allow for single assignment — whatever the original data structure was. Left-hand sides are then simply a mapping from the instruction's control word to the tree. As an example, let us consider the program of Figure 3.12, shown here again in Figure 8.14.

Because it is doubly recursive, its call graph is a tree, as discussed in Chapter 3, whose nodes correspond to instances of the procedure and can be labeled by words in

. . . .

```
1   procedure P
2   do
3     v := foo(v);
4     if c1 then P() endif;
5     if c2 then P() endif
6   end
```

. . . . *Figure 8.14. A simple recursive procedure.* . . . .

the regular language $(4 + 5)^*$. In the procedure shown in Figure 8.14, each procedure invocation writes into v, so converting into single-assignment form requires replacing scalar v by a tree-shaped data structure—a data structure isomorphic to the call tree. This tree will be called v3, to stress the fact it corresponds to statement **3**. (There might be more than one tree corresponding to scalar v, as several arrays x1, x2, etc. correspond to scalar x in Figure 8.4.) As discussed earlier, changing left-hand expressions is the first step in converting to single-assignment form. The result of this first step is shown in Figure 8.15, where the notation [. .] is used to index tree-like structures *à la* array. Because statement **4** goes along left children and statement **5** toward right children, a node in v3 is denoted by v3 [*w*], where $w \in (4 + 5)^*$. In other words, the left child of a node *w* of v3 is referenced by v3 [*w*.**4**] and the right child by v3 [*w*.**5**].

. . . .

```
0   Type "word" captures the regular language (4 + 5)*
1   procedure P(word w)
2   do
3     v3[w] := foo(...);
4     if c1 then P(w.4) endif;
5     if c2 then P(w.5) endif
6   end
```

. . . . . . *Figure 8.15. First step toward a conversion to single-assignment form.* . . . . . .

In the second step, we replace references to v by ϕ-functions each time there might be more than one reaching definition, as illustrated in Figure 8.16. The program in Figure 8.16 can be compared with the one in Figure 8.6.

Furthermore, applying the result of the reaching definition analysis done in Chapter 5 gives more details. We saw that one way to express the result of this analysis is given by the following three equations:

$$\mathrm{RD}(3) = \{\bot\} \qquad\qquad\qquad (8.11)$$

. . . .

```
1   procedure P(w)
2   do
3     v3[w] := foo(φ(write(RD(3ʷ))));
4     if c1 then P(w.4) endif;
5     if c2 then P(w.5) endif
6   end
```

. . . . . . *Figure 8.16. Single-assignment form for the procedure of Figure 8.14.* . . . . . .

$$\forall w \in \mathcal{D}(3), w' \in (4+5)^* : (w = w'43) \Rightarrow (\mathrm{RD}(w) = \{w'3\}) \tag{8.12}$$

$$\forall w \in \mathcal{D}(3), w' \in (4+5)^* : (w = w'53) \Rightarrow (\mathrm{RD}(w) = w'(4+\varepsilon)(4+5)^*3) \tag{8.13}$$

Equation (8.11) gives the definition reaching the root instance in the call tree, (8.12) provides the exact definition reaching a given left child, whereas (8.13) is not as definite since it maps right children to sets (regular languages) of writes.

. . . .

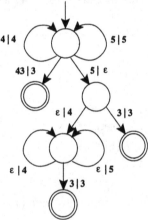

. . . . *Figure 8.17. Reaching definition transducer for the program in Figure 8.14.* . . . .

The equivalent transducer appears in Figure 5.28, reproduced here in Figure 8.17. Taking the image by this relation of the current instance of statement **3** gives the set of all possible definitions reaching that instance. Applying mapping write to that set gives the labels of all elements of tree v3 that possibly contain the value we need. The abstract transformed program is shown in Figure 8.18. (In Figure 8.18, we drop the final "**3**" in words w.) The `matches` operator is a pattern matching operator, as in the PERL language. That is, the following expression

```
w matches w'4
```

if true, means that w ends with **4** and that w' is the corresponding prefix.

....

```
1   procedure P(w)
2   do
3     v3[w] :=
          foo( (if w=ε then v3[ε]
                else (if w matches w'4 then v3[w']
                      else φ(write(RD(3ᵂ)))) )));
4     if c1 then P(w.4) endif;
5     if c2 then P(w.5) endif
6   end
```

.... *Figure 8.18. Refinement of Figure 8.16.* ....

You can notice that the case-by-case expression in Figure 8.18 represents a refinement of the program shown in Figure 8.16. In the first two cases, there is a direct mapping to the appropriate element of tree v3. However, the expression for single-assignment form cannot be derived beyond this point. Indeed, there is no simple expression for the ϕ in Figure 8.16 because there is no simple closed-form expression for the relation captured by the transducer in Figure 5.28. A dedicated run-time support is required to restore the data flow in the final case of statement **3**.

8.1.4 Array Single Assignment

So far, all data structures in input programs have been scalars. However, single assignment applies as well to more general structures, and to arrays in particular. We then call it *array single assignment*.

Array single assignment has exactly the same purpose as single assignment: It makes the data flow explicit in imperative programs, extending this idea to programs manipulating arrays. Thanks to this property, array single assignment has been used for a long time in many fields, including parallelizing compilers and VLSI array design [59].

To see how array single assignment helps transform programs, consider the example in Figure 8.19. Its single-assignment counterpart is shown in Figure 8.20. As you can notice, by definition of single assignment, all anti- and output dependencies are removed. The benefit of this property is that any reference to, say, a4[3,2] anywhere in the program refers not only to the same memory location but also to the same value. The second benefit for parallelizing compilers is of course that fewer dependencies means more parallelism. A parallelizing compiler might then want to use the array SA form as a draft for the code actually generated.

. . . .

```
1   a[..]   := ...
2   for i := 1 to n do
3     for j := 1 to n do
4         a[i+j] := 1 + a[i+j-1]
5     end for
6   end for
```

. . . . Figure 8.19. Single assignment extended to arrays. . . . .

. . . .

```
1   a1[..]   := ...
2   for i := 1 to n do
3     for j := 1 to n do
4       a4[i,j] := 1 +
              (if j>=2 then a4[i,j-1]
              else (if i>=2 then
              a4[i-1,j] else a1[i+j-1] ))
5     end for
6   end for
```

. . . . Figure 8.20. Program in Figure 8.19 in single-assignment form. . . . .

Another point is that it really is difficult to visualize how data flow in the course of an execution. In contrast, Figure 8.20 shows how regular the flow of data actually is. The regularity of the data flow of the program in Figure 8.19 appears even more clearly in Figure 8.21. For instance, the graph makes clear that, for j greater than 1, the source of the data flow is the immediate neighbor down the vertical axis. Notice that the data flow in the program in Figure 8.19 is, in fact, identical. However, its data flow is lost among many memory-based dependencies that are not relevant to the actual algorithm. In contrast, the simplicity of the algorithm of the program in Figure 8.19 shows up very well in Figure 8.20.

What Is New Here?   Notice that we stress "array" in the expression "array single assignment" for pedagogical reasons only. By emphasizing "array," we underline the difference between the material of this section and what can be found elsewhere in the literature. But there is in fact nothing new, and we should not even need to mention the word "array": Single assignment is a general concept not limited to scalars or arrays. Indeed, it is important to realize that, whatever the control-flow structures or the data structures, conversion to single-assignment form can be automated as long as an adequate instancewise reaching definition analysis is available. Feautrier was the first researcher to realize this and to present an algorithm for single-assignment conversion in the presence of nonscalar data structures [29]. The instancewise reaching definition analysis presented in this book gives a means to transform a program, even if it includes

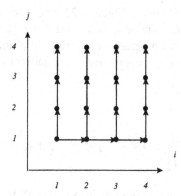

.... *Figure 8.21. Flow of data in the programs in Figures 8.19 and 8.20.* ....

arrays, to single-assignment form.

In fact, the alert reader may have noticed that, in all the material of this chapter, the original data structure is *not* relevant in converting to single-assignment form. What matters is the *domain* of the statement. More precisely, whatever the data structure in the original programs, single-assignment form in the transformed program *only* requires the new data structure to be isomorphic to (i.e., in one-to-one mapping with) the set of write instances, that is, the domain of the assignment.

```
1   a[..]   := ...
2   for i := 1 to n do
3     if P(i) then
4       for j := 1 to n do
5         a[i+j] := 1 + a[i+j-1]
6       end for
7     end if
8   end for
```

.... *Figure 8.22. Program in Figure 8.19 with additional test.* ....

How General Is Conversion to Array Single-Assignment Form?   As stated earlier, conversion to single-assignment form (or the "array" version, for that matter) only requires us (1) to be able to create data structures that are isomorphic to the control flow and (2) to have an instancewise reaching definition. If some control structures have no bound, like while loops in general, then requisite (1) is an issue and some tricks need to be applied, when possible. If control structures include conditionals, then the difficulty lies more in (2), that is, the reaching definition analysis. However, we have seen in previous chapters that this is not a difficult issue.

Consider the example shown in Figure 8.22, which adds a conditional to the program in Figure 8.19. For illustration purposes, we assume the first statement initializes all elements of array a in that program. A reaching definition analysis is done in Exercise 5.9 page 108. This analysis reports that the definitions reaching $5^{i,j}$ are

$$
\begin{aligned}
\text{RD}(5^{i,j}) = \quad &\textbf{if } j \geq 2 \\
&\textbf{then } \{5^{i,j-1}\} \\
&\textbf{else } \textbf{if } i \geq 2 \\
&\quad\quad \textbf{then } \{1\} \cup \{5^{i',j'} : 1 \leq i' < i, 1 \leq j' \leq n, i' + j' = i + j - 1\} \\
&\quad\quad \textbf{else } \{1\}
\end{aligned}
$$

Again, instancewise reaching definitions give nearly all the information we need: In two cases, there is one and only one definition reaching the read of a[i+j-1]. These two cases are, on the one hand, all iterations of the inner loop except the first one (j greater than or equal to 2) and, on the other hand, the very first execution of statement 5. Therefore, no ϕ-function is needed in either case. However, when $i > 1$ and $j = 1$, many definitions may reach a[i+j-1], and the right one cannot be selected at compile time. A ϕ-function is then (and only then) needed to abstract (or actually implement!) this selection. The single-assignment form of Figure 8.22 is shown in Figure 8.23.

· ·

```
1   a1[..]   := ...
2   for i := 1 to n do
3     if P(i) then
4       for j := 1 to n do
5         a5[i,j] := 1 +
              if j>=2 then a5[i,j-1]
              else
                if i>=2 then
                  φ({a1[i+j-1]}∪
                    {a5[i',j'] : 1 ≤ i' < i, 1 ≤ j' ≤ n, i' + j' = i+j-1})
                else
                  a1[i+j-1]
                end if
              end if
6       end for
7     end if
8   end for
```

· · · · · · · Figure 8.23. Single-assignment form of the program in Figure 8.22. · · · · · · ·

Exercise 8.1   Convert the program shown in Figure 8.24 to single assignment form. (We assume $1 \leq foo \leq n + 1$.) Hint: The reaching definitions in this program are studied in Exercise 5.8.

....

```
1   for i = 1 to n do
2      a[i] := ...;
3      if(..)  a[i+1]:=...   end if
4   end for
5   a[n+1] := ..
6   ..   := a[foo]
```

.... Figure 8.24. Program used in Exercise 8.1. ....

Solution   The reaching definitions given by (5.24) page 108 are:

$$RD(6) = \begin{array}{l} \textbf{if } foo = n + 1 \\ \textbf{then } \{5\} \\ \textbf{else } \{2^{foo}\} \end{array}$$

This expression directly yields the transformed program shown in Figure 8.25. Notice that $a3$ does not appear in the right-hand expression of **6** thanks to the result of reaching definition analysis.

....

```
1   for i = 1 to n do
2      a2[i] := ...;
3      if(..)  a3[i+1]:=...   end if
4   end for
5   a5[n+1] = ..;
6   ..   := if (foo=n+1) then a5[n+1] else a2[foo] end if
```

.... Figure 8.25. Single-assignment form for the program in Figure 8.24. ....

Notice that, for the purpose of conversion to single-assignment form, reaching definition analysis should not be too aggressive in eliminating execution-time constants. For instance, since the analysis knows little about the value of foo (just that $1 \leq foo \leq n + 1$), it might be tempted to collapse the conditional, yielding

$$RD(6) = \{2^{foo}\} \cup \{5\} \tag{8.14}$$

The corresponding transformed program would then be the one in Figure 8.26. ∎

....

```
1   for i := 1 to n do
2     a2[i] := ...
3     if(..) a3[i+1] := ...
4   end for
5   a5[n+1] := ..
6   .. := φ(a2[foo],a5[n+1])
```

.... *Figure 8.26. Single-assignment form for the program in Figure 8.24.* ....

Exercise 8.2   Convert the program skeleton shown in Figure 5.15, shown here again in Figure 8.27, to single-assignment form.

....

```
1   a[1] := 0
2   for i := 1 to n do
3     for j := 1 to n
4       a[i+j] := ...
5       a[i] := ...  a[i+j-1]
6     end for
7   end for
```

.... *Figure 8.27. Program used in Exercise 8.2.* ....

....

```
1   a1[1] := 0
2   for i := 1 to n
3     for j := 1 to n
4       a4[i,j] := ...
5       a5[i,j]:=.. if j>=2 then a4[i,j-1]
                    else  if i>=2 then a4[i-1,j]
                          else a1[1]
                          end if
                    end if
6     end for
7   end for
```

.... *Figure 8.28. Single-assignment form for the program shown in Figure 8.27.* ....

Solution   We see in (5.9) that the definitions reaching a[i+j-1] are

$$\text{RD}(5^{i,j}) = \quad \textbf{if } j \geq 2$$
$$\textbf{then } \{4^{i,j-1}\}$$
$$\textbf{else if } i \geq 2$$
$$\textbf{then } \{4^{i-1,j}\}$$
$$\textbf{else } \{1\}$$

This tells us that definitions in the left-hand side of statement **5** never reach the right-hand side. Therefore, private array a5 of **5** does not appear as an argument to the ϕ-function. An expression for the ϕ-function that depends only on loop counters can also be derived from (5.9). The end result appears in Figure 8.28. ■

Exercise 8.3   Consider the program below:

```
0    x[0] := 0
1    for i:= 1 to 2*n do
2      t := x[2*n-i+1];
3        x[i] := x[i-1] + t
4    end for
```

Convert it to single-assignment form. Hint: We compute the definition reaching x in statement **2**, page 92.

Solution   On page 92, we see that the definitions of x reaching 2^i are

$$\text{RD}(\langle 2^i, x[2*n-i+1]\rangle) = \quad \textbf{if } 1 \leq i \leq n$$
$$\textbf{then } \{\bot\}$$
$$\textbf{else } \{3^{2n-i+1}\}$$

The definitions reaching x[i-1] and t in statement **3** are easier to find:

$$\text{RD}(\langle 3^i, x[i-1]\rangle) = \quad \textbf{if } i = 1$$
$$\textbf{then } \{0\}$$
$$\textbf{else } \{3^{i-1}\}$$

and

$$\text{RD}(\langle 3^i, t\rangle) = \{2^i\}$$

A single-assignment equivalent of this program is, therefore,

```
0    x0[0] := 0
1    for i:= 1 to 2*n do
2      t2[i]:= if 1<=i<=n then x[2*n-i+1]
                    else x3[2*n-i+1] end if;
3        x3[i]:= (if i=1 then x0[0] else x3[i-1] end if)
                    + t2[i]
4    end for
```

Notice that the "bottom" $\perp$ in $RD(\langle 2^i, x \rangle)$ means that the corresponding reference is not defined in the given program fragment. Therefore, the transformation should plug in the original reference, verbatim, for this particular case. This is why the right-hand expression in statement **2** begins with

```
if 1<=i<=n then x[2*n-i+1]
```

even though array x is not defined anywhere in the transformed program. Indeed, we should not forget that more statements, including definitions to array x, may precede statement **0**. This single-assignment program is used in Chapter 11. ∎

A Few More Tricks   So far, conversion to single-assignment form can be done in an automatic or semiautomatic way. However, there are cases where automatic conversion fails. Alternatively, when the reaching definition analysis returns a very approximate result, the transformed program may be too complex to be useful. In these cases, conversion by hand is a very useful option. Indeed, some applications do not absolutely require an automatic tool to transform a program. A case in point is systolic array design [59] for which designers are willing to spend hours on the specification (the program to be mapped to a systolic array) if this can improve the area, the throughput, or the power consumption of the final circuit. (The next section is dedicated to systolic array design.)

Transforming a program by hand also allows us to play more tricks. Consider the simple loop below:

```
1   for i := 1 to n do
2     if p(i) then
3         x := x+1
4     end if
5   end for
```

Converting the loop to single-assignment form using the method described earlier in this chapter would consist of two steps. First, find the instancewise reaching definitions of x in **3**:

$$RD(3^i) = \quad \textbf{if } i = 1$$
$$\textbf{then } \{\perp\}$$
$$\textbf{else } \{3^{i'} \, : \, 1 \leq i' < i\}$$

Second, expand left-hand expressions and plug the reaching definitions in right-hand sides:

```
for i := 1 to n do
  if p(i) then
    x[i] := (if i=1 then x else φ({x[i'] : 1 ≤ i' < i}))
             + 1
  end if
end for
```

which is correct but quite intricate. In particular, we lost the fact that the value of x in the right-hand side comes was produced by the last instance of **3**.

On the other hand, the initial program can equivalently be seen as

```
1  for i := 1 to n do
2    if p(i) then
3      x := x+1
4    else
5      x := x
6    end if
7  end for
```

Of course, the new assignment in the "else" branch of the conditional is just a copy that serves to propagate the value of x from one iteration to the next. Data such as x, which are propagated without being modified, are called *transmittent data* [59].

The big asset of the modified loop is that the definition reaching x in statement **3** at a given iteration i, for $i > 1$, comes from one of *exactly* two definitions: 3^{i-1} or 5^{i-1}. Then, converting the loop to single-assignment form is pretty simple:

```
for i := 1 to n do
  if p(i) then
    x[i] := x[i-1]+1
  else
    x[i] := x[i-1]
  end if
end for
```

Notice that, in the latter loop, we did not duplicate array x into two different arrays x3 and x5. In other words, we did not change the left-hand expressions of **3** and **5** into x3[i] and x5[i], respectively. This allows us to keep simple right-hand sides. We revisit this idea in Chapter 9.

8.1.5   Single Assignment and Systolic Array Design

For instance, single assignment is of the utmost importance in *systolic array* design. In that context, transforming the input program or algorithm in any way—by a tool or by the designer—can make sense because the time available to the design of a circuit, including compilation, is much longer than the time considered to be acceptable in the classical compilation context (where the user is staring at the screen waiting for his or her compilation to finish). In circuit design, the user has the freedom to change the input program to make the systolic implementation faster.

In particular, it would make no sense for a systolic array designer to keep the output dependencies of the original algorithm or program. These dependencies would only reduce the amount of parallelism in the circuit. Second, systolic arrays need local, regular data flow.

The best way to exhibit this locality and this regularity is to put the program into single assignment [59]. Pieces of the program can then be considered as functional building blocks that can be composed at will as very well illustrated in [1]. These pieces become circuit parts, more often the cells of the systolic array, and can be laid out more easily on the circuit.

....

```
1   Lmax := 0;
2   Iopt := 0;
3   for i := 0 to n-Ls-1 do
4     L[i] := 0;
5     E[i] := 1;
6     for j := 0 to Ls-1 do
7       if(M[j]=B[i+j] and E[i]=1) then
8          L[i] := L[i]+1
9       else
10         E[i] := 0
11      end if
12    end for
13    if Lmax <= L[i] then Iopt:=i; Lmax:=L[i] endif
14  end for
```

.... *Figure 8.29. Code for LZ compression.* ....

An example in point given in recent literature [50] is the code for LZ data compression shown in Figure 8.29. The LZ algorithm, designed by Lempel and Ziv in 1977, is one of the most popular algorithms for data compression. A lot of work has been devoted to optimized implementations, in software, of numerous versions of the LZ algorithm, but their speeds are often too slow for some applications. Therefore, researchers are trying to synthesize specialized circuits in a semiautomatic way from a high-level description (in a language like C); for instance, Hwang and Wu recently presented a VLSI systolic array implementation of LZ compression [50].

The SA form of the program in Figure 8.29 is shown in Figure 8.30. The trick described earlier is applied twice, once for L and once for E.

This SA form has several benefits. First, output dependencies have disappeared. Therefore, more parallelism is available is the transformed program. This becomes apparent when deriving a systolic circuit out of this program. An elementary cell of our circuit consists of statements **7** through **11**. This "mini-program" has four inputs (M[j], B[i+j], E[i,j], and L[i,j]) and two outputs (L[i,j+1] and E[i,j+1]). We really can consider L[i,j+1] and E[i,j+1] as the two output signals, as opposed to storage location, thanks to the single-assignment property.

8.2   Static Single Assignment

Static single assignment (SSA) is a limited form of single-assignment form. This limitation is on purpose and is an advantage in many cases, especially for its original goal as an intermediate representation of programs using scalars. The usefulness and applicability of the SSA framework [23] are undisputed, and SSA is still the subject of active research (e.g., [82]).

. . . .

```
1   Lmax := 0;
2   Iopt := 0;
3   for i := 0 to n-Ls-1 do
4      L[i,0] := 0;
5      E[i,0] := 1;
6      for j := 0 to Ls-1 do
7         if (M[j]=B[i+j] and E[i,j]=1) then
8            L[i,j+1] := L[i,j]+1;
8b           E[i,j+1] := E[i,j]      // E[i,j] equals one
9         else
10           E[i,j+1] := 0;
10b          L[i,j+1] := L[i,j];
11        end if
12     end for
13     if Lmax <= L[i,Ls-1] then
          Iopt:=i; Lmax:=L[i,Ls-1]
       endif
14  end for
```

. . . . *Figure 8.30. Handwritten SA form for the code in Figure 8.29.* . . . .

The goal of SSA is to give each *statement* its own private data structure. Formally, SSA can be defined as

$$\forall \mathbf{S} \in \mathcal{S}, \mathbf{T} \in \mathcal{S}, u \in \mathcal{D}(\mathbf{S}), v \in \mathcal{D}(\mathbf{T}):$$
$$(\mathbf{S} \neq \mathbf{T}) \;\Rightarrow\; (\overline{\mathsf{write}}(u) \cap \overline{\mathsf{write}}(v) = \emptyset) \tag{8.15}$$

That is, in the transformed program (indicated by the line over write), two instances spawned by two distinct statements are guaranteed to write to different memory locations. If they are spawned by one statement, then SSA does not make any requirement. In other words, what matters is that the two statements **S** and **7** are different, not that the instances (u and v) are.

In contrast, plain SA gives each statement *instance* its data structure, so for straight-line codes without loops, SSA and SA are no different. Therefore, the program in Figure 8.2 also serves as a valid SSA form for Figure 8.1. (Notice, however, that the "official" SSA form, as defined by its inventors, does not use ϕ in expressions but inserts additional explicit assignments to new temporary variables. An example of the "official" form, as applied to the running example, appears in Figure 8.31. Conceptually, this makes no difference, so we stick to the version with ϕ-expressions. These additional assignments in SSA form, however, are helpful to simplify the construction of SSA.)

To see how SSA really differs from plain SA, let's consider a simple example with loops, like the program in Figure 8.4 on page 170. In contrast to SA, which expands scalar x into an array shown in Figure 8.4, SSA just duplicates x into two scalars.

. . . .

```
1   if (..)  then
2      x2 := 0
3   else
4      x4 := 1
5   end if
6   x6 := φ(x2,x4);
6'  y6 := x6+1;
7   x7 := 11
8   if (..)  then
9      x9 := 2
10  else
11     x11 := 3
12  end if
13  x13 := φ(x7,x9,x11);
13' z13 := x13
```

. . . . . . *Figure 8.31. An SSA version that complies with the original definition.* . . . . . .

The resulting program appears in Figure 8.32. Does the difference matter? It depends on the program properties you want to capture. In a basic block, SSA has the useful property that two occurrences of the same name represent the same value. Outside a block, you lose that property. For instance, there are two occurrences of $x2$ in the SSA form in Figure 8.32, and each represents a different value. In contrast, in the SA form in Figure 8.7, two references to the same element of array $x2$ are guaranteed to represent the same value.

. . . .

```
0   x0 := 0
1   for i := 1 to 10
2      x2 := φ(x0,x2) + i
3   endfor
```

. . . . *Figure 8.32. Figure 8.4 in static single-assignment form.* . . . .

Notice that the "official" SSA definition does not try to give a closed-form expression to the ϕ-function in Figure 8.32. Indeed, we could mimic Figure 8.7 and consider the program in Figure 8.33 as the SSA form for Figure 8.4. It all depends on the assumptions made on the reaching definition analysis. Figure 8.32 assumes a representation of def-use chains that is not based on instances, whereas Figure 8.33 assumes an instancewise representation.

. . . .

```
0   x0 := 0
1   for i := 1 to 10
2      x2 := (if i=1 then x0 else x2) + i
3   endfor
```

.... *Figure 8.33. SSA form for Figure 8.4 with a closed-form expression for φ.* ....

Array SSA Array SSA, an extension of SSA to arrays, is introduced in [56]. As in SSA, array SSA enforces that each statement writes into its own data structure. Therefore, array SSA is also defined by Eq. (8.15)—the implicit difference from classical SSA is that original structures (the mapping write) are of array "type." Indeed, (8.15) does not specify whether the original data structure is a scalar, an array, or a graph. Therefore, constructing the left-hand sides of an Array SSA form is easy: We just have to give a new, unique array name to each statement. Usually, the name of the new array is the old name plus the statement number.

As an example, consider the program in Figure 8.27 on page 184. In the first step, converting to array SSA form consists of providing new array names to assignments, so the left-hand expressions in statements **1**, **4**, and **5** simply become a1[1], a4[i+j], and a5[i], respectively. The outcome of this first step appears in Figure 8.34.

. . . .

```
1   a[1] := 0
2   for i := 1 to n do
3      for j := 1 to n
4         a[i+j] := ...
5         a[i] := ...  ?
6      end for
7   end for
```

. . . . *Figure 8.34. First step of array SSA conversion for Figure 8.27.* . . . .

Concerning right-hand sides, all the necessary information is once again provided by instancewise reaching definitions. Equation (5.9) on page 96 tells us that the definitions reaching a[i+j-1] are

$$RD(2^{i,j}) = \quad \textbf{if } j \geq 2 \qquad\qquad\qquad (8.16)$$
$$\textbf{then } \{4^{i,j-1}\}$$
$$\textbf{else if } i \geq 2$$
$$\textbf{then } \{4^{i-1,j}\}$$
$$\textbf{else } \{1\}$$

```
1  a1[1] := 0
2  for i := 1 to n do
3    for j := 1 to n do
4       a4[i+j] := ...
5       a5[i]:=.. if j>=2
                  then
                     a4[i+(j-1)]
                  else  if i>=2
                          then a4[(i-1)+j]
                          else a1[1]
                          end if
                  end if
6    end for
7  end for
```

.... *Figure 8.35. Array SSA for the program in Figure 8.27.* ....

This expression of reaching definitions can be plugged into the transformed code nearly verbatim, as you can see in Figure 8.35. All that remains to be done is to map definitions to the array elements they define. This is not hard, since we know the values of the loop counters (like $(i, j-1)$ when $j \geq 2$) and since subscripts in left-hand sides are the same as in the original program. As an example, when j is greater than 1, we know the loop counters of the reaching definition are $(i, j-1)$, and since the syntactic expression of that definition is a4[i+j], we know we have to read from a4[i+(j-1)].

You can also notice that no ϕ-function is needed: For any given instance of statement 5, (8.16) tells at compile time which definition to read from. There is no run-time ambiguity, as can be shown by the very fact we can peel the loops, as shown in Figure 8.36. Notice also that a second pass of renaming must be applied on the program in Figure 8.36 to restore the array SSA property.

8.3 Further Reading

Conversion to single assignment removes all output and antidependencies. This approach might be an overkill. How to selectively remove such dependencies for the purpose of scheduling is detailed in [11].

Many techniques allow us to reduce the size of arrays in single-assignment programs [17, 61] or, in other words, to go out of an array single-assignment intermediate representation. The simplest idea is to first compute a schedule function for statement instances and to compute the last use of a definition according to (7.14) in Section 7.3. The scheduled time step for this last reference is then known as well, and the associated memory location can be deallocated just after this time step.

....

```
a1[1] := 0;
a4[1] := ...;
a5[1] := ...  a1[1];
for j := 2 to n do
   a4[1+j] := ...;
   a5[1] := ...a4[1+(j-1)]
end for
for i := 2 to n do
   a4[i+1] := ...;
   a5[i] := ...a4[(i-1)+1]
   for j := 2 to n do
      a4[i+j] := ...;
      a5[i] := ...a4[i+(j-1)]
   end for
end for
```

.... *Figure 8.36. Figure 8.35 after loop peeling.* ....

Regarding static single assignment, [13] extends SSA to *predicated code*. Predicated codes are a type of assembly-level programs where instructions are guarded by Boolean predicates indicating whether or not the instruction's side effects should be committed. Predicates appear in the instruction set of recent microprocessors, including the Itanium(R) processor [51].

Classical SSA can be extended to include more sophisticated ϕ-functions that preserve more information. Indeed, the selection a ϕ must perform can be gated by the conditions of if statements or by predicates on loop iteraSuctions. This *gated SSA* is studied in [86].

8.4 Conclusion

Single assignment and static single assignment are two program forms that capture the data flow, or at least a part of it in the case of SSA. This property makes imperative programming closer to functional programming, as illustrated by the SISAL language, among others.

Transforming a program to either form boils down to modifying all left-hand expressions and updating right-hand sides accordingly. Rules to change left-hand sides are pretty simple. However, how to change the right-hand sides is hard because we have to make sure the original data flow is preserved. Changing right-hand sides often requires us to use oracle ϕ-functions, whose implementation can be involved. Fortunately, we saw that right-hand sides, with both forms, can be obtained easily once an instancewise reaching definition analysis is done. Such an analysis also detects cases where ϕ-functions are, in fact, not needed.

Don't be misled, however: Using instancewise reaching definition analysis is no guarantee that *all* ϕ-functions disappear from the array SSA form. When a leaf in the expression of reaching definitions is a set with more than one element, there is an ambiguity — perhaps because the analysis wasn't precise enough, or perhaps because the ambiguity is intrinsic to the program. To see why, consider again the program in Figure 8.24 on page 183. More than one definition possibly reaches statement **6**, as given by (8.14). Without information on the condition of the if in statement **3**, no compile-time analysis will ever be able to lift this ambiguity, and therefore a ϕ *has* to appear in both the array SA and the array SSA equivalents of Figure 8.24. Actually, for that particular program, the array SA and array SSA forms coincide, and the SSA form is the code appearing in Figure 8.25.

Chapter 9

Maximal Static Expansion

We have seen that data dependencies hamper automatic parallelization of imperative programs. We have also seen that a general method to reduce the number of dependencies is to change writes so that they access distinct memory locations, that is, to *expand* data structures. However, expanding data structures has a cost. The increase in memory is an obvious cost. However, other costs discussed below may also be incurred. Therefore, a general problem arises: Given a cost criterion, what expansion provides maximum parallelism at the lowest cost?

As we said, the mere size of required memory is a cost, and this might be the chief optimization criterion on systems with little available memory, like embedded systems. Another optimization criterion can be the removal of dependencies that hamper parallel execution [11]. However, the criterion we address in this chapter is related to performance when available memory is not an issue.

To see where this cost comes from, consider again single assignment or static single assignment, and imagine we keep this representation in the generated code: ϕ-functions must be materialized to "merge" multiple reaching definitions. These ϕ-functions represent a run-time overhead, especially for nonscalar data structures or when replicated data are distributed across processors. As detailed in Chapter 8, a symbolic instancewise reaching definition analysis can help significantly reduce the number of ϕ-functions. However, as discussed in Section 8.4, the data flow may be intrinsically dynamic—that is, it is sometimes impossible to predict data flow at compile time. Therefore, even excellent analyses will not be able to avoid ϕ-functions in single-assignment and static single-assignment forms.

There is thus an apparent catch-22. On the one hand, both single-assignment forms expose some of the program's data flow and therefore allow some optimizations like parallelization. On the other hand, they introduce these "oracle" ϕ-functions whose overhead may defeat the purpose of parallelization. Maximal static expansion [8], or MSE for short, solves this contradiction by offering a tradeoff.

However, MSE should not be considered as the *only* or the *best* tradeoff between parallelism and memory usage, but just as *one* possible solution. It does provide, however, a theoretical upper bound on the parallelism in a program. This upper bound is derived under the following two assumptions: The transformed program must be free of ϕ-functions, and the result of reaching definitions is fixed (i.e., it is an input to our MSE algorithm).

This chapter is by far the most technical in this book, so don't be surprised if you find it harder to read. However, the following section is a self-contained, bird's-eye overview of the techniques. It contains nearly no math, so you might want to read it and then skip to Section 9.5. Overall, the whole chapter applies and builds on nearly all the concepts discussed so far, so you might find it interesting to see how each piece fits in the puzzle.

9.1 Motivating Examples

Let us consider two writes u and v that may both reach some read r. If we draw a figure to represent u, v, and r, then we obtain the drawing on the left of Figure 9.1. Edges represent data flowing from either u or v to r.

Now assume we assign two distinct memory locations to u and v. Then a ϕ-function is needed to restore the data flow since we do not know which of the two locations has the value needed by r. The left part of Figure 9.1 shows that u and v are in a sense "related" through r. Because of this relation, which we call R, expanding them would imply introducing a ϕ.

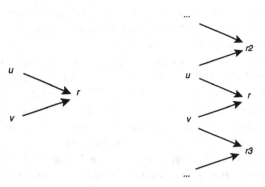

. . . . *Figure 9.1. Relation R (left) and its transitive closure (right).* . . . .

Instead, we want a *static expansion*, that is, a (data structure) expansion that does not need a ϕ-function.[1] Coming back to our example, a static expansion enforces that u and v, in the transformed program, write in fact to the same memory location.

But now we can suspect there are other reads, call them $r2$ and $r3$, and other writes reaching these reads. These additional reads and writes appear on the right side of Figure 9.1, with the convention that writes appear to the left (aligned vertically with u and v) and reads to the right (aligned with r). The new writes are independently "related" to u and v, through $r2$, $r3$, or some other reads. As depicted on the right

---

[1]Notice that according to this definition, an expansion in the SSA framework may *not* be "static."

part of Figure 9.1, a chain of writes builds up. This chain corresponds to the transitive closure of the relation sketched earlier. (See Section 7.4.1 on page 156 for the definition of transitive closure.)

If we pause for a moment, we see that two types of relations emerge as key instruments for static expansion: the relation among writes built through shared reached uses, and another relation which is the transitive closure of the first one.

We will push this concept to its limits and introduce *maximal* static expansion, or MSE. Indeed, there is not a unique static expansion of a given program. But there is only one maximal static expansion, which is the static expansion exposing the maximum amount of parallelism.

To see how these ideas apply to real-life programs, the rest of this section presents three examples. The sections that follow are quite involved, so remember you might want to skip to the wrap-up (Section 9.5) if this is your first read.

. . . .

```
1   real x, A[N]
2   for i := 1 to N do
3     x := foo(i)
4     while (..)  do w := 1 begin
5       x := bar(x)
6     endwhile
7     A[i] := x
8   endfor
```

. . . . *Figure 9.2. Illustrating maximal static expansion on a* while *loop.* . . . .

First Example: Dynamic Control Flow   Consider again the program in Figure 8.11, shown here again in Figure 9.2. The while .. do construct is just a counted while loop and was introduced page 12.

In Chapter 8 on page 175, we derive the single-assignement form of this program, reproduced here in Figure 9.3. This single-assignment program has two shortcomings. First, the array associated with statement **5** cannot be allocated statically. Second, a ϕ-function is needed, and we know ϕ-functions in generated code introduce run-time penalties. The goal of maximal static expansion, therefore, is to expand x as much as possible without having to insert a ϕ-function.

A possible static expansion is to expand all left-hand-side occurrences of x into a single array x3 and to make iterations of the for loop write to distinct array elements. (Note the data structure is renamed. The "old" name x is reserved for possible reference to the initial value of the original variable x.) Figure 9.4 shows the resulting code. The new left-hand sides make sure there is no output dependence carried by the outer loop. Because the while loop is sequential anyway, the transformed program has the same degree of parallelism and is simpler than the program in single assignment.

....

```
2   for i := 1 to N do
3      x1[i] := foo(i)
4      while (..)  do w := 1 begin
5         x5[i,w] := if w>1 then bar(x5[i,w-1])
                            else bar(x3[i])
                    end if
6      end while
7      A7[i] := φ({x3[i]}∪{x5[i,w] : w ≥ 1})
8   end for
```

.... *Figure 9.3. Single-assignment form of Figure 9.2.* ....

....

```
1   real x3[N], A[N]
2   for i := 1 to N do
3      x3[i] := ···
4      while ··· do
5         x3[i] := x3[i] ···
6      end while
7      A[i] := x3[i] ···
8   end for
```

.... *Figure 9.4. Maximal static expansion of the program in Figure 9.2.* ....

Notice that it should be easy to adapt the array privatization techniques by Maydan et al. [66] to handle the program in Figure 5.20. These techniques would tell us that x can be privatized along i. However, we want to do more than privatization along loops, as illustrated in the following examples.

Second Example: Array Expansion   Let us give a more complex example: the program in Figure 5.24, shown again here in Figure 9.5.

The corresponding reaching definitions are given in equations (5.25) through (5.27):

$$RD(\langle 5^{i,j}, B[j]\rangle) = RD(\langle 4^{i,j}, B[j]\rangle) = \begin{array}{l} \textbf{if } i > 1 \\ \textbf{then } \{5^{i-1,j}\} \\ \textbf{else } \{\bot\} \end{array}$$

$$RD(\langle 5^{i,j}, A[i]\rangle) = \{4^{i,j'} : 1 \leq j' \leq j\} \cup \{2^i\}$$

$$RD(\langle 4^{i,j}, A[i]\rangle) = \{4^{i,j'} : 1 \leq j' < j\} \cup \{2^i\}$$

. . . .

```
1  for i := 1 to N
2    A[i] := ..
3    for j := 1 to N
4      if B[j]>A[i] then A[i] := B[j];
5      B[j] := foo (B[j], A[i])
6    end for
7  end for
```

. . . . *Figure 9.5. Second example of maximal static expansion* . . . .

Because the expressions for definitions reaching A in both **5** and **4** contain non-singleton sets, converting this program to single-assignment form would require ϕ-functions. Therefore, MSE forbids expanding array A. On the other hand, expanding array B along the inner loop does not require ϕ-functions, because the reaching definition expressions for references to B[j] in **5** and **4** are unambiguous: We know the definition, if it exists, can only be $5^{i-1,j}$.

So expanding array B does not need any ϕ, whereas expanding A should be avoided. This "selective" expansion is in fact a salient feature of maximal static expansion, and the corresponding transformed program is shown in Figure 9.6.

. . . .

```
1  for i := 1 to N do
2    A2[i] := ..
3    for j := 1 to N do
4      if((if i>1 then B5[i-1,j] else B[j]) > A2[j]) then
         A2[i] := (if i>1 then B5[i-1,j] else B[j])
       end if
5      B5[i,j]:=foo((if i>1 then B5[i-1,j] else B[j]),
                     A2[i])
6    end for
7  end for
```

. . . . *Figure 9.6. Maximal static expansion for the program in Figure 9.5.* . . . .

Possible schedules for the transformed program includes mapping all instances $4^{i,j}$ and $5^{i,j}$ to logical time step $t = i + j$ (see Section 3.2). The resulting program has as much parallelism as the single-assignment form without the run-time cost.

Third Example: Nonaffine Array Subscripts Consider the program in Figure 5.25, shown here again in Figure 9.7. *foo* and *bar* are arbitrary subscripts. Array A is assumed to be of size N, that is, valid elements range from A[1] to A[N]. Definitions

. . . .

```
1   for i := 1 to N do
2     for j := 1 to N do
3       A[j] := ...
4     end for
5     A[foo(i)] = ...
6       ...  = ...  A[bar(i)]
7   end for
```

. . . . *Figure 9.7. Third example illustrating maximal static expansion.* . . . .

reaching the use in statement **6** are given in (5.28):

$$\forall i \in \mathbb{N}, 1 \le i \le N : \quad \mathrm{RD}(6) = \{5^i\} \cup \{3^{i,j} : 1 \le j \le N\}$$

Maximal static expansion adds a new dimension to A subscripted by i, as shown in Figure 9.8. This allows the outer loop to potentially execute in parallel. Indeed, all loop-carried dependencies are removed. In this case, MSE boils down to privatizing array A.

. . . .

```
1   for i = 1 to N do
2     for j = 1 to N do
3       A3[j,i] := ...
4     end for
5     A3[foo(i),i] := ...
6       ... := ...  A3[bar(i),i]
7   end for
```

. . . . . *Figure 9.8. Maximal static expansion form of the program in Figure 9.7.* . . . . .

9.2 Problem Statement

In the previous chapter, we saw in (8.4) page 169 that a ϕ-function is needed for a read instance r when two or more definitions possibly reach r:

$$(8.4) \iff \exists u, v \in \mathcal{W}, \ u \ne v \wedge u \in \mathrm{RD}(r) \wedge v \in \mathrm{RD}(r)$$

We can also take the opposite point of view, not from the reads' standpoint but from the writes'. What we then see is that there is a relation between u and v, in the mathematical sense. We call this relation R and define it as

$$\forall u, v \in \mathcal{W} : \quad u \mathrel{R} v \iff \exists r \in \mathcal{R} : u \in \mathrm{RD}(r) \wedge v \in \mathrm{RD}(r) \qquad (9.1)$$

We can even eliminate r from (9.1):

$$\forall u, v \in \mathcal{W} : \quad u \, \mathsf{R} \, v \iff u \in \mathsf{RD}(\mathsf{RD}^{-1}(v)) \tag{9.2}$$

If u and v write into the same memory location for some execution e of the input program, then expanding the data structure associated with u and v means inserting a ϕ-function somewhere. We "lost" track of where in (9.2.

Since our goal is to eliminate ϕ-functions, we *decide* not to expand the data structures of writes related by R. Putting all this together, we can formally state the property a static expansion must follow, for any execution e:

$$\forall u, v \in \mathcal{W}, (u \, \mathsf{R} \, v \wedge \mathsf{write}_e(u) = \mathsf{write}_e(v)) \implies \overline{\mathsf{write}}_e(u) = \overline{\mathsf{write}}_e(v)$$

The fact that the "old" and "new" storage mappings write_e and $\overline{\mathsf{write}}_e$, respectively, map both writes to the same location means there is no expansion.

However, we now face a technical hurdle: Relation R is *not* an equivalence relation, since it has only two of the three required properties. Reflexivity, since we clearly have $u \in \mathsf{RD}(\mathsf{RD}^{-1}(u))$ for all us. Symmetry, since $u \in \mathsf{RD}(\mathsf{RD}^{-1}(v))$ is equivalent to $v \in \mathsf{RD}(\mathsf{RD}^{-1}(u))$. But not transitivity, since there may be, on the one hand, a read r relating u and v and, on the other hand, another read $r2$ relating v and some write w, but in general there is not *one* read $r3$ relating u and w, so u and w do not comply with (9.1).

However, even if u and w are not in relation "through" $r3$, they might independently be in relations with other writes. The right part of Figure 9.1 page 196 illustrates the point. So it is natural to consider R^*, the transitive closure of R. This relation is an equivalence relation since we added the missing property, transitivity, by definition of transitive closure!

Interestingly, R^*, the transitive closure of R, is reminiscent of *webs* [68] even if, strictly speaking, webs include definitions *and* uses, whereas R^* apply to definitions only.

Thanks to R^*, we can now give the formal definition of static expansion. Given an execution $e \in \mathcal{E}$, an expansion $\overline{\mathsf{write}}_e$ is *static* if

$$\forall u, v \in \mathcal{W} : \quad u \, \mathsf{R}^* \, v \wedge \mathsf{write}_e(u) = \mathsf{write}_e(v) \implies \overline{\mathsf{write}}_e(u) = \overline{\mathsf{write}}_e(v) \tag{9.3}$$

Now, we are interested in removing as many dependencies as possible, without introducing ϕ-functions. We are looking for the *maximal* static expansion (MSE), assigning the largest number of memory locations while verifying (9.3): Given an execution $e \in \mathcal{E}$, a static expansion $\overline{\mathsf{write}}_e$ is *maximal* on the set of writes $\mathcal{W}$ if for any *static* expansion write'_e,

$$\forall u, v \in \mathcal{W} : \quad \overline{\mathsf{write}}_e(u) = \overline{\mathsf{write}}_e(v) \implies \mathsf{write}'_e(u) = \mathsf{write}'_e(v) \tag{9.4}$$

Intuitively, if $\overline{\mathsf{write}}_e$ is maximal, then write'_e cannot do better: It maps two writes to the same memory location each time $\overline{\mathsf{write}}_e$ does.

9.3   Constructing the Maximal Static Expansion

All the above discussion is pretty theoretical. But from a practical standpoint, how can we construct maximal static expansion?

Let us give step-by-step guidelines. Step 1 is clearly to compute RD, and step 2 to compute RD^*.

To simplify code generation, we enforce a certain pattern to expansion storage mapping: We look for an expansion $\overline{\text{write}_e}$ of the form (write_e, ν). That is, a left-hand array reference

```
A[foo]
```

becomes

```
newA[foo,ν]
```

The problem of constructing $\overline{\text{write}_e}$ thus becomes the problem of constructing function ν. (Note that ν may be empty, in which case static expansion boils down to renaming.) This new problem is simpler. However, we are still facing the main hurdle: In practice, we cannot decide expression

$$\text{write}_e(u) = \text{write}_e(v)$$

that appears in (9.3) for all u's, v's and e's. In general, we have only an approximation of write_e, which is relation **Alias** defined in (4.2) page 60. Because of this approximation, we cannot be sure to find the "best" possible expansion. Again, the expansion we are about to construct is "maximal" only with respect to this given approximation.

A second issue is that **Alias** is not transitive in general and therefore is not an equivalence relation. Intuitively, we still want to partition the set of all writes $\mathcal{W}$ into subsets of aliasing writes. To that purpose, we compute the transitive closure $\textbf{Alias}^*$ of **Alias** and consider equivalence classes $\mathcal{W}/_{\textbf{Alias}^*}$.

Still, we can state that, on the one hand, the expansion must be static:

$$\forall v, w \in \mathcal{W} : v \ \textbf{Alias}^* \ w \wedge v \ \textbf{R}^* \ w \implies \nu(v) = \nu(w) \tag{9.5}$$

and, on the other hand, the expansion must be maximal:

$$\forall v, w \in \mathcal{W} : v \ \textbf{Alias}^* \ w \wedge \neg(v \ \textbf{R}^* \ w) \implies \nu(v) \neq \nu(w) \tag{9.6}$$

Notice that (9.5) and (9.6) build a graph coloring problem: Two writes cannot have the same "color" if related.

We still don't know how to construct ν. For the class of programs we are most interested in, write_e is an index to an array. It thus makes sense to construct expansion (write_e, ν) as another subscript to a potentially different array. Function ν should then be a mapping from writes to integer tuples.

There are many different but valid ways to construct ν. The method we describe here may sound intricate but is relatively easy to implement. This method has two steps: First we pick a distinguished element, or *representative*, in each equivalence class of $^C/_{\textbf{R}^*}$, where C is itself an equivalence class of $\mathcal{W}/_{\textbf{Alias}^*}$. Let us stress that any unambiguous way to select one representative for each class is fine. The way we use here is only a suggestion: For a set S, the representative we pick is the first executed element in this set, that is,

$$\rho(S) = \min_{\prec} S$$

We saw in Chapter 5 how to compute extrema. This concludes step 3.

In step 4 we give a "number" (an integer tuple) to each of these representatives. This number is, of course, ν. There are many ways to build function ν, the simplest being to take the very label of the representative.

Step 5 actually changes the code. A left-hand side is replaced by a reference to a newly created array. The name of this array is the concatenation of the old name and the label of the representative's statement. The subscripts of the reference are the original subscripts augmented by ν if the expression for ν is not already subscripting an array dimension in the original expression.

More Theoretical Considerations We can deduce that, given a program execution $e \in \mathcal{E}$, a storage mapping $\mathsf{write}'_e = (\mathsf{write}_e, \nu)$ is a maximal static expansion iff for each equivalence class $\mathbf{C} \in {}^W/_{\mathsf{Alias}^*}$, ν is constant on each class in ${}^{\mathbf{C}}/_{\mathsf{R}^*}$ and takes distinct values between different classes: $\forall v, w \in \mathbf{C} : v \; \mathsf{R}^* \; w \Leftrightarrow \nu(v) = \nu(w)$.

This answers two other interesting questions. First, how much is each individual memory location expanded by MSE? From what we just saw, we can state that this *expansion factor* for any memory location assigned by writes in $\mathbf{C}$ is the number of equivalence classes in ${}^{\mathbf{C}}/_{\mathsf{R}^*}$.

Second, notice that ν is only constrained within the same class $\mathbf{C}$: For two distinct equivalence classes $\mathbf{C}_1$ and $\mathbf{C}_2$, both belonging to ${}^W/_{\mathsf{Alias}^*}$, and two instances u_1, u_2 in each of these sets ($u_1 \in \mathbf{C}_1$ and $u_2 \in \mathbf{C}_2$), nothing forbids that $\nu(u_1) = \nu(u_2)$. As a consequence, two maximal static expansions write'_e and write''_e are identical on a class of ${}^W/_{\mathsf{Alias}^*}$ up to a one-to-one mapping between constant values.

9.4 Back to the Examples

First Example Let us consider the program in Figure 9.2 on page 197. Using the Omega Calculator, we describe a step-by-step execution of the expansion algorithm.

To begin, notice that only one memory location is written into in this program: the one referred to by variable x. Therefore, all write instances are related via relation Alias, and there is only one class $\mathbf{C}$ in ${}^W/_{\mathsf{Alias}^*}$.

Step 1. Equations (5.22) and (5.23), repeated here, give the reaching definitions:

$$\mathsf{RD}(5^{i,w}) = \begin{array}{l} \textbf{if } w > 1 \\ \textbf{then } \{5^{i,w-1}\} \\ \textbf{else } \{3^i\} \end{array} \tag{9.7}$$

and

$$\mathsf{RD}(7^i) = \{3^i\} \cup \{5^{i,w} : w \geq 1\} \tag{9.8}$$

We can lump these reaching definitions together into one Omega relation we call rd. If you are actually using Omega when reading this book, a straightforward expression would be

```
# rd := {[5,i,1]->[3,i] : 1<=i<=N}
#   union {[5,i,w]->[5,i,w-1] : 1<=i<=N && 2<=w}
#   union {[7,i]->[3,i] : 1<=i<=N}
#   union {[7,i]->[5,i,w] : 1<=i<=N && 1<=w};
```

However, the above relation has an arity problem. Both the input and output tuples are of unequal dimensions, so Omega does not accept this expression. One trick is to pad short tuples with a trailing zero to make all tuples of dimension 3:

```
# rd := {[5,i,1]->[3,i,0] : 1<=i<=N}
#   union {[5,i,w]->[5,i,w-1] : 1<=i<=N && 2<=w}
#   union {[7,i,0]->[3,i,0] : 1<=i<=N}
#   union {[7,i,0]->[5,i,w] : 1<=i<=N && 1<=w};
```

Step 2. We compute R defined in (9.1). Doing so is straightforward:

```
# rd' := inverse rd;
# R := rd( rd' );
# R;
```

```
{[3,i,0]->[3,i,0] : 1<=i<=N} union
{[5,i,w]->[3,i,0] : 1<=i<=N && 1<=w} union
{[3,i,0]->[5,i,w'] : 1<=i<=N && 1<=w'} union
{[5,i,w]->[5,i,w'] : 1<=i<=N && 1<=w' && 1<=w}
```

This Omega output can be rephrased as follows:

$$3^i \mathrel{\mathsf{R}} 3^i \iff 1 \le i \le N \tag{9.9}$$

$$5^{i,w} \mathrel{\mathsf{R}} 3^i \iff 1 \le i \le N \wedge w \ge 1 \tag{9.10}$$

$$3^i \mathrel{\mathsf{R}} 5^{i,w'} \iff 1 \le i \le N \wedge w' \ge 1 \tag{9.11}$$

$$5^{i,w} \mathrel{\mathsf{R}} 5^{i,w'} \iff 1 \le i \le N, w \ge 1, w' \ge 1 \tag{9.12}$$

Of course, this result looks a bit verbose to us humans. First, (9.9) was obvious from the beginning, since we know that R is reflexive. Also, we know that R is symmetrical, so (9.10) implies (9.11), and vice versa.

Interestingly, relation R is already transitive ($R=R^*$), so no closure computation is necessary. We deduce from the above that

$$^C\!/_{\mathsf{R}^*} = \left\{ \left(\{3^i\} \cup \{5^{i,w} : w \ge 1\} \right) : 1 \le i \le N \right\}$$

In other words, one equivalence class in $^C\!/_{\mathsf{R}^*}$ is $\{3^1\} \cup \{5^{1,w} : w \ge 1\}$, for i equals 1. Another class is $\{3^2\} \cup \{5^{2,w} : w \ge 1\}$, for $i = 2$, etc. Since there are N equivalence classes in $^C\!/_{\mathsf{R}^*}$, variable x is expanded N times.

Step 3. Let us choose representatives as the first executed instances in each equivalence class $\{3^i\} \cup \{5^{i,w} : w \geq 1\}$.

To do this, here is a trick to compute the minimum element with respect to an order. Here, the order is the lexicographical order, which, on the relevant elements, is

```
Lex := {[3,i,0] -> [3,i',0] : 1<=i,i'<=N && i'>i}
   union {[3,i,0] -> [5,i',w] : 1<=i,i'<=N
            && w>=1 && i'>=i}
   union {[5,i,w] -> [5,i',w'] : 1<=i,i'<=N
            && w>=1 && w'>=1
            && (i'>i || (i=i' && w'>w)) }
   union {[5,i,w] -> [3,i',0] : 1<=i,i'<=N && w>=1
            && i'>i};
```

Notice we write the order as a relation from an element to elements that *follow*. (If we were to compute maxima, we would write the order as a relation from elements to elements that precede.) Then we compose this order after the relation of interest. The result should be thought of as the relation from elements of the relation to elements that follow *at least* the source element. Now, if we subtract the result relation from the original relation, we obtain elements in the original relation that are *not* successors of *any* other element in the relation—which is exactly the definition of a minimum! We express this as follows:

```
# Repr := R - (Lex compose R);
# Repr;
```

```
{[3,i,0] -> [3,i,0] : 1 <= i <= N} union
 {[5,i,w] -> [3,i,0] : 1 <= i <= N && 1 <= w}
```

In other words, all elements in a class are mapped to the single instance of **3** in the class:

$$\forall i \in \mathbb{N},\ 1 \leq i \leq N : \quad \rho(\{3^i\} \cup \{5^{i,w} : w \geq 1\}) = 3^i$$

Step 4. There is an obvious label for representatives 3^i:

$$\forall i \in \mathbb{N},\ 1 \leq i \leq N : \quad \nu(3) = i \tag{9.13}$$

Step 5. All left-hand-side references to x are transformed into an array subscripted by ν, that is, by [i]. Consistent with previous chapters, the name of the new array is the name of the original data structure concatenated with the statement label of the representative, which is **3**. All references to x in the right-hand side are transformed into x3[i], too, since their reaching definitions are instances of **5** or **3** for the same i. The size declaration of the new array is x3[1..N]. The expanded code is thus exactly the one found intuitively in Figure 9.4.

Second Example We now consider the program in Figure 9.5. Instances 2^i, $4^{i,j}$ and $5^{i,j}$ are denoted by [2,i,0], [4,i,j], and [5,i,j], respectively.

Step 1. From (5.27), reproduced on page 198, the reaching definitions relations rda and rdb for arrays A and B, respectively, can be expressed as follows:

```
rda := {[4,i,j]->[2,i,0] : 1<=i,j<=N}
  union {[5,i,j]->[2,i,0] : 1<=i,j<=N}
  union {[4,i,j]->[4,i,j'] : 1<=i,j,j'<=N && j'<j}
  union {[5,i,j]->[4,i,j'] : 1<=i,j,j'<=N && j'<=j};

rdb := {[4,i,j]->[5,i-1,j] : 2<=i<=N && 1<=j<=N}
  union {[5,i,j]->[5,i-1,j] : 2<=i<=N && 1<=j<=N};
```

It is easy to compute relations **Aliasa** and **Aliasb** since all array subscripts are affine:

```
Aliasa := {[2,i,0]->[2,i,0] : 1<=i<=N}
    union {[4,i,j]->[4,i,j'] : 1<=i,j,j'<=N}
    union {[2,i,0]->[4,i,j] : 1<=i,j<=N}
    union {[4,i,j]->[2,i,0] : 1<=i,j<=N};

Aliasb := {[5,i,j]->[5,i',j] : 1<=i,i',j<=N};
```

Notice that these relations are transitive.

Step 2. As in the first example, we can easily compute relations **Ra** and **Rb**:

```
# rda' := inverse rda;
# Ra := rda( rda' );
# Ra;

{[2,i,0] -> [2,i,0] : 1<=i<=N} union
 {[4,i,j] -> [2,i,0] : 1<=j<=N && 1<=i<=N} union
 {[2,i,0] -> [4,i,j'] : 1<=j'<=N && 1<=i<=N} union
 {[4,i,j] -> [4,i,j'] : 1<=j'<=N && 1<=i<=N
                        && 1<=j<=N}

# rdb' := inverse rdb;
# Rb := rdb( rdb' );
# Rb;

{[5,In_2,j] -> [5,In_2,j] : 1 <= j <= N && 1 <= In_2 < N}
```

Computing (R compose R) - R shows that both relations are already transitive:

```
# (Ra compose Ra) - Ra;

{[In_1,i,j] -> [Out_1,i',j']  : FALSE }

# (Rb compose Rb) - Rb;

{[In_1,In_2,j] -> [Out_1,Out_2,j']  : FALSE }
```

Step 3. For a given u, the equivalence class S it belongs to is $\{u' : u' \text{ Aliasa}^* u \wedge u' \text{ Ra}^* u\}$:

```
# RelAliasa := Aliasa intersection Ra;
```

The representative of this class is now chosen to be the first element in S according to lexicographic order. This order is

```
# Lexa := {[2,i,0]->[2,i',0] : 1<=i<i'<=N}
#    union {[2,i,0]->[4,i',j'] : 1<=i<=i'<=N && 1<=j'<=N}
#    union {[4,i,j]->[2,i',0] : 1<=i<i'<=N && 1<=j<=N}
#    union {[4,i,j]->[4,i',j'] : 1<=i<i'<=N
#           || (1<=j<j'<=N && i=i' && 1<=i,i'<=N)};
```

So the representative mapping can be computed as

```
# Repr := RelAliasa - (Lexa compose RelAliasa);
# Repr;
```

```
{[2,i,0] -> [2,i,0] : 1 <= i <= N} union
 {[4,i,j] -> [2,i,0] : 1 <= j <= N && 1 <= i <= N}
```

which can be interpreted as

$$\rho\left(\{2^i, 4^{i,j} : 1 \le i \le N, 1 \le j \le N\}\right) = 2^i$$

The same can be done for writes to array B:

```
# Lexb := {[i,j,5]->[i',j',5] : 1<=i<i'<=N
#    || (1<=j<j'<=N && i=i' && 1<=i,i'<=N)};
#
# RelAliasb := Rb intersection Aliasb;
# Reprb := RelAliasb - (Lexb compose RelAliasb);
# Reprb;
```

```
{[5,i,j] -> [5,i,j] : 1 <= j <= N && 1 <= i < N}
```

That is,

$$\forall i, j,\ 1 \le i \le N, 1 \le j \le N: \qquad \rho(\{5^{i,j}\}) = 5^{i,j}$$

Step 4. A natural labeling for representatives 2^i of the first group of classes $\{2^i, 4^{i,j} : 1 \le i \le N, 1 \le j \le N\}$ is

$$\nu(2^i) = i$$

For the second group,

$$\nu(5^{i,j}) = (i, j)$$

Step 5.   Concerning Array A, function ν is identical to the current subscript, so adding a second dimension to A and indexing it with i would not help disambiguate dependencies. So A is unchanged, except for its renaming to A2 since the statement label of the representative is **2**.

Regarding array B, function ν provides only one new subscript: Since $\nu(\mathbf{5}^{i,j}) = (i,j)$ and B is already indexed by j, only one dimension needs to be added. This new dimension is indexed by i, whose values range from 1 to N. Array B is therefore expanded into B5 [1..N,1..N]. The static expansion code appears in Figure 9.6 on page 199.

Third Example: Nonaffine Array Subscripts   We now turn to the program in Figure 9.7.

Step 1.   From (5.28), reproduced on page 200, we build the relation of reaching definitions:

```
# rd := {[6,i,0]->[3,i,j] : 1<=i,j<=N}
#    union {[6,i,0]->[5,i,0] : 1<=i<=N};
```

Since some subscripts are nonaffine, we cannot compute at compile time the exact relation between instances writing in some location A[x]. We can only make the following conservative approximation of **Alias**: All instances are related together (because they *may* assign the same memory location).

Step 2.

```
# rd' := inverse rd;
# R := rd( rd' );
# R;
```

```
{[3,i,j] -> [3,i,j'] : 1<=j'<=N && 1<=i<=N
                       && 1<=j<=N} union
 {[5,i,0] -> [3,i,j'] : 1<=j'<=N && 1<=i<=N} union
 {[3,i,j] -> [5,i,0] : 1<=j<=N && 1<=i<=N} union
 {[5,i,0] -> [5,i,0] : 1<=i<=N}
```

R is already transitive: $R=R^*$.

Step 3.   There is only one equivalence class for **Alias***. Computing ρ yields:

$$\rho\left(\{\mathbf{5}^i\} \cup \{\mathbf{3}^{i,j} : 1 \le j \le N\}\right) = \mathbf{3}^{i,1}$$

Note that every instance $\mathbf{3}^{i,j}$ is in relation with $\mathbf{3}^{i,1}$.

Step 4.   Since there are N representatives of the form $\mathbf{3}^i$, the maximal static expansion of variable x requires N memory locations. We can use i to label these representatives:

$$\nu(\mathbf{3}^{i,1}) = i$$

Step 5. Using this labeling, a left-hand-side reference A[..] becomes A3[..,i] in the expanded code. Since the definition reaching 6^i is an instance of **5** or **3** at the same iteration i, the right-hand side of **6** is expanded the same way. Array A[1..N] becomes A3[1..N,1..N]. Expanding the code thus leads to the intuitive result given in Figure 9.8.

| **Exercise 9.1** | In the program below, A is an array of size N and Perm is a permutation. The definition reaching 3^i is exactly 2^i. |

```
1   for i = 1 to N do
2       A[Perm(i)] := ···
3       ··· := A[Perm(i)]
4   end for
```

What is the maximal static expansion of this program?

Solution We can imagine MSE would expand into

```
1   for i = 1 to N do
2       A[Perm(i),i] := ···
3       ··· := A[Perm(i),i]
4   end for
```

However, MSE leaves the program unchanged. There is no loop-carried dependence, and the loop can be parallelized without transforming the array.

Indeed, Perm is a permutation, which means

$$\forall i, i' \in \{1, \ldots, N\} : 2^i \text{ Alias } 2^{i'} \iff i = i'$$

Therefore, there are N equivalence classes $\mathbf{C}_i$ in $^W/_{\text{Alias}^*}$, each being a singleton: $\mathbf{C}_i = \{2^i\}$, $1 \le i \le N$. (Therefore, there also are N equivalence classes $^{C_i}/_{R^*}$, each again a singleton, but we don't even have to investigate the equivalence classes for R^*.) As noted in the paragraph "More Theoretical Considerations," page 203, we can give the same labels ν across all these classes, say "1." A smart implementation detects this special case and does not modify the subscripts. A not-so-smart implementation would transform the loop into

```
1   for i = 1 to N do
2       A2[Perm(i),1] := ···
3       ··· := A2[Perm(i),1]
4   end for
```

transforming a one-dimensional array of size N into a two-dimensional array of size $N \times 1$, that is, a zero memory overhead. ∎

9.5   Conclusion

Expanding data structures removes dependencies and therefore leads to more parallelism. It comes, however, at a cost: When the data flow cannot be predicted at compile time, this flow has to be restored by a run-time mechanism that adversely impacts performance.

This chapter gives a formal and general definition of the problem. When the use of a data element has no unique instancewise reaching definition (either because the analysis wasn't powerful enough or because the question cannot be answered until run time), then expanding this data element yields a run-time overhead. Basically, we expand as much as possible without ever needing a run-time support. (That remedy makes no compromise. Tuning this criterion and finding smarter ones is the subject of related research.) To do so, we lump together all uses that share an ambiguous definition. Because this sharing relation can yield to chains of uses and definitions, we take the transitive closure of the relation. The "lumps" we intuitively see, accepting one expanded copy of the data element without run-time cost, correspond to equivalence classes of the transitive closure.

Finding the transitive closure can be done automatically in some cases. In any case, it serves as a useful conceptual tool to tune tradeoffs between parallelism and memory usage.

Chapter 10

Parallel Languages

After decades of parallel processing, few programming languages can claim to be used on a wide range of parallel machines. One of the reasons probably lies in the difficulty of efficiently compiling a general language on an ever-widening spectrum of architectures.

In turn, one reason parallel programming does not always deliver is that the compiler has a hard time figuring out which data can safely be kept by one processor and which have to be passed around. When the compiler doesn't know for sure, it conservatively chooses to pass the data, and it inserts communications to that purpose. Unfortunately, the cost of communications in parallel computers, at least in the current state of technology, is extremely high compared to processor speed. To detect when data transfers are an overkill, a compiler has to understand which values produced (or owned) by a processor are needed by another. The compiler can then send exactly these data, thereby limiting the volume of communication.

The purpose of this chapter is not to present parallel languages, not even an introduction. The goal is not to describe compilation techniques either. Both topics would require entire volumes. The goals are, using a very simple toy language, to illustrate the challenges of analyses and optimizations for parallel languages and to show that the concepts and techniques studied earlier extend naturally. In particular, we will see that the data flow in a parallel program is a key property even if, unfortunately, very few reaching definition analyses for parallel languages exist in the literature.

10.1 Parallel Languages

Unordered Execution   As discussed in the Chapter 1, parallelism is just about unordered computations. If you require A to be computed before B, your program is sequential. If you don't require an order, that is, if B may be computed before A, or A before B, or A and B at the same time, then your program is parallel. Let us point out that the simultaneous execution of A and B at the same time is only one of the three possibilities.

In our toy language, the simplest way to express parallelism is to use *parallel sec-*

. . . .

```
par
  section
    x := ...
  end section
  section
    x := ...
  end section
end par
..   := x
```

. . . . *Figure 10.1. Parallel sections.* . . . .

tions. The program shown in Figure 10.1 is easy to understand. The programmer made explicit that the final value x may come from either assignment to x.

. . . .

```
1   for i := 1 to n
2     par
3       section
4         x := ...
5       end section
6       section
7         ...   := x
8         x := ...
9       end section
10    end par
11  end for
```

. . . . . . *Figure 10.2. Illustrating the influence of memory consistency models.* . . . . . .

Memory Consistency   The parallel languages we consider have a weak model of memory consistency. In a weak model, a consistent view of memory is restored at the exit of parallel constructs only, except where required specifically (typically, flush in OpenMP [69]). Consider the program in Figure 10.2. The par construct is executed n times. Each time, two parallel threads are spawned, both writing in x and one reading x. Because of the weak model, the value set in x by the first thread cannot be immediately seen by the second. Therefore, the definition reaching the ith instance of statement **7** is the $(i - 1)$th instance of either **4** or **8**. (This holds for $i > 1$; otherwise, the reaching definition is undefined.)

In contrast, with a strong model of memory consistency, the definition in **4** would be immediately visible by the other thread. Therefore, the ith instance of **4** may (or may not, depending on the execution) reach **7** in the same iteration i.

Indexed Parallel Constructs   So far, the programs we looked at describe only two parallel computations. Clearly, we can easily change these programs to describe three parallel computations, or four. But this is not general enough. We need the parallel equivalent of loops that create an arbitrary number of simultaneous computations. To that purpose, we introduce two indexed parallel constructs: `doall` and `forall`.

```
1   doall i = 0, n
2     a[i] := ..
3       ... := a[..]
4   end doall
```

.... *Figure 10.3. Simple example of* `doall`. ....

Several languages [37, 27] have indexed parallel constructs whose semantics correspond to what we call `doall`: A statement instance is spawned for each possible value of the index variable. An example program appears in Figure 10.3. Conceptually, each instance has its own copy of shared data structures, and all reads and writes are applied to this copy. This corresponds to the FIRSTPRIVATE directive in OpenMP. A consistent view of memory is provided on exiting the parallel construct. The simple Fortran program in Figure 10.4 illustrates the directive.

```
!$omp parallel do firstprivate(a)
        do i = 0, n
1           a(i) = ..
2           ...
        end do
```

.... *Figure 10.4. A Fortran OpenMP equivalent of Figure 10.3.* ....

Notice that we consider that all instances of both arms of the `where` parallel conditional structure are executed in parallel.

Similarly, a `forall` construct spawns as many instances as there are possible values for the index variable. An example is given in Figure 10.5. The semantics of `forall` we consider are reminiscent of the HPF semantics [58]: In a multistatement `forall`, "the array assignment semantics are applied to each statement in turn." Note that in compliance to HPF's rules H404 and H406 [58], the only accepted parallel constructs inside `forall`s are `forall`s and `where`s.

. . . .

```
1   forall i = 0, n
2     a[i] := ..
3     ...  := a[..]
4   end forall
```

. . . . *Figure 10.5. Simple example of* `forall`. . . . .

Data structures in a `forall` are shared and are updated before any instance of following statements begins. Therefore, the instances of statements in the body of a `forall` loop always work on the most recently updated shared data, even if a different iteration did the update (in contrast to `doall` loops).

. . . .

```
!$omp parallel do shared(a)
      do i = 0, n
1         a(i) =
!$omp barrier
2         ...
      end do
```

. . . . *Figure 10.6. A Fortran OpenMP equivalent of Figure 10.5.* . . . .

The program in Figure 10.5 can be written in OpenMP as shown in Figure 10.6. Notice that, in OpenMP, `barrier` implies that shared variables are `flushed` to memory to provide a consistent view of memory.

10.2   Execution Order

The purpose of this section is not to give a complete semantical description of a parallel language. As far as data flows are concerned, we are mainly interested in the order $\prec$ in which computations, and their corresponding writes and reads to memory, occur.

To deal with these language constructs, we use the following definitions. First, we extend the definition of an *iteration vector*. The iteration vector of a statement **S** is the vector built from the counters of `for`, `forall`, `doall`, and `while` constructs surrounding **S**.

The *depth* of a statement or construct is the number of surrounding `for`, `forall`, `doall`, or `while` constructs. So, the depth of **S** equals the dimension of its iteration vector. Let x be this vector. If x_p, $p \geq 0$, is a counter of a `for`, `forall`, or `doall` construct then the lower and upper bounds are known. If x_p is a counter of a `while` loop, then its upper bound is unknown at compile time.

. . . .

```
1     a[1] := ..
2     for i := 1 to n
3       par
4         section
5           for j := 1 to i
6             par
7               section
8                 a[i+j] := ...
9               end section
10              section
11                  ... := ..a[i+j-1]..
12              end section
13            end par
14          end for
15        end section
16        section
17          a[i+1] := ...
18        end section
19      end par
20    end for
```

. . . . Figure 10.7. Interleaving sections and parallel loops. . . . .

We define $C_p(\mathbf{S})$ as the iterative (for, while, forall, or doall) construct surrounding $\mathbf{S}$ at depth p. (When clear from the context, $\mathbf{S}$ is omitted.) We also define $P(\mathbf{S}, \mathbf{R})$ to be the par construct surrounding both $\mathbf{S}$ and $\mathbf{R}$ such that $\mathbf{S}$ and $\mathbf{R}$ appear in distinct sections of the par construct. (Notice that there is at most one such construct.)

Moreover, let $M(\mathbf{S}, \mathbf{R})$ be the depth of $P(\mathbf{S}, \mathbf{R})$. If $P(\mathbf{S}, \mathbf{R})$ does not exist, then $M(\mathbf{S}, \mathbf{R})$ is the number of for, forall, doall, or while constructs surrounding both $\mathbf{S}$ and $\mathbf{R}$.

Consider for example the program in Figure 10.7: $P(\mathbf{8}, \mathbf{11}) = \mathbf{6}$, so $M(\mathbf{8}, \mathbf{11}) = 2$. Also, $P(\mathbf{17}, \mathbf{11}) = \mathbf{3}$, so $M(\mathbf{17}, \mathbf{11}) = 1$.

We also define predicate $\Delta(\mathbf{S}, \mathbf{R})$. This predicate is true if two statements $\mathbf{S}$ and $\mathbf{R}$ appear in opposite arms of an if..then..else or where..elsewhere construct, or in distinct sections of a par construct. Predicate $T(\mathbf{S}, \mathbf{R})$ is true if $\mathbf{S}$ textually precedes $\mathbf{R}$ and $\Delta(\mathbf{S}, \mathbf{R})$ is false.

For a second example, consider the program in Figure 10.5. There is no par construct surrounding both $\mathbf{2}$ and $\mathbf{3}$, so $P(\mathbf{2}, \mathbf{3}) = \emptyset$. Therefore, applying the preceding rules, $M(\mathbf{2}, \mathbf{3})$ equals the number of surrounding iterative constructs, so $M(\mathbf{2}, \mathbf{3}) = 1$. Also, the outermost (and only) iterative construct is $C_0 = $ forall. Furthermore, $\mathbf{2}$ textually precedes $\mathbf{3}$, so $T(\mathbf{2}, \mathbf{3}) = \textbf{true}$.

Execution order $\prec$ can now be expressed in closed form:

$$\mathbf{S}^x \prec \mathbf{R}^y \Leftrightarrow \left(\begin{array}{cc} \bigvee \\ p = 0..M(\mathbf{S},\mathbf{R})-1, & Pred(p,x,y) \\ C_p = \texttt{for} \vee C_p = \texttt{while} \end{array} \right)$$

$$\vee \left(\left(\bigwedge_{p=0..(M(\mathbf{S},\mathbf{R})-1)} Equ(p,x,y) \right) \wedge T(S,R) \right) \quad (10.1)$$

Note that $\forall P$, $\bigvee_{i \in \emptyset} P(i) = \textbf{false}$ and $\bigwedge_{i \in \emptyset} P(i) = \textbf{true}$. Note also that the lexicographical order in sequential programs comes as a special case of (10.1).

We also state the following definitions, one for each "loop" construct. They formally tell us when two incarnations of the loop bodies are "equal" with respect to the execution order at depth p.

$$C_p = \texttt{for} : Equ(p,x,y) \quad \Leftrightarrow \quad x_p = y_p \qquad (10.2)$$
$$C_p = \texttt{while} : Equ(p,x,y) \quad \Leftrightarrow \quad x_p = y_p \qquad (10.3)$$
$$C_p = \texttt{forall} : Equ(p,x,y) \quad \Leftrightarrow \quad \textbf{true} \qquad (10.4)$$
$$C_p = \texttt{doall} : Equ(p,x,y) \quad \Leftrightarrow \quad x_p = y_p \qquad (10.5)$$

We can then state one condition telling us if x is a predecessor of y:

$$Pred(p,x,y) \Leftrightarrow \left(\bigwedge_{i=0..p-1} Equ(i,x,y) \right) \wedge x_p < y_p \qquad (10.6)$$

Obviously, (10.1) is a partial order on instances. (In particular, it has no cycle.) Intuitively, predicate $Pred$ in (10.1) formalizes the sequential order of a given `for` or `while` loop at depth p. Such a loop enforces an order up to the first `par` construct encountered at depth $M(\mathbf{S},\mathbf{R})$ while traversing the nest of control structures, from the outermost level to the innermost. The order of sequential loops is given by the strict inequality in (10.6), under the condition that the two instances at hand are not ordered up to level $p-1$; hence the conjunction on the p outer predicates Equ. Notice that the instances of two successive statements inside a `forall` at depth p are always ordered at depth p due to (10.4), but are ordered inside a `doall` only if they belong to the same task i.e., the values of the `doall` index are equal, cf. (10.5).

As an example, consider the program in Figure 10.5. We know that $P(2,3) = \emptyset$, $M(2,3) = 1$, $C_0 = \texttt{forall}$, and $T(2,3) = \textbf{true}$. Thus,

$$2^{i'} \prec 3^i \Leftrightarrow \left(\bigvee_{p \in \emptyset} Pred(p,i',i) \right) \vee (Equ(0,i',i) \wedge T(2,3))$$

$$\Leftrightarrow \quad \textbf{false} \vee (\textbf{true} \wedge \textbf{true})$$

$$\Leftrightarrow \quad \textbf{true} \qquad (10.7)$$

Notice that $5^{i'} \prec 3^i$ is also always true.

As far as Figure 10.3 is concerned, we have $P(2,3) = \emptyset$, so $M(2,3) = 1$. $C_0 =$ doall and $T(2,3) = \textbf{true}$. Thus,

$$2^{i'} \prec 3^i \quad \Leftrightarrow \quad \left(\bigvee_{p \in \emptyset} Pred(p, i', i) \right) \vee (Equ(0, i', i) \wedge T(2,3))$$

$$\Leftrightarrow \quad \textbf{false} \vee (i' = i \wedge \textbf{true})$$

$$\Leftrightarrow \quad i' = i \tag{10.8}$$

Let us come back to the program shown in Figure 10.7. We have $P(8,11) = 6$, so $M(8,11) = 2$. Thus, the execution order between instances of statements $\textbf{8}$ and $\textbf{11}$ is given by

$$8^{i',j'} \prec 11^{i,j} \quad \Leftrightarrow \quad \bigvee_{p=0..1, C_p = \texttt{for}} Pred(p, (i',j'), (i,j))$$

$$\vee \left(\bigwedge_{p=0..1} Equ(p, (i',j'), (i,j)) \wedge T(8,11) \right)$$

$$\Leftrightarrow \quad Pred(0, (i',j'), (i,j)) \vee Pred(1, (i',j'), (i,j))$$

$$\vee (i' = i \wedge j' = j \wedge \textbf{false})$$

$$\Leftrightarrow \quad i' < i \vee (i' = i \wedge j' < j) \vee (i' = i \wedge j' = j \wedge \textbf{false})$$

so finally,

$$8^{i',j'} \prec 11^{i,j} \quad \Longleftrightarrow \quad i' < i \vee (i' = i \wedge j' < j) \tag{10.9}$$

Similarly, we have

$$8^{i',j'} \prec 8^{i,j} \quad \Longleftrightarrow \quad i' < i \vee (i' = i \wedge j' < j) \tag{10.10}$$

Regarding statement $\textbf{17}$, we know that $P(17,11) = 3$, so $M(17,11) = 1$. Thus, the execution order between instances of statements $\textbf{17}$ and $\textbf{11}$ is given by

$$17^{i'} \prec 11^{i,j} \quad \Leftrightarrow \quad Pred(0, (i'), (i,j))$$

$$\vee (Equ(0, (i'), (i,j)) \wedge T(17,11))$$

$$\Leftrightarrow \quad \textbf{true} \wedge i' < i$$

$$\vee (i' = i \wedge \textbf{false})$$

that is,

$$17^{i'} \prec 11^{i,j} \quad \Longleftrightarrow \quad i' < i \tag{10.11}$$

10.3 Reaching Definition Analysis

All the material of Chapter 5 still applies. We simply have a new definition of execution order $\prec$, since execution is now parallel.

To compute the definitions $8^{i',j'}$ in Figure 10.7 reaching a[i+j-1] in $11^{i,j}$, we subtract instances $8^{i3,j3}$ and 17^{i4} that may be kills:

$$\{8^{i',j'} \quad : \quad 1 \leq i' \leq n \wedge 1 \leq j' \leq i'$$
$$\wedge \quad i' + j' = i + j - 1, (i' < i \vee (i' = i \wedge j' < j))$$
$$\wedge \quad (\nexists \, 8^{i3,j3} : i + j - 1 = i3 + j3 \wedge 8^{i',j'} \prec 8^{i3,j3} \prec 11^{i,j})$$
$$\wedge \quad (\nexists \, 17^{i4} : i + j - 1 = i4 + 1 \wedge 8^{i',j'} \prec 17^{i4} \prec 11^{i,j})\}$$

Equations (10.9), (10.10) and (10.11) provide the inequalities we miss. The set is a Presburger expression and can thus be expressed, nearly verbatim, in Omega. Since no confusion can arise, we omit statement numbers:

```
# symbolic n;
# rd811 := {[i,j] -> [i',j'] : 1<=i<=n && 1 <=j<= i
#             && 1<=i'<=n && 1<=j'<=i'
#             && i'+j' = i+j-1
#             && (i'<i or (i'=i && j'<j))
#             && not exists( i3,j3 : 1<=i3<=n && 1<=j3<=i3
#                   && i3+j3 = i+j-1
#                   && (i'<i3 or (i3=i' && j'<j3))
#                   && (i3<i  or (i3=i  && j3< j)))
#             && not exists( i4 : 1<=i4<=n && i4+1 = i+j-1
#                   && i'<i4<i) };
```

Omega solves this into

```
# rd811;

{[i,1] -> [i-1,1] : 2 <= i <= n} union
 {[i,j] -> [i,j-1] : 2 <= j <= i <= n}
```

The first part of this relation can be read as

$$\forall i \in \mathbb{N}, \, 2 \leq i \leq n : \text{RD}(11^{i,1}) = \{8^{i-1,1}\} \tag{10.12}$$

and the second as

$$\forall i,j \in \mathbb{N}, \, 2 \leq j \leq i \leq n : \text{RD}(11^{i,j}) = \{8^{i,j-1}\} \tag{10.13}$$

Notice that j implicitly equals 1 in (10.12).

We now compute the definitions $17^{i'}$ that reach a given $11^{i,j}$. To do this, we eliminate instances of 8 and other instances of 17 that kill $17^{i'}$:

```
# symbolic n;
# rd1711 := {[i,j]->[i'] : 1<=i,i'<=n && 1<=j<=i
#             && i' + 1 = i + j - 1 && i' < i
#             && not exists(i3,j3 : 1<=i3<=n && 1<=j3<=i3
```

```
#                           && i3 + j3 = i + j - 1
#                           && i3 > i'
#                           && (i3<i or (i3=i && j3<=j)))
#              && not exists(i4 : 1<=i4<=n && i4+1=i+j-1
#                           && i4 > i' && i4 < i  )};
```

The Omega Calculator derives

```
# rd1711;
{[i,1] -> [i-1] : 2 <= i <= n}
```

That is:,

$$\forall i \in \mathbb{N},\ 2 \le i \le n : \text{RD}(\mathbf{11}^{i,1}) = \{\mathbf{17}^{i-1}\} \tag{10.14}$$

In conclusion, after merging (10.12), (10.13), and (10.14), we get

$$\forall i,j \in \mathbb{N}, 1 \le j \le i \le n : \quad \text{RD}(\mathbf{11}^{i,j}) = \quad \textbf{if } i \ge 2 \tag{10.15}$$
$$\textbf{then} \quad \textbf{if } j \ge 2$$
$$\textbf{then} \ \{\mathbf{8}^{i,j-1}\}$$
$$\textbf{else} \ \{\mathbf{8}^{i-1,1}, \mathbf{17}^{i-1}\}$$
$$\textbf{else} \ \{\mathbf{1}\}$$

In one case $(i,j) = (1,1)$, the value doesn't come from either **8** or **17**, but from **1**. Notice there is only one such case since i is the upper bound of loop j. Notice also that there are $n - 1$ cases where two definitions may reach a use. These cases are clearly indicated: They correspond to $2 \le i \le n$ and $j = 1$. Indeed, because we are consiering the first iteration of an instance of the j-loop, reaching definitions cannot come from statement **8** in that loop instance. If we consider the preceding iteration of the outer i-loop, however, two definitions, $\mathbf{8}^{i-1,1}$ and $\mathbf{17}^{i-1}$, do execute and do write to the same element of array a. Because of the par construct starting line **3**, however, we cannot tell which definition executes last.

10.4   (S)SA Forms for Explicitly Parallel Programs

In what follows, we use the reaching definition analysis presented ealier in this chapter to derive a precise *parallel array single-assignment* form. This form is a natural extension of either array SSA or array SA. The only additional hurdle, of course, is parallelism.

Let us consider the program in Figure 10.8. Parallel array (S)SA form first renames arrays in all left-hand expressions. Not surprisingly, the real problem is then to modify right-hand expressions correctly: Since the two parallel sections execute in any order, the value read in the last statement is not determined. Because of array renaming, an auxiliary function is inserted to restore the flow of data. As in [60], this function is called a π-function.

As in the sequential case, we have two possibilities: Where a π-function is needed, either the π-function is plugged in directly is the right-hand expression (as in Figure 10.9), or a new array is created to store the "merged" values coming from the

. . . .

```
1  par
2     section
3        a[1] := ...
4     end section
5     section
6        a[1] := ...
7     end section
8  end par
9  ..  := a[1]
```

. . . . Figure 10.8. Challenges of parallel array (S)SA forms. . . . .

. . . .

```
1  par
2     section
3        a3[1] := ...
4     end section
5     section
6        a6[1] := ...
7     end section
8  end par
9  ..  := π(a3[1],a6[1])
```

. . . . Figure 10.9. Parallel array (S)SA form of the program in Figure 10.8. . . . .

various reaching definitions, and a pseudo-assignment to this new array is inserted.
Such pseudo-assignments using π-functions are typically inserted at the earliest point
guaranteed to be executed before the read and after all its possible reaching definitions. These pseudo-assignments do not bring much, however. We therefore use the
first method, as illustrated in the transformed program shown in Figure 10.9.

Let us convert the programs in Figure 10.7 to single-assignment form. The left-
hand sides now write into three arrays, a1, a8, and a17. There is one right-hand
expression, in statement **11**. Thanks to the instancewise reaching definitions in (10.15),
replace this reference by

```
if (i >= 2)
then if (j >= 2) then a8[i+j-1]
        else π(a8[i],a17[i])
          end if
else a1[1]
end if
```

Notice how some expressions are simplified. For instance, when $i \geq 2$ and $j = 1$, Eq. (10.15) tells us the definitions reaching $\mathbf{11}^{i,1}$ are $\mathbf{8}^{i-1,1}$ and $\mathbf{17}^{i-1}$. The subscript of a8 in **8** is i+j, which equals $(i - 1) + 1 = i$ at $\mathbf{8}^{i-1,1}$. Similarly, the subscript of a17 in **17** is i+1, which equals i when evaluating $\mathbf{17}^{i-1}$. The transformed program is shown in Figure 10.10. Notice that only one π-function on two array elements is needed.

. . . .

```
1    a1[1] := ..
2    for i := 1 to n
3      par
4        section
5          for j := 1 to i
6            par
7              section
8                a8[i+j] := ...
9              end section
10             section
11               ..:= if (i >= 2)
                       then if (j >= 2)
                            then a8[i+j-1]
                            else π(a8[i],a17[i])
                            end if
                       else a1[1]
                       end if
12             end section
13           end par
14         end for
15       end section
16       section
17         a17[i+1] := ...
18       end section
19     end par
20   end for
```

. . . . *Figure 10.10. Array SSA form for the program in Figure 10.7.* . . . .

10.5   Further Reading

The first part of this chapter studies a reaching definition analysis for parallel programs. Another approach for control-parallel programs, based on regular section descriptors and the iterative solving of data flow equations, was proposed by Ferrante et al. [36].

Another important related work is [43]. Array distribution in data-parallel languages is addressed in [14], among other papers.

Finally, even if they are a bit outside the scope of this chapter, [38] and [63] are excellent articles worth reading. [38] details the formal derivation of data-parallel programs using skeletons, and [63] discusses the link between data parallelism and functional programming.

10.6 Conclusion

This chapter presents a data-flow analysis that can be applied to data- and/or task-parallel programs, with dynamic flows of control. The framework expresses data flows as linear equations and inequalities, instead of classical flow equations that are solved by iterative means. In other words, this analysis does not rely on control-flow graphs to capture the relative order of computation, but on symbolic constraints instead. This has several benefits, such as precise information on accesses to array elements. The price to pay, however, is that parallel programs are supposed to be structured and, in particular, that control cannot enter within or exit from the body of a parallel construct. But interestingly enough, this assumption is made in most related work anyway.

In a second part, this framework is extended to define an array SSA form for explicitly parallel programs. For the same reasons, placing ϕ- and π-functions (the parallel counterpart of ϕ-functions in SSA) is not based here on dominance frontiers, but on symbolic (in)equalities.

Chapter 11

Conclusion: Toward Algorithm Recognition

What should be the ultimate goal of a compiler? Perhaps a weird question, isn't it? But consider this: If the compiler had a perfect understanding of both the program and the target computer, then it could ideally translate the former into the best possible code for the latter, couldn't it? So what is the best possible understanding of a program? Wouldn't it be to extract the algorithm the programmer had in mind when he or she originally wrote his or her program?

Imagine you are the compiler and are facing the following program (taken from [80]):

```
0   x[0] := 0
1   for i := 1 to 2*n do
2     t := x[2*n-i+1];
3     x[i] := x[i-1] + t
4   end for
```

Wouldn't it be nice to recognize that this program actually means to compute

$$x_{2n} = \sum_{i=1}^{n} (n - i + 2)x_{2n-i+1} \qquad (11.1)$$

The algorithm to compute this sum, as implemented in this program, may be surprising. Nevertheless, it is a correct implementation of the equation as you might check with pen and paper.

To detect this, the method suggested in [80] relies on instancewise reaching definitions. In Figure 5.11 on page 92, we saw that the definitions of x[2*n-i+1] reaching 2^i are

$$\mathrm{RD}(\langle 2^i, \mathtt{x[2*n-i+1]} \rangle) = \begin{array}{l} \textbf{if} \ \ 1 \leq i \leq n \\ \textbf{then} \ \ \{\bot\} \\ \textbf{else} \ \ \{3^{2n-i+1}\} \end{array}$$

The definitions reaching $x[i-1]$ and t in statement **3** are easy to find:

$$RD(\langle 3^i, x[i-1]\rangle) = \quad \textbf{if } i = 1$$
$$\textbf{then } \{0\}$$
$$\textbf{else } \{3^{i-1}\}$$

and

$$RD(\langle 3^i, t\rangle) = \{2^i\}$$

We then saw in Exercise 8.3 on page 186 that a single-assignment equivalent of this program is

```
0   x0 := 0
1   for i := 1 to 2*n do
2       t2[i]:= if 1<=i<=n then x[2*n-i+1]
                else x3[2*n-i+1] end if;
3       x3[i]:= (if i=1 then x0 else x3[i-1] end if)
                + t2[i]
4   end for
```

As we know, the single-assignment form gives a system of recurrence equations, here on variables $t2$ and $x3$:

$$t2_i = \begin{cases} x2_{n-i+1} & \text{if } 1 \leq i \leq n \\ x3_{2n-i+1} & \text{if } n+1 \leq i \leq 2n \end{cases}$$

and

$$x3_i = \begin{cases} x0 + t2_1 & \text{if } i = 1 \\ x3_{i-1} + t2_i & \text{if } i \geq 2 \text{ and } i \leq 2n \end{cases}$$

Pay attention to indices: $x3_{2n-i+1}$, $x0$ and $t2_1$ refer, respectively, to the $(2n-i+1)$th term of series $x3$, the 0th term of series $x0$, and the term indexed by 1 in series $t2$.

If we use the fact that $x0 = 0$, and, after substituting for $t2$ in the expression of $x3$, we get

$$x3_i = \begin{cases} x2_n & \text{if } i = 1 \\ x3_{i-1} + x2_{n-i+1} & \text{if } 2 \leq i \leq n \\ x3_{i-1} + x3_{2n-i+1} & \text{if } n+1 \leq i \leq 2n \end{cases}$$

The tough part then is to detect and correctly handle the recurrence on $x3$. How to do this is detailed in [79, 80]. Once the recurrence is detected, however, simple algebraic transformations allow us to yield the closed-form expression (11.1).

The process we just described is similar in spirit to detecting the equality of variables [2]. In both cases, the imperative program is replaced by a single-assignment or functional equivalent that better represents the flow of value. However, we can leverage the techniques described throughout this book to address much more complex programs. The fact that the work of Redon and Feautrier is based on closed-form descriptions of precise reaching definition information is one more reason for our focus, in this book, on symbolic reaching definition analysis.

Notice that deriving a mathematical equation from the source code is far more difficult than deriving a program that implements an equation. In addition, even if there are several mathematical ways to write the preceding equation, there are so many ways to write a program implementing this equation that we can claim the equation is a more "canonical" form. One more argument is that the equation is a pretty good description of the programmer's intent, and that an automated tool, or programmers themselves, can later decide which algorithm to use and even later which code to generate for that algorithm. (Actually, when a high-level mathematical computation is recognized, the compiler or programmer might want to use specialized, fine-tuned libraries, like BLAS routines in the case of numerical analysis, to get top performance.) To top it off, a mathematical equation is technology-independent: It doesn't have to rely on the fact that computers have memory and that we use side effects through an imperative language.

Those more interested in the bottom line than in high-level discussions will be happy, too. The performance benefit we can get from recognizing the equation from the program is clear. The preceding equation is indeed a sum, which is a type of scan, and we saw that it can be executed in a logarithmic number of steps, here $\log_2 n$ steps (n being the number of elements being summed) instead of $2n$ steps as in the preceding program.

Exercise 11.1 Consider the following program:

```
1   x := 0;
2   for i := 1 to n do
3       x := x + i;
4       a[i] := some expression depending on x
5   end for
```

Why can't this loop be parallelized? How can the techniques outlined above help?

Solution This loop can't be parallelized because of the loop-carried dependence on x in statement **3**.

However, that statement implements a reduction on i. Not only can this reduction be recognized automatically, but it also can be replaced by a closed-form expression with respect to i. Indeed, the value of x after **3** (i.e., at statement **4**) at a given iteration i is

$$[x]_{4^i} = \frac{i(i+1)}{2}$$

The above loop can then be rewritten as

```
1   x := 0;
2   for i := 1 to n do
3       x := (i*(i+1))/2;
4       a[i] := some expression depending on x
5   end for
```

The output dependence on x can easily be removed by expanding x into an array indexed by i. The final loop can be executed in parallel. ∎

Now we can get even one step further. Wouldn't it be nice to recognize that the similar program

```
x[0] := 1
for i := 1 to 2*n do
   t[i] := x[2*n-i+1];
   x[i] := x[i-1] * t[i]
end for
```

has exactly the same flow of data as the summation program we just saw, and that, in addition, it computes a similar expression:

$$x_{2n} = \prod_{i=1}^{n} x_{2n-i+1}^{n-i+2}$$

So apparently different programs can have the identical underlying data flows. Therefore, some optimizations apply to both. Of course, data values are different, because the operators applied to these values are different.[1] However, both programs above are instances of a more general "meta-" program:

```
x[0] := e
for i := 1 to 2*n do
   t[i] := x[2*n-i+1];
   x[i] := x[i-1] ⊙ t[i]
end for
```

where ⊙ is some operator with e a neutral element for ⊙. This abstract program can be implemented as a procedure that takes two arguments: the initial value of x[0] (in the examples above, this value is e) and the operator to be applied.[2] If ⊙ is commutative and associative, the meta-program is an implementation of an algorithm that computes

$$x_{2n} = \bigodot_{i=1}^{n} \left(\odot_{k=1}^{n-i+2} x_{2n-i+1} \right)$$

that is,

$$x_{2n} = \bigodot_{i=1}^{n} \left(\underbrace{x_{2n-i+1} \odot x_{2n-i+1} \odot \ldots \odot x_{2n-i+1}}_{n-i+2 \text{ times}} \right)$$

As a matter of fact, the study of "meta-algorithms" dates back at least to the work by Tarjan [85, 84], which shows that several classical algorithms (including shortest-path computation, flow analysis, and conversion of finite automata into regular expressions) were instances of a more general one called the algebraic path problem. In retrospect, the existence of meta-algorithms is of no surprise, since they are a mere consequence of algebra.

---

[1]Otherwise the algorithm would be the same. Algorithm recognition therefore cannot rely on reaching definitions only.

[2]When a procedure takes another procedure or operator as an argument, we say the procedure is "higher-order" because it is not limited to "first-order" data [1]. Probably all functional languages provide higher-order procedures. Some imperative languages like C provide support for higher-order procedures through function pointers.

To wrap up, our point here is twofold. First, data flows are the signatures of algorithms, and instancewise reaching definitions are the right concept to express them. Once the data flow is expressed, a part of algorithm recognition is done, enabling optimizations such as replacement by specialized or finely tuned library functions. Second, we can go one step further: Data flows are the signature of the underlying meta-algorithm. Recognizing that a piece of code implements an instance of a meta-algorithm, and recognizing which concrete operators incarnate the abstract "meta-" operators, enable optimizations such as replacement of the code by a library call.

Perhaps one day single-assignment languages will be mainstream languages. But until that day comes, understanding the data flow of imperative programs and extracting algorithms from them will both require challenging research and pave the way to exciting optimizations. These fruits are not hanging low, but I hope you are now convinced they are worth catching.

References

[1] H. Abelson and G. J. Sussman. *Structure and Interpretation of Computer Programs (2nd edition).* MIT Press, 1996.

[2] B. Alpern, M. N. Wegman, and F. K. Zadeck. Detecting equality of variables in programs. In *ACM Sym. on Prin. of Prog. Lang. (PoPL)*, pages 1–11, January 1988.

[3] C. Ancourt and F. Irigoin. Scanning polyhedra with DO loops. In *Proc. of the ACM SIGPLAN Symp. on Prin. and Practice of Parallel Prog. (PPoPP)*, pages 39–50, June 1991.

[4] Th. Ball and J. R. Larus. Using paths to measure, explain and enhance program behavior. *IEEE Computer*, 33(7):57–65, July 2000.

[5] U. Banerjee. *Dependence Analysis for Supercomputing.* Kluwer Academic Publishers, 1988.

[6] U. Banerjee. *Loop Transformations for Restructuring Compilers: The Foundations.* Kluwer Academic Publishers, 1992.

[7] D. Barthou. *Array Dataflow Analysis in Presence of Non-affine Constraints.* Ph.D. thesis, Univ. Versailles, February 1998.

[8] D. Barthou, A. Cohen, and J.-F. Collard. Maximal static expansion. In *ACM Sym. on Prin. of Prog. Lang. (PoPL)*, pages 98–106, San Diego, CA, January 1998.

[9] A. J. Bernstein. Analysis of programs for parallel processing. *IEEE Trans. on El. Computers*, EC-15, 1966.

[10] R. Bodík and S. Anik. Path-sensitive value-flow analysis. In *ACM Sym. on Prin. of Prog. Lang. (PoPL)*, pages 237–251, San Diego, CA, January 1998.

[11] P.-Y. Calland, A. Darte, Y. Robert, and F. Vivien. Plugging anti and output dependence removal techniques into loop parallelization algorithms. *Parallel Computing*, 23(1-2):251–266, 1997.

[12] D. C. Cann. *SISAL 1.2: A Bief Introduction and Tutorial.* Lawrence Livermore Nat. Lab., Livermore, CA. ftp://sisal.llnl.gov/pub/sisal/.

[13] L. Carter, B. Simon, B. Calder, L. Carter, and J. Ferrante. Predicated static single assignment. In *Proc. Intl. Conf. on Parallel Architectures and Compilation Techniques*, Newport Beach, CA, October 1999.

[14] S. Chaterjee, J. R. Gilbert, R. Schreiber, and T. J. Sheffler. Array distribution in data-parallel programs. Technical report.

[15] Ph. Clauss. Counting solutions to linear and nonlinear constraints through ehrhart polynomials: Applications to analyze and transform scientific programs. In *Proc. ACM Intl. Conf. on Supercomputing*, Philadelphia, May 1996.

[16] A. Cohen. *Program analysis and transformation: From the polytope model to formal languages*. Ph.D. thesis, Univ. Versailles, December 1999.

[17] J.-F. Collard. Code generation in automatic parallelizers. In C. Girault, ed., *Proc. Intl. Conf. on Applications in Parallel and Distributed Computing, IFIP W.G 10.3*, pages 185–194, Caracas, Venezuela, April 1994. North Holland.

[18] J.-F. Collard and J. Knoop. A comparative study of reaching definitions analyses. Technical Report 1998/22, PRiSM, U. of Versailles, 1998.

[19] P. Cousot and R. Cousot. Temporal abstract interpretation. In *Proc. ACM Conf. on Princ. of Prog. Lang. (PoPL)*, pages 12–25, Boston, MA, 2000.

[20] P. Cousot and N. Halbwachs. Automatic discovery of linear restraints among variables of a program. In *ACM Sym. on Prin. of Prog. Lang. (PoPL)*, pages 84–96, January 1978.

[21] B. Creusillet. *Array Region Analyses and Applications*. Ph.D. thesis, Ecole des Mines de Paris, December 1996.

[22] B. Creusillet and F. Irigoin. Interprocedural array region analysis. *Intl. J. of Parallel Prog.*, 24(6):513–545, 1996.

[23] R. Cytron, J. Ferrante, B. K. Rosen, M. N. Wegman, and F. K. Zadeck. Efficiently computing static single assignment form and the control dependence graph. *ACM Trans. on Prog. Lang. Sys.*, 13(4):451–490, October 1991.

[24] A. Darte, Y. Robert, and F. Vivien. *Scheduling and Automatic Parallelization*. Birkhäuser, 2000.

[25] A. Dolzmann and Th. Sturm. *REDLOG User Manual: A REDUCE Logic Package*. Univ. Passau, Germany, www.fmi.uni-passau.de/~redlog.

[26] E. Duesterwald, R. Gupta, and M.-L. Soffa. A practical data flow framework for array reference analysis and its use in optimization. In *ACM SIGPLAN'93 Conf. on Prog. Lang. Design and Implementation*, pages 68–77, June 1993.

[27] B. Chapman et al. Extending Vienna fortran with task parallelism. In *Proc. Intl. Conf. on Parallel and Distributed Systems*, pages 258–263, Hsinchu, Taiwan, December 1994.

[28] P. Feautrier. *Solving Systems of Affine (In)Equalities: PIP's User's Guide.* Univ. Versailles. `http://www.prism.uvsq.fr/~paf`.

[29] P. Feautrier. Array expansion. In *ACM Intl. Conf. on Supercomputing, St. Malo*, pages 429–441, 1988.

[30] P. Feautrier. Parametric integer programming. *RAIRO Recherche Opérationnelle*, 22:243–268, September 1988.

[31] P. Feautrier. Dataflow analysis of scalar and array references. *Intl. J. of Parallel Prog.*, 20(1):23–53, February 1991.

[32] P. Feautrier. Some efficient solution to the affine scheduling problem, Part I, One-dimensional time. *Intl. J. of Parallel Prog.*, 21(5):313–348, October 1992.

[33] P. Feautrier. Some efficient solution to the affine scheduling problem, Part II, Multidimensional time. *Intl. J. of Parallel Prog.*, 21(6), December 1992.

[34] P. Feautrier. Automatic parallelization in the polytope model. In G.-R. Perrin and A. Darte, eds., *The Data Parallel Programming Model*, volume 1132 of *LNCS*, pages 79–103. Springer-Verlag, June 1996.

[35] P. Feautrier. A parallelization framework for recursive tree programs. In *Europar'98*, number 1470 in LNCS, pages 470–479. Springer-Verlag, September 1998.

[36] J. Ferrante, D. Grunwald, and H. Srinivasan. Computing communication sets for control parallel programs. In *W. on Lang. and Comp. for Par. Comp. (LCPC)*, volume 892 of *LNCS*, pages 316–330, Ithaca, NY, August 1994. Springer-Verlag.

[37] M. Gerndt and R. Berrendorf. *SVM-Fortran, Reference Manual, Version 1.4.* Research Center Jülich, May 1995.

[38] S. Gorlatch and H. Bischof. A generic MPI implementation for a data-parallel skeleton: Formal derivation and application to FFT. *Parallel Proc. Lett.*, 8(4):447–458, December 1998.

[39] Ph. Granger. *Analyses semantiques de congruence.* Ph.D. thesis, Ecole Polytechnique, 1991.

[40] Ph. Granger. Static analysis of linear congreunce equalities among variables of a program. 1991.

[41] M. Griebl and C. Lengauer. On scanning space-time mapped while loops. In B. Buchberger, ed., *Parallel Processing: CONPAR 94 – VAPP VI*, Lecture Notes in Computer Science 854, pages 677–688, Linz, Austria, 1994. Springer-Verlag.

[42] D. Gries. *The Science of Programming.* Springer-Verlag, 1981.

[43] D. Grunwald and H. Srinivasan. Data flow equations for explicitly parallel programs. In *Proc. ACM Conf. on Prin. of Prog. Lang. (PoPL)*, pages 159–168, May 1993.

[44] J. Gu, Z. Li, and G. Lee. Symbolic array dataflow analysis for array privatization and program parallelization. In *ACM Supercomputing'95*, San Diego, CA, December 1995.

[45] J. Gu, Z. Li, and G. Lee. Experience with efficient array data flow analysis for array privatization. In *ACM SIGPLAN Sym. on Princ. and Prac. of Par. Prog. (PPoPP)*, Las Vegas, June 1997.

[46] E. M. Gurari. *An Introduction to the Theory of Computation*. Computer Science Press, 1989.

[47] N. Heintze, J. Jaffar, and R. Voicu. A framework for combining analysis and verification. In *Proc. ACM Conf. on Princ. of Prog. Lang. (PoPL)*, pages 26–39, Boston, MA, 2000.

[48] L. J. Hendren and A. Nicolau. Parallelizing programs with recursive data structures. In *Intl. Conf. on Parallel Proc.*, pages II–49 – II–56, 1989.

[49] C. A. Herrmann and C. Lengauer. On the space-time mapping of a class of divide-and-conquer recursions. *Parallel Proc. Lett.*, 6(4):525–537, 1996.

[50] S.-A. Hwang and C.-W. Wu. Unified VLSI systolic array design for LZ data compression. *IEEE Trans. on VLSI Systems*, 9(4):489–499, August 2001.

[51] Intel Corp. *Intel IA-64 Application Developer's Architecture Guide*, 2000.

[52] J. L. Jensen, M. E. Jorgensen, M. I. Schwartzbach, and N. Klarlund. Automatic verification of pointer programs using monadic second-order logic. In *ACM SIGPLAN Conf. on Prog. Lang. Design and Implem. (PLDI)*, 1997.

[53] R. M. Karp, R. E. Miller, and S. Winograd. The organization of computations for uniform recurrence equations. *J. ACM*, 14(3):563–590, July 1967.

[54] W. Kelly, V. Maslov, W. Pugh, E. Rosser, T. Shpeisman, and D. Wonnacott. *The Omega Calculator and Library, version 1.1.0*. Univ. Maryland, November 1996. http://www.cs.umd.edu/projects/omega/index.html.

[55] W. Kelly, W. Pugh, E. Rosser, and T. Shpeisman. Transitive closure of infinite graphs and its applications. *Intl. J. of Parallel Prog.*, 24(6):579–598, 1996.

[56] K. Knobe and V. Sarkar. Array SSA form and its use in parallelization. In *ACM Sym. on Prin. of Prog. Lang. (PoPL)*, pages 107–120, San Diego, CA, January 1998.

[57] J. Knoop and B. Steffen. The interprocedural coincidence theorem. In *Proc. of the 4th Intl. Conf. on Compiler Construction (CC'92)*, number 641 in LNCS, Paderborn, Germany, 1992.

[58] C. H. Koelbel, D. B. Loveman, R. S. Schreiber, G. L. Stelle Jr., and M. E. Zosel. *The High Performance Fortran Handbook*. The MIT Press, 1994.

[59] S. Y. Kung. *VLSI Array Processors*. Prentice Hall, 1998.

[60] J. Lee, S. Midkiff, and D. A. Padua. Concurrent static single assignment form and constant propagation for explicitly parallel programs. In *W. on Lang. and Comp. for Par. Comp. (LCPC)*, August 1997.

[61] V. Lefebvre and P. Feautrier. Automatic storage management for parallel programs. *J. Parallel Comp.*, 24:649–671, 1998.

[62] C. Lengauer. Loop parallelization in the polytope model. In E. Best, ed., *CONCUR '93*, LNCS 715, pages 398–416. Springer-Verlag, 1993.

[63] B. Lisper. Data parallelism and functional programming. In G.-R. Perrin and A. Darte, eds., *The Data Parallel Programming Model*, volume 1132 of *LNCS*, pages 220–251. Springer-Verlag, June 1996.

[64] V. Maslov. Global value propagation through value flow graph and its use in dependence analysis. Technical Report CS-TR-3310, CS Dept, Univ. of Maryland, 1994.

[65] V. Maslov. Enhancing array dataflow dependence analysis with on-demand global value propagation. In *Proc. Intl. Conf. on Supercomputing*, pages 265–269, Barcelona, 1995.

[66] D. E. Maydan, S. P. Amarasinghe, and M. S. Lam. Array dataflow analysis and its use in array privatization. In *Proc. ACM Conf. on Prin. of Prog. Lang. (PoPL)*, pages 2–15, January 1993.

[67] S. Moon and M. W. Hall. Evaluation of predicated array data-flow analysis for automatic parallelization. In *Proc. ACM SIGPLAN Symp. on Princ. and Prac. of Parallel Prog. (PPoPP)*, Atlanta, GA, May 1999.

[68] S. S. Muchnick. *Advanced Compiler Design & Implementation*. Morgan Kaufmann, 1997.

[69] OpenMP Architecture Review Board. *OpenMP Fortran application program interface, 2.0*, November 2000.

[70] G. D. Plotkin. *Structural operational semantics*. Lecture Notes, DAIMI FN-19. Aarhus Univ., Denmark, 1981.

[71] W. Pugh. The omega test: A fast and practical integer programming algorithm for dependence analysis. *Comm. of the ACM*, 8:102–114, August 1992.

[72] W. Pugh. A practical algorithm for exact array dependence analysis. *Comm. of the ACM*, 35(8):27–47, August 1992.

[73] W. Pugh. Counting solutions to Presburger formulas: How and why. Technical Report CS-TR-3234, Univ. Maryland, March 1994.

[74] W. Pugh and E. Rosser. Iteration space slicing and its application to communication optimization. In *International Conference on Supercomputing*, Vienna, Austria, July 1997. Springer-Verlag.

[75] W. Pugh and E. Rosser. Iteration space slicing for locality. In L. Carter and J. Ferrante, eds., *Workshop on Lang. and Compilers for Parallel Comp. (LCPC)*, volume 1863 of *LNCS*, pages 164–184, La Jolla, CA, 1999. Springer-Verlag.

[76] W. Pugh and D. Wonnacott. Eliminating false data dependences using the omega test. In *Proc. ACM SIGPLAN Conf. on Prog. Lang. Design and Implem. (PLDI)*, 1992.

[77] W. Pugh and D. Wonnacott. Constraint-based array dependence analysis. *ACM Trans. on Prog. Lang. and Systems*, 1891, 1998.

[78] J. Ramanujam. Non-unimodular transformations of nested loops. In *Supercomputing'92*, pages 214–223, November 1992.

[79] X. Redon. *Détection et exploitation des récurrences dans les programmes scientifiques en vue de leur parallélisation*. Ph.D. thesis, Univ. Versailles, 1995.

[80] X. Redon and P. Feautrier. Detection of reductions in sequentials programs with loops. In A. Bode, M. Reeve, and G. Wolf, eds., *Proc. 5th Intl. Parallel Architectures and Lang. Europe*, pages 132–145, June 1993.

[81] B. K. Rosen, M. N. Wegman, and F. K. Zadeck. Global value numbers and redundant computations. In *ACM Sym. on Prin. of Prog. Lang. (PoPL)*, pages 12–27, 1988.

[82] A. V. S. Sastry and R. D. C. Ju. A new algorithm for scalar register promotion based on SSA form. In *ACM SIGPLAN Conf. on Prog. Lang. Design and Implem. (PLDI)*, pages 15–25, Montreal, June 1998.

[83] A. Schrijver. *Theory of linear and integer programming*. Wiley, 1986.

[84] R. E. Tarjan. Fast algorithms for solving path problems. *J. ACM*, 28(3):594–614, July 1981.

[85] R. E. Tarjan. A unified approach to path problems. *J. ACM*, 28(3):577–593, July 1981.

[86] P. Tu and D. Padua. Gated SSA-Based demand-driven symbolic analysis for parallelizing compilers. In *ACM Intl. Conf. on Supercomputing*, pages 414–423, Barcelona, July 1995.

[87] M. Weiser. Program slicing. *IEEE Trans. on Software Eng.*, pages 352–357, 1984.

[88] D. Wonnacott. *Constraint-based Array Dependence Analysis*. Ph.D. thesis, Univ. Maryland, 1995.

[89] D. Wonnacott. Extending scalar optimizations for arrays. In *Workshop on Lang. and Compilers for Parallel Comp. (LCPC)*, 2000.

[90] D. Wonnacott and W. Pugh. Nonlinear array dependence analysis. In *Proc. 3rd Workshop on Lang., Compilers and Run-Time Systems for Scalable Comp.*, 1995. Troy, NY.

Index